CROSSING THE STAGE

Cross-dressing in theatrical performance has generated a controversial, and at times contentious, debate during the last decade. Are cross-dressed women making politicized statements about gender hierarchies? Are male drag artists subverting traditional masculinity, or are they cruelly parodying a hackneyed and stereotypical vision of female beauty?

This volume brings together for the first time essays which focus on cross-dressing in theater, cabaret, opera, and dance. The essays raise issues which range from the significance of the cross-dressed classical Greek actor to the Renaissance tradition of adolescent boys playing female roles; from Restoration breeches roles to the contemporary phenomenon of "voguing."

Crossing the Stage illuminates the way in which current theoretical and pedagogical scholarship on the politics and discourse of the body bears on the significance of the cross-dressed performer from psychoanalytical, social, historical and feminist perspectives. *Crossing the Stage* is a major source book on theatrical cross-dressing and includes a full bibliography to supplement the collection. It will be essential reading for all performance specialists and those interested in issues of gender and representation.

Contributors include Jean Howard, Jill Campbell, Lynn Garafola, Laurence Senelick, Marybeth Hamilton, Elizabeth Drorbaugh, Peggy Phelan and Alisa Solomon.

Lesley Ferris is Director of Theater at Memphis State University. She lived and worked in London for twelve years, has directed on the London Fringe and the Edinburgh Festival and was a Senior Lecturer and Acting Head of the School for Drama at Middlesex Polytechnic (now University). She has published various articles and her book *Acting Women: Images of Women in Theatre* was published in 1990.

CROSSING THE STAGE
Controversies on cross-dressing

Edited by Lesley Ferris

London and New York

First published in 1993
by Routledge
11 New Fetter Lane, London EC4P 4EE

Simultaneously published in the USA and Canada
by Routledge
29 West 35th Street, New York, NY 10001

Editorial material and Introduction
© 1993 Lesley Ferris;
individual chapters © 1993 individual contributors;
this collection © Routledge

Typeset in 10 on 12 Baskerville by Florencetype Ltd, Kewstoke, Avon
Printed in Great Britain by Biddles Ltd, Guildford and King's Lynn

British Library Cataloguing in Publication Data
A catalogue record for this book is available from the British Library

Library of Congress Cataloging in Publication Data
Crossing the Stage : Controversies on cross-dressing / edited by Lesley Ferris.
p.   cm.
Includes bibliographical references and index.
1. Impersonation.   2. Theater—Casting.   3. Transvestism.   4. Female
impersonators.   5. Male impersonators.   6. Theater and society.   7. Sex role
in literature.   8. Feminism and theater.
I. Ferris, Lesley.
PN2071.I47C76   1993
792′.028—dc20   93–6894

ISBN 0–415–06268–3 (hbk)
ISBN 0–415–06269–1 (pbk)

This book is dedicated to
Kitty Mrosovsky,
whose friendship and writing
have been an inspiration to me over the years

The most horrifying experiences and the cruelest of pleasures are entirely valuable if they contribute to the development of a real understanding of what it is to be human. Only a puritan would disagree, seeing in the body only gross matter and a despicable magma of viscera, rather than a mysterious theater which provides a stage for all exchange – whether of matter, mind or the senses – between inner and outer worlds.

Michel Leiris, "Le Corps enjeu," *Documents*, 1930

Vain trifles as they seem, clothes have, as they say, more important offices than merely to keep us warm. They change our view of the world and the world's view of us.

Virginia Woolf, *Orlando*, 1928

And clothes are the last frontier.

Kate Bornstein, 1989

CONTENTS

CONTENTS

ILLUSTRATIONS

NOTES ON CONTRIBUTORS

Jill Campbell is an Associate Professor of English at Yale University. Her teaching and publications have concentrated on eighteenth-century British literature, exploring, in particular, representations of gender and sexuality. The essay in this volume is adapted from a part of her book *Natural Masques: Gender and Identity in Fielding's Plays and Novels* (forthcoming, Stanford University Press). She has also published articles on Lady Mary Wortley Montagu's letters, portraits of John, Lord Hervey, *Joseph Andrews*, and *Tom Jones*. She was awarded the American Society for Eighteenth-Century Studies Teaching Prize for her course on "Problems of Gender in Early Eighteenth-Century Literature."

Elizabeth Drorbaugh is a Ph.D. candidate in the Department of Performance Studies at New York University and a member of the adjunct faculty at Hofstra University. She is a member of the Editorial Board of *Women and Performance: A Journal of Feminist Theory*. Prior to coming to New York City, she was an Assistant Professor in the Wells College Theatre Department during which time she was also a Teaching Artist with the Cultural Arts Council in Syracuse, New York, involved in developing arts programs for children in cooperation with city schools. Elizabeth is a playwright, a director, and a performer. She has appeared in drag in productions at New York University and the WOW Café in New York City.

Lynn Garafola is the author of *Diaghilev's Ballets Russes*, coeditor of *André Levinson on Dance: Writings from Paris in the Twenties*, and translator/editor of *The Diaries of Marius Petipa*. A contributing editor and critic for *Dance Magazine*, she is also the editor of the journal *Studies in Dance History*. Her articles have appeared in *Ballet Review*, *Dance Research Journal*, *The Nation*, *The Women's Review of Books*, *The Times Literary Supplement*, and in various collections such as *New York: Culture Capital of the World, 1940–1965* and *Breakthroughs: Avant-garde Artists in Europe and America, 1950–1990*. The recipient of fellowships from the Social Science Research

Council, the Getty Center for the Study of Art and the Humanities, and the National Endowment for the Humanities, she is working on a book about Ida Rubinstein.

Marybeth Hamilton was born in California and holds a Ph.D. in history from Princeton University. She now lives in London, where she works as a writer and lecturer. Currently she is a lecturer in American history at Birkbeck College, University of London. Her book, *"When I'm Bad, I'm Better": Mae West, Sex and American Entertainment*, is being published in America by Harper Collins.

Jean E. Howard teaches early modern literature at Columbia University. She has written a number of essays on Renaissance drama and on contemporary literary theory. Her first book, *Shakespeare's Art of Orchestration*, was published in 1984, and she subsequently coedited, with Marion O'Connor, *Shakespeare Reproduced: The Text in History and Ideology* (Methuen, 1987). Her forthcoming book *The Stage and Social Struggle in Early Modern England* will be published by Routledge in 1993, and she is currently completing, with Phyllis Rackin, a feminist study of Shakespeare's history plays.

Peggy Phelan is an Associate Professor of Performance Studies at New York University. She contributes to *TDR* (*The Drama Review*) in the areas of race, gender, and performance. Her book *Unmarked* appeared in 1993 from Routledge. With Lynda Hart she has co-edited *Acting Out: Feminist Performances* (University of Michigan Press, 1983).

Isa Ragusa, who received her Ph.D. from the Institute of Fine Arts at New York University, is an art historian specializing in the medieval period and in iconography. She has been a Research Art Historian in the Department of Art and Archaeology at Princeton University, a reader at the Index of Christian Art for Princeton for many years, retiring as Acting Director of the Index, and Visiting Lecturer in iconography at the Università Cattolica, Milan, Italy. She has published widely on the medieval period, most recently in *Arte Medievale* and *Miniatura*.

Laurence Senelick is Fletcher Professor of Drama at Tufts University, a former Fellow of the Guggenheim Foundation and the Institute for Advanced Studies in Berlin, and author of many works of theater history. The most recent include *Cabaret Performance: Europe 1890–1940* (2 vols), and *National Theatre in Northern and Eastern Europe 1746–1900*. He has edited *Gender in Performance: The Presentation of Difference in the Performing Arts* and *Wandering Stars: Russian Emigré Theatre*. His writing on eroticism, gender, and theater have appeared in *Journal of the History* *of Sexuality, Russian Review, Theatre History Studies*, etc. He is currently working on a cross-cultural history of theatrical transvestism.

Alisa Solomon is a Staff Writer at the *Village Voice*, where she writes theater criticism as well as essays, news analysis, and reportage on such topics as the Middle East, reproductive rights, gay and lesbian issues, New York City politics, and women's sports. Her work has also appeared in *Theater, American Theater, Performing Arts Journal, The Drama Review*, the *New York Times, New York Newsday, Ms., Glamour*, and other publications. She is also an Assistant Professor of English at Baruch College–City University of New York.

ACKNOWLEDGMENTS

A great many people have contributed, in various ways, to the making of this book. My thanks go to: my students who have helped me enormously, first by asking questions, and second by acting in my cross-dressed productions of Eve Merriam's *The Club* and Bertolt Brecht's *Man is Man*; the Department of Theater and Communication Arts, Memphis State University who in various ways supported my research; my Faculty Research Grant, Memphis State University which made it possible for me to have the excellent services of Linda Brigance as a research assistant; Helena Reckitt, who originally commissioned the book; Talia Rodgers and Julia Hall, who enthusiastically encouraged the project; Marjorie Bowman and Phillip Baumgarner, who both provided astute and invaluable editorial assistance; Deborah Brackstone, Inter-Library Loan Librarian extraordinaire at Memphis State University Library; Sharon Chesher, whose expertise on the AppleMac was inestimable; Brian Rotman, whose rigorous suggestions and support provided invaluable intellectual sustenance.

I want to thank the following publications who gave me permission to reprint the following previously published essays: *Shakespeare Quarterly* (1988) for Jean E. Howard's "Cross-dressing, the theatre, and gender struggle in early modern England"; *Medieval English Theatre* (1984) for Isa Ragusa's translation of Goethe's "Women's parts played by men in the Roman theatre" (6, 2); Methuen's *The New Eighteenth Century: Theory, Politics, English Literature* (1987), eds Felicity Nussbaum and Laura Brown, for Jill Campbell's "'When men women turn': gender reversals in Fielding's plays"; *Dance Research Journal* (1985–6) for Lynn Garafola's "The travesty dancer in nineteenth-century ballet."

1

INTRODUCTION
Current crossings
Lesley Ferris

VARIETIES OF SHAKESPEAREAN ILLUSION

In the fall of 1991 Declan Donnellan's London Cheek By Jowl Theatre Company produced *As You Like It* with an all-male cast. Hailed by some as a bold experiment, others as a misguided disappointment, and still others as insensitive to the politics of theater employment (always more actresses are "resting" and out of work than actors), the production echoed a similar London undertaking more than twenty years earlier. In 1967 the National Theatre produced an all-male *As You Like It*. Why this apparent longing for a theater convention long dead? Do such experiments attempt to capture – however ephemerally – a Shakespearean authenticity, a sense of how it really was back then, during one of the so-called "golden ages" of theater?

A much more radical departure from the all-male casting of *As You Like It* is Neil Bartlett's production of *Twelfth Night* which opened at the Goodman Theater in Chicago in January, 1992 (Plate 1). Bartlett primarily reversed the all-male-actor convention of Shakespeare's England. Although Viola and her twin brother Sebastian were played by two 16-year-old boys, all the men, except the clown Feste, were played by women. Bartlett comments on his innovative reading of Shakespeare:

> If you did *Twelfth Night* as it was written, as an all-male production, it would be the "gay" *Twelfth Night* even before it opened. . . . The piece would be about whether the characters in the play are really homosexual and it would be about whether gay love is as good as straight love. And quite frankly, these are questions which are behind us.
>
> (Raymond 1992: 34)

In 1991 Stage West in Springfield, Massachusetts, produced *Hamlet* with an actress in the title role (Plate 2). Despite the director's claim that he did not cast the role to "make a sexual statement," at least one critic disagrees with this intention:

1

By casting Kelly Maurer in the role, director Eric Hill had ignited the anguish of Hamlet's psycho sexual crisis like a Molotov cocktail. By turns masculine, feminine, androgynous, Maurer's great Dane, like Marcel Duchamp's mustachioed *Mona Lisa*, smiled inscrutably at the audience from a no-man's-land of sexual equivocation.

(Holmberg 1992: 12)

Stage West's *Hamlet* follows an historically well established casting choice. The tradition of female Hamlets apparently began in 1776 when Sarah Siddons, the great tragedienne of the English stage, initiated this theatrical experiment (Edmonds 1992: 59). By the middle of the nineteenth century, it was commonplace for the actress to have a selection of acceptable male Shakespearean roles – principally Hamlet and Romeo – in her repertoire.

Eva Le Gallienne supported her 1936 interpretation of the role by stressing the role's suitability for actresses:

If one thinks of Hamlet as a man in his thirties, the idea of a woman's attempting to play the part is of course ridiculous. But Hamlet's whole psychology has always seemed to me that of a youth rather than of a mature man . . . It is possible for an actress at the height of her powers to give the impression of being a boy, while having at her command all the craft, range, force, and subtlety which such great roles require. This has always been true of Rostand's *L'Aiglon*, which, with a few insignificant exceptions, has always been played by women; also DeMusset's Lorenzaccio, and – in a very different mood – Barrie's Peter Pan.

(Le Gallienne 1983: 51)

Le Gallienne's Hamlet is part of a theater tradition primarily undertaken to give accomplished actresses an opportunity to play significant Shakespearean roles, in effect to show off the actress's range.

Erika Munk critiques the cross-dressed Hamlet as a reaffirmation of the prevailing gender system:

Hamlet, stereotyped as a waffling neurotic prone to violent fits, is considered proper for women to enact, unlike Lear, Henry V, Caesar, Coriolanus, or Falstaff . . . Basically such casting comes from producers' gimmickry and actresses' frustration, from the fact that most playwrights and most big roles are male; as long as men aren't clamoring to play Mother Courage or Juliet or Amanda Wingfield, Hamlet as a woman reemphasizes the universalist pretensions of maleness, the specific limitations of femaleness, in our culture.

(Munk 1985b: 80)

2

But what happens when the role of Lear *is* played by a woman? Writing in 1985 Munk could not foresee that five years later two *King Lear* productions would cast females in the title role. In May, 1990, Robert Wilson cast the 77-year-old actress Marianne Hoppe as King Lear in his production in Frankfurt. One of the significant features of this unusual casting choice is that Hoppe does not attempt to create the illusion of masculinity by disguising herself as a man, although the text remained consistent with Shakespeare.

In contrast to Wilson's single instance of cross-gender casting, Lee Breuer's production of *Lear* which opened in the same year attempted to rework the gender hierarchy of the play. Breuer and his company Mabou Mines began working on the Lear project in 1987 in Atlanta. The southern locale convinced the company to update the script to Georgia in the 1950s with Lear as a southern matriarchal figure with three sons.

Despite difficulties in justifying all the gender switches and updates, the company found enough intrigue, excitement, and contemporary resonance in these ideas to pursue them through a series of residencies in which they developed their concept until they presented their final interpretation of *Lear* in New York City. Ruth Maleczech, who played the role of Lear, described the astonishing effect this gender switch had for her: "When a man has power, we take it for granted. But when a woman has power, we're forced to look at the nature of power itself." Breuer, in considering Maleczech's desire to speak Lear's lines, said:

> It took me a while to understand that there were certain political imperatives inherent in that desire. What's one of the first things you see? That Lear's story, at least in part, is about the relationship between power and love. A man can be powerful and still be loved, but it's rare to see a woman loved for her power – women must be powerless. So as women gain power in our society, they also find love more difficult to attain.
>
> (Wetzsteon 1990: 40)

BACCHIC RITES AND WRONGS

In 1986 the Royal Court Theatre, London, produced Caryl Churchill's and David Lan's *A Mouthful of Birds* which reworked several thematic elements of Euripides' *The Bacchae* (Plate 3). In this contemporary script the androgynous god Dionysus is a character who encourages and oversees a variety of metamorphoses. One of these metamorphic manifestations centers on the life of Herculine Barbin, a nineteenth-century hermaphrodite. In the Royal Court production, a woman entered the stage cross-dressed in the clothes of a nineteenth-century French man. During her moving monologue, she slowly, ritually opens her small

3

suitcase removing her lace shawl, her petticoat, a rose, which she is now forced – by French law – to discard. She says: "Was I really Herculine Barbin, playing by the sea, starting school at the convent, nobody doubted I was a girl. Hermaphrodite, the doctors were fascinated, how to define the body, does it fascinate you, it doesn't fascinate me, let it die" (Churchill and Lan 1986: 51).

This interest in Herculine Barbin was initiated by Michel Foucault's republication of his/her memoirs in 1980. In his introductory essay to the memoirs Foucault asks, "Do we *truly* need a *true* sex?" (Foucault 1980: vii). Foucault provides a brief historical overview of the status which medical authority and law granted to hermaphrodites. He points out that records surviving from the Middle Ages display a much more tolerant attitude toward hermaphrodites, who were free to decide themselves which sex they preferred to maintain through their adult life. By the time of Herculine's story, which took place in the 1860–70s, the medical profession was obsessed with investigating and determining the true and only sex. As Foucault explains:

> Henceforth, everybody was to have one and only one sex. Everybody was to have his or her primary, profound, determined and determining sexual identity; as for the elements of the other sex that might appear, they could only be accidental, superficial, or even quite simply illusory. From the medical point of view, this meant that when confronted with a hermaphrodite, the doctor was no longer concerned with recognizing the presence of the two sexes, juxtaposed or intermingled, or with knowing which of the two prevailed over the other, but rather with deciphering the true sex that was hidden beneath ambiguous appearances.
>
> (Foucault 1980: viii)

This medical insistence on one true sex and the Herculine Barbin story have provided other theater artists with potentially fascinating performance material. Kate Bornstein performed a work-in-progress based on the life of Herculine Barbin at the Ninth Annual Conference for Women in Theater in San Diego, August, 1988. The significant, perhaps startling, aspect of this performance of the nineteenth-century hermaphrodite is that Kate Bornstein is a transsexual.

Her performance at the conference – a kind of autobiographical collage – encompassed a variety of scenes from her acting past in addition to her new work on Barbin. (For example, the first scene she performed was from her previous – male – life as an actor. It was the role of the macho make-out artist in Ann Jellicoe's play *The Knack*.) An important aspect of Bornstein's Herculine Barbin piece, entitled *Hidden: A Gender*, examines the suicide of Barbin. Bornstein states that her sense of humor has kept her from ending up like Barbin:

[T]he journey I want to portray is, did [Barbin] really have to be a he or a she? We he really some other gender that was trying to survive? And that's the way I feel myself. . . . I certainly don't feel I'm a man, and many times I question whether I'm a woman. I laugh at a world that permits me to be only one or the other.

(Wolff-Wilkinson 1989: 29–30)

Bornstein and her performance work center on her personal journey through masculinity to the feminine, a journey that overtly questions our culture's rigid gender system; these concerns starkly contrast another transsexual performing artist recently analyzed in Morris Meyer's provocative essay, "I dream of Jeannie: transsexual striptease as scientific display" (Meyer 1991: 25–42). Jeannie is a striptease artist who performs solo several times a year as part of a Milwaukee drag revue. Unlike other female impersonators in the show who manipulate clothing and makeup to create and maintain an illusion of femininity, "Jeannie's art was marked by a process of costume reduction that terminated in a theatrical display of her nude body" (25). At the end of the performance the show's director enters the stage and announces "Don't get yourself too worked up over her. It's all man-made" (29). This announcement is made for those audience members who have not "read" Jeannie's trans-sexual body correctly.

Lindsay Kemp returned to Sadlers Wells in April, 1992, to perform his production of *Onnagata*. The title of this performance piece refers to the term applied to the male actor in Japanese Kabuki theater whose specialty is playing female roles. Kemp is best known for his roles as Salomé and Divine (from his Genet-inspired production *Flowers*) and his performance in this most recent work continues his aesthetic of over-the-top theatricality created by his elaborate cross-dressed roles. In *Onnagata* Kemp's first stage entrance was from above the stage itself. He descended on invisible wires wearing an elaborate Japanese gown and carrying a parasol. During the rest of the performance he impersonated Isadora Duncan, Lady Macbeth, Loië Fuller, and the Virgin Mary.

Kemp's work in Britain is often considered the radical excess of a long theatrical tradition of comic cross-dressed men. It is a tradition that comes alive seasonally with Christmas pantomime and the comic Dame role. Popular entertainment – both in live and in televised performances – has promulgated the outrageous Dame figure with the most recent work of Barry Humphries as Dame Edna Everage. It is a tradition with which commercial producers often attempt to create a money-making theater event. Witness the two recent shows in London's West End which opened in 1992. One is the reworking of the Jules Styne/Bob Merrill musical *Sugar*, now titled *Some Like It Hot* after Billy Wilder's 1959 film comedy and taking the same storyline but adding a musical score.

Tommy Steele and Billy Boyle play the roles that Tony Curtis and Jack Lemmon originated in the film – two on-the-run musicians who disguise themselves as women to join an all-female band. The second piece is a rock version of *Moby Dick* which takes place in a girls' school under the tutelage of a transvestite headmistress. One reviewer, bemoaning the failures of both productions, commented, "It has not been a good week for drag" (Hirschorn 1992: 26).

Running parallel to these mainstream drag images is the alternative or experimental form of drag performance. Charles Ludlam, who founded his Ridiculous Theatrical Company in 1967, considered himself the pioneer of a new kind of performance – a female impersonation that could be serious acting, in the same way that Sarah Bernhardt playing Hamlet was considered serious acting. Ludlam is best known for his role as Marguerite Gautier in *Camille* (Plate 4). He stated: "*Camille* is a profoundly feminist work. There is a prejudice against a man dressing up as a woman because women are considered inferior beings. For a man to dress as a woman is a step down" (Ludlam 1992: 19). Ludlam's innovations appear to offer an important direction for those performers and theatre practitioners who seek a new meaning in female impersonation other than the tendency to parody and degrade. Other performers who have taken Ludlam's lead are Charles Busch, Ethyl Eichenberger, and Lypsinka.

Much of the available material on cross-dressing has a straightforward bias for male-to-female transformations, as several authors in this collection make clear.[1] Elizabeth Drorbaugh suggests that "women's cross-dressing is comparatively underexplored." And Alisa Solomon says "to make male-to-female drag the point from which all discussion of cross-dressing follows simply reinstates the presumption of the male as universal."[2] With some significant exceptions, discussed above, examples of contemporary female-to-male performance are harder to come by, mostly confined mainly to actor-training or educational theater. Rhonda Blair, for example, employed cross-gender casting in Albee's *Zoo Story* at the University of Kentucky for the purpose of examining connections between gender and aggression. The production used a round robin performance mode in which two men and two women rotated in and out of Jerry and Peter's roles (Jenkins and Ogden-Malouf 1985: 68). In two productions at Bryn Mawr and Haverford, Susan Ogden-Malouf cast women in all the roles of Molière's *The School for Wives* with the exception of Arnolphe in order to shift focus on the female characters (Jenkins and Ogden-Malouf 1985: 68). Another production of a "classic" text using an all-female cast to highlight male oppression of women was Julia Fischer's production of Aphra Behn's *The Rover* at the University of Minnesota (Walen 1991). As a director, I have produced Brecht's *Man is Man* with an all-women cast in 1984 at Middlesex Polytechnic, London. I wanted to experiment with gendered body language as a way of staging Brecht's connection between militarism and masculinity. As Sande Zeig says: "Gestures are material, as material as clothing which one may 'put on' and 'take off.' Gestures are a concrete means of producing meaning, both the gestures that have been assigned to us and those that have not been assigned to us" (Zeig 1985: 13). In addition to examining the gestural language of men, the actresses/soldiers toted batons. This displacement of a key prop – rifle as baton – created an alienating stage image juxtaposing the frivolous nature of the twirling female majorette with the serious masculine stance of the soldier.

DIFFERENCE AND MEANING IN PERFORMANCE

In June, 1991, a production titled *Sarrasine* by the British Gloria company opened in London (Plate 5). The production was a post-modern performance based on Balzac's 1830 short story (which is supposedly based on historical events that took place in the eighteenth century). Sarrasine is a young, impetuous, talented sculptor who, in Rome for the first time, sees La Zambinella at the opera. He considers her to be the epitome of feminine perfection, falls madly in love with her, and is blind to the fact that "she" is a castrato, a male actor performing female roles owing to the ban on actresses in the papal states. Sarrasine's illusion is shattered and he dies at the hands of hired assassins who are protecting La Zambinella for the Cardinal, who claims to own "her." This story is framed by another telling, that of an anonymous young man trying to seduce Madame de Rochefide by telling her the story of La Zambinella and Sarrasine. In the Gloria production the story of La Zambinella is framed by the Comtesse who becomes obsessed with finding the aged La Zambinella in order to hear his celebrated singing voice.

The Gloria production unfolded as a series of interwoven monologues, songs from both opera and cabaret, and ensemble moments. The role of La Zambinella was played by three different performers: François Testory, a drag performer with Bloolips, played La Zambinella as the young, beautiful creature beloved by Sarrasine; Bette Bourne, a majestically aging actor known for his drag roles with the Lindsay Kemp company, played La Zambinella as an ancient, broken-down diva; and Beverly Klein, an actress known for her deep throaty voice, played the castrato as a softened middle-aged cabaret singer.

The interest in *Sarrasine* goes beyond this critically acclaimed production that toured parts of Europe and the United States. Balzac's story has entered contemporary literary criticism with the publication of Roland Barthes's *S/Z* in 1972. For Barthes, Balzac's short story serves as a literary paradigm for the development of his own critical value system, a system based on a major polarity that Barthes discerns as a way of evaluating texts: the readerly and writerly. Barthes distinguishes between the readerly text as a work merely consumed by the reader; the writerly text, however, pursues his concept of reader as producer, an active participant in determining the multiple possibilities for meaning. In other words, the reader of a writerly text "writes" his/her own plural play of meaning onto the text; the text is no longer one-dimensional, unified, or in any final sense "closed."

Barthes's theoretical stance is grounded in his belief in rereading, a critical activity that can turn all texts into writerly ones:

> Rereading, an operation contrary to the commercial and ideological habits of our society, which would have us "throw away" the story once it has been consumed ("devoured"), so that we can then move on to another story, buy another book, and which is tolerated only in certain marginal categories of readers (children, old people, professors), rereading is here suggested at the outset, for it alone saves the rest from repetition (those who fail to reread are obliged to read the same story everywhere).
>
> (Barthes 1974: 15–16)

How can this concept of rereading and the readerly/writerly text apply to performance, specifically cross-dressed performance? I propose that transvestite theater – cross-dressing in performance – is an exemplary source of the writerly text, a work that forces the reader/spectator to see multiple meanings in the very act of reading itself, of listening, watching a performance. Unlike the stationary, handheld, literary text, a performance text operates in dimensions of real time and real space. Its primary mode of communication is not the spoken or written word; communication occurs through the use of the human body: its movement, gestural language, physicality, costume. One of the first readings we are taught in our lives is gender. Is it a man? Is it a woman? We are taught these as bedrock definitions, with no possibility for multiple meanings, no playful ambiguity. As spectators of transvestite theater we are the Barthesian "producers" of text extraordinaire. We are forced to concede to multiple meanings, to ambiguities of thought, feeling, categorization, to refuse closure.

Sarrasine, the sculptor with an idealized vision of femininity, can only read La Zambinella as a woman. His immersion in the binary, rigidly authoritative logic of gender leads to his downfall. Indeed, his failure to reread is fatal.

Returning to the production of *Sarrasine*, three actors played the single role of La Zambinella. We are given glimpses of the operatic world of the castrati juxtaposed with the music hall world of the drag artist. Are they so different? Two men and one woman move in and out of the role of La Zambinella. All three at various times create an illusion of haunting eroticism. Does the erotic rely on clear definitions of male and female? Or is the blurring of these distinctions its very source? If, for Sarrasine, La Zambinella embodies the perfect woman, is not the hollowness of this ideal made clear in this performance?

Because theater requires a public forum, performance can become a kind of battleground for shifting moral dilemmas and social and cultural change. Within that battleground, cross-dressing becomes, in Bruce Smith's words, "a particularly volatile symbol of liminality, a relaxation of the social rules that hold man's animal passions in check" (Smith 1991: 153). This very sense of playing with thresholds has been a source of controversy since the very beginnings of western theater. From Plato's condemnation of playing the other (a fear that mimetic freedom was formative, men might tend to become the women they imitate on stage) to the Puritanical anti-theatrical tracts of the English Renaissance, the human body has been a site for repression and possession. Theatrical cross-dressing has provided one way of playing with liminality and its multiple possibilities and extending that sense of the possible to the spectator/reader; a way of play, that while often reinforcing the social mores and status quo, carries with it the possibility for exposing that liminal moment, that threshold of questioning, that slippery sense of a mutable self. As spectators we are invited to read the transvestite body crossing the stage in more than one way. An investment in rereading the cross-dressed body both links and underscores the majority of the essays in this collection.

CONTROVERSIES AND CONUNDRUMS

Cross-dressing in performance is riddled with dissension and ambiguity. Contemporary drag, for example, answers to a viable gay aesthetic while simultaneously promulgating misogynistic images of women. Significantly, according to Erika Munk, men do not impersonate women by putting on jeans and tennis shoes; the staple image-making of male drag performers relies on grotesque caricature. In 1985 Munk examined the contemporary modes of cross-dressing:

> At the moment, most men in drag are no more subversive than whites in blackface were when minstrel shows were America's most popular form of entertainment. Before the abolitionist movement grew strong, blackface minstrels scattered bits of anti-slavery sentiment in their portrayals; during the Civil War they became more actively hostile to blacks though remaining pro-Union; but from Reconstruction on they were thoroughly and vehemently racist. There is an instructive parallel here, however inexact: first the women's movement showed us that this particular imitation wasn't

9

the sincerest form of flattery, then Reaganism gave drag performers an embattled interest in defending an image of femininity
which had become a weapon of reaction.

(Munk 1985a: 93)

In another vein Jill Dolan identifies the absence central to the commodity exchange of women in male drag performance:

both spectator and performer conspire to construct a male-
identified subject that is left out of the terms of exchange: women
are non-existent in drag performance, but woman-as-myth, as a
cultural, ideological object, is constructed in an agreed upon
exchange between the male performer and the usually male spectator. Male drag mirrors women's socially constructed roles.

(Dolan 1985: 8)

Peggy Phelan, in the essay that concludes this collection, pursues a
similar theoretical point: "Within the economy of patriarchal desire
which frames – though does not completely define – gay male cross-
dressing, the figure of the woman is appropriated as a sign to validate
male authority."

Is it possible to articulate the differences between what Munk, Dolan,
and Phelan might call a reactionary drag performance and cross-
dressing by men used as social and political commentary? For many,
Charles Ludlam's portrayal of Camille transposed the clichéd, reactionary drag queen's knowing winks and double entendres to a different
mode of cross-dressed performance. Ludlam – considered the father
figure of this "new drag" – claimed to have played Camille "straight." He
stated, "I pioneered the idea that female impersonation could be serious
acting, an approach to character. I became known as the actor who does
real acting in drag" (Ludlam 1992: 16). David Drake articulated this line
of thought on female impersonation by saying that with this new
approach the actor says, "It's not 'Oh, I'm in a dress – get me." It's not
about that. The audience is in on the joke but the people onstage aren't'
(Harris 1991: 23). For Drake, a gay activist actor whose drag career took
off when he took over Charles Busch's role in *Vampire Lesbians of Sodom*,
wearing women's clothing is an essential part of his theatrical vision.
Drake, who in 1991 was performing Miss Deep South in the popular off-
Broadway beauty contest revue *Pageant*, is convinced that with cross-
dressing, "[I am] part of a long line of people expressing themselves in
this way, for comedic and societal purposes. . . . Wearing a dress onstage
is part of a gay aesthetic. It's how one expresses oneself theatrically
through a heterosexual society" (Harris 1991: 19).

Ludlam, Busch, and Drake, all openly homosexual men in theater,
connect their personal life with their theatrical endeavors. In contrast,

10

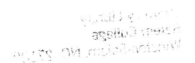

Barry Humphries, the Australian comic who has taken Britain by storm with his creation of Dame Edna Everage, is avowedly heterosexual. (Can this heterosexual proclamation have anything to do with the fact that Humphries's performance has vaulted him into mainstream performance venues and major television appearances?) Humphries, who has been impersonating Dame Edna sporadically since 1955, describes his approach to her as a unique break from the more traditional forms of female impersonation – pantomime Dames and drag queens:

> It's a clown in the form of an Australian housewife. It belongs a bit to the pantomime-dame tradition, though it doesn't exploit the pantomime dame, which is generally a rather sturdy man. The joke of the pantomime dame is the tension between the female of the clothes and the stocky footballer's legs and boots. The drag queen is the other extreme, really a man on the one hand mocking a woman and at the same time trying to titillate the audience. Edna is somewhere in between – closer, really, to character acting: a man playing a woman and making points about life.
>
> (quoted in Lahr 1991: 39)

Significantly Humphries's creation has a life of her own. Not only has Dame Edna Everage authored her own autobiography but she makes regular celebrity appearances beyond her sold-out Drury Lane solo performances. Dame Edna has turned on the Christmas lights in Regent Street, taken a cameo role in the ever popular radio soap opera "the Archers," and even been a guest on BBC radio's "Desert Island Discs." (Lahr 1991: 38). As John Lahr, who has written extensively about Barry Humphries, has it, "Dame Edna is a celebration of contradictions: hilarious and malign, polite and lewd, generous and envious, high and low comic. But the most sensational of all Dame Edna's contradictions is that she is a he" (Lahr 1991: 39). Pointing out that the most sensational contradiction is the cross-dressed Humphries himself, Lahr challenges a previous claim that describes Dame Edna as "amazingly actual . . . a person soon loses the sense that this is a man-as-woman, and accepts her as real." Indeed, Dame Edna Everage is so "real" that she is impersonated at gay drag parties (Lahr 1991: 42). So which is it? Dame Edna's "realness" makes us forget Humphries underneath? By looking at Dame Edna do we read the cross-dressed Humphries? Or do we experience a liminal moment ourselves in moving from one spectatorial interpretation to another? A moment that perhaps suggests to us the impossibility of stable meanings and definitive answers.

Even in the classical Greek period, arguably the one time in which the theatrical convention of cross-dressing was apparently unquestioned, the unstable meaning of the transvestite was used as a thematic underscoring of some of the playwrights' vital concerns. Aristophanes, for

11

example, used cross-dressing to expose the comic hypocrisy of tragic poets – Agathon and Euripides – in his *Thesmophoriazusae*. Euripides in *The Bacchae* uses the transvestite image of Dionysus and the cross-dressed Pentheus as, in Froma I. Zeitlin's words, "an instructive spectacle of the inclusive functions of the feminine in the drama" (Zeitlin 1985: 64). Zeitlin, in her stunning essay "Playing the other: theater, theatricality, and the feminine in Greek drama," analyzes the ambiguous function of the feminine by pointing out that while Dionysus wields power by manipulating a feminized persona, Pentheus is destroyed when he finally succumbs to women's clothing. Zeitlin's essay reaches beyond Euripides' dramatic stagings of cross-dressed men to ask if there is an intrinsic connection between the phenomenon of Athenian tragedy – the first theater of the west – and the feminine. Zeitlin argues that the tragic impulse grounds itself in Greek notions of gender: "the final paradox may be that theater uses the feminine for purposes of imagining a fuller model for the masculine self, and 'playing the other' opens that self to those often banned emotions of fear and pity" (Zeitlin 1985: 80). Tragedy, then, allows the masculine, virile self to undergo an emotional range denied men in normal, civic life. Emotions are gender-identified as feminine. To empathetically experience fear and pity – either as a male audience member observing the instructive spectacle of the tragic character at an Athenian festival, or as the actor himself playing a role in a tragedy – is both a cornerstone to the tragic impulse and a pathway through an emotional minefield culturally defined as feminine.

As Zeitlin points out, Pentheus dressed in women's clothing discovers for the first time the significance of his corporeal self – a flesh and blood body that is ultimately vulnerable and, without its normal masculine accoutrements, defenseless:

> it is perhaps not an accident that only when Pentheus dresses as a woman does he see double for the first time – two suns, two Thebes. This is a symptom of madness, to be sure, attributed by the ancient commentators to inebriation, but madness is the emblem of the feminine, and seeing double is also the emblem of a double consciousness that a man acquires by dressing like a woman and entering into the theatrical illusion. The very fact of that dressing up already demonstrates the premise in unequivocal and theatrical terms.
>
> (Zeitlin 1985: 80)

Zeitlin's premise of theatrical illusion has a Barthesian doubleness of vision to it. Dressing as a woman makes Pentheus see double; the spectators of Euripides' theatrical illusion also participate in this doubling of vision by witnessing the convention of the cross-dressed male

12

actor. Contemporary parallels between Zeitlin's vision of a Greek feminine gendered theater can be found in contemporary drag performance. Charles Ludlam, for example, confirmed this with his performance of Marguerite Gautier in *Camille*:

> You're looked down on if you feel becoming a woman is something to be attained. To defiantly do that and say women are worthwhile creatures, and to put my whole soul and being into creating this woman and to give her everything I have, including my emotions (*remember that the greatest taboo is to experience feminine emotions*), and to take myself seriously in the face of ridicule was the highest statement.
>
> (Ludlam 1992: 19; italics mine)

Theater, then, becomes a kind of playground of feminine emotions for men. The problem, however, is that once the cross-dressed male actor leaves that playground he gets to step back into a patriarchal world that supports and elevates him for his maleness. As Jill Dolan states, "the stakes in the gender game aren't as high for these particular gay men. They can easily assume female roles, knowing that offstage, they wear the clothes of the social elite" (Dolan 1985: 8).

What then about women who cross-dress in performance? What is rendered by the female body in male dress on the stage? Or, as Elizabeth Drorbaugh says later in this collection, "When we see a woman cross-dress as a man, the 'real' in our culture, what do we see?" Three of the following essays focus exclusively on female-to-male impersonation: Lynn Garafola's "The travesty dancer in nineteenth-century ballet," Drorbaugh's "Sliding scales: notes on Stormé DeLarverié and the Jewel Box Revue, the cross-dressed woman on the contemporary stage, and the invert" and Alisa Solomon's "It's never too late to switch: crossing toward power." Solomon examines recent female-to-male cross-dressing during the last two decades in American theater. Solomon's essay contends that "men dressed as women often *parody* gender, women dressed as men, on the other hand, tend to *perform* gender." Her analysis confirms the commentary made by Gerald Rabkin, Bonnie Marranca, and Elinor Fuchs in their published discussion of the 1990–1 New York theater season. Of the many productions under discussion, the critics consider – as does Solomon – the cross-dressing found in the Split Britches/Bloolips coproduction of *Belle Reprieve*, a reworking of Tennessee Williams's *Streetcar Named Desire* (Plate 6). This collaboration between the lesbian/feminist company and the gay drag performers, considered a radical theatrical event, juxtaposed contrary cultural assumptions about male and female drag. Rabkin states: "Notice the difference in the stage names – the men are called 'Precious Pearl' and 'Bette Bourne' while the women use their own names; they create themselves much less in the images of dream iconography" (Marranca, Fuchs, and Rabkin 1991: 13). And Marranca points out another variance between the gendered interplay of cross-dressing found in this pro- duction: "It seems to me that men strive for a kind of androgynous utopia in transvestism. Women, on the other hand, tend to make a critique of maleness, and the quality of admiration is missing in their portrayal of the other sex" (Marranca, Fuchs, and Rabkin 1991: 14). Men strive for idealized feminine perfection and women critique images of masculinity. But even this analysis finds controversial counterpoint in the following essays by Garafola and Drorbaugh that address male impersonation.

THE COLLECTION: A MULTI-VOCAL REPERTOIRE

This collection brings together for the first time a range of recent essays – the majority of which are being published for the first time – which examine and articulate particular aspects of cross-dressing in western culture. The one exception to this is the inclusion of Goethe's essay, "Women's parts played by men in the Roman theater," recently trans- lated by Isa Ragusa and for which I have provided a contemporary commentary. It is admittedly unusual to include a single primary source among contemporary essays. My interest in including this historical document is twofold. First, Goethe's premise of the superiority of male mimesis is central to much of the discussion on cross-dressing. Second, the essay has often been referred to by various scholars to support cross- dressing claims and, as Ragusa points out, it is not part of Goethe's regularly reissued work. It is reprinted here to serve as a touchstone to the historical past and to provide a primary context for much of the work discussed here.

The book's overarching focus is determinedly pluralistic, recognizing as Tracy C. Davis does in her pioneering *Actresses as Working Women: Their Social Identity in Victorian Culture*, "that the topic is multifaceted and that conventional subject boundaries are meaningless" (Davis 1991: xi). Thus, for example, Jean E. Howard's essay utilizes materialist feminism as a critical gridwork; Peggy Phelan's critical perspective relies on femi- nist psychoanalytic theory; and Marybeth Hamilton offers a more straightforward and no less penetrating narrative history of newly re- covered cross-dressing material. Though they do not invoke the term, the essays ask us to view cross-dressing as Barthesian writerly texts, imbued with a doubleness of vision. The authors question the cultural and social assumptions of gender by examining the public display of the performing body and they generally agree that the theater is an import- ant locus for cultural transformation.

Without intending to be a definitive historical account of cross-dressing in western culture, the pluralistic function is furthered by the variety of historical periods under discussion. The Renaissance, eighteenth, nineteenth, and twentieth centuries all serve as particular historical epochs in which cross-dressing in some form proved to be the rule as opposed to the exception. Marjorie Garber makes a claim that "transvestite theater is the *norm*, not the aberration" in spite of the fact that "aberration" is often the accepted view (Garber 1992: 39).

The first essay of the collection, "Cross-dressing, the theatre, and gender struggle in early modern England" by Jean E. Howard, examines a period where perhaps cross-dressing has been most vigorously pursued by contemporary scholars: the English Renaissance. The combination of an active, popular transvestite stage with the puritanical abhorrence of theater created a hotbed of cross-dressing controversy, and a range of historical and literary scholars have examined this period.[3] In this essay she points out that a number of women actually cross-dressed themselves – not in the theater where the convention was decidedly one-way, but daringly on the streets of London. Howard explores the transgressive potential of this practice, delineating its various forms and differences in both the social and the stage practice. Howard provides a refreshing analysis and rereading of four plays where women cross-dress as men: Shakespeare's *Twelfth Night*, *The Merchant of Venice*, and *As You Like It* and Middleton and Dekker's *The Roaring Girl*. Her reading of the cross-dressed Viola, in contrast to many recent analyses of this role, argues for a reinforcement of the gender roles. (Compare Neil Bartlett's contemporary production discussed earlier.)

The exclusionary ethics of the superiority of male mimesis, such as that discussed by Goethe, perhaps finds its most extreme manifestation in the use of castrati in opera.[4] The female soprano voice became very popular in the early seventeenth century but the women were forced to sing privately in courts or salons, never taking to the public stage. The church's ban on women performing in public led to the tacit condoning of castration of young boys. The first recognized castrati performed in the Sistine Chapel Choir in 1599 and though the church publicly forbade castration, it clandestinely practiced it, providing the best musical training in Europe for these young mutilated boys. Castrati dominated opera in the seventeenth and eighteenth centuries and these singers were introduced to the English public in 1667 by theatrical entrepreneur Thomas Killigrew. The castrati perhaps serve as *the* emblem of the contradictions of social and cultural gender anxiety. They were revered for their supreme vocal qualities and their performances were often exuberantly greeted with the shout, "Long live the knife!" (Melicow and Meyer 1983: 761). Simultaneously their mutilated bodies were targets of disgust and derision.[5] Their hold on the English imagination was prodigious and they began to perform there regularly in the early eighteenth century.

The puritanical fear of theater as a feminizing agent for both spectators and performers alike must have been thought to be finally realized when castrated males began to sing on the English stage. Jill Campbell in her essay " 'When men women turn': gender reversals in Fielding's plays" demonstrates, by examining Fielding's plays, how Fielding articulated his anti-theatrical prejudice. Farinelli, considered by many to be the most magnificent castrato in the history of this practice, was often a target of Fielding's satire. Indeed, Fielding blamed the decline of theater on the ambiguous gender and foreign birth (Farinelli was Italian) of the castrato. Another target of Fielding's sexual satire was his view that women were wrongly appropriating male power for their own ends. Campbell shows that Fielding's gender anxiety leads him to compare the castrated male with the cross-dressed woman. Just as Jean Howard has demonstrated the fear of cross-dressed women in the culture and values of the Elizabethan period, so Campbell pursues a parallel theme through her acute analysis of Fielding's pamphlet account of *The Female Husband* (1746).

An important element to the dilemma of the castrati centers on class. Most of the boys who went under the knife came from backgrounds of such extreme poverty that their parents' only choice for survival was to secretly sell their child to the musical academies who trained the young singers. Class is, of course, central to the way in which the dominating cultural hegemony exploits and contains its gender neurosis. Like the young boys offered up to the Catholic priests, young female children were the mainstay of the corps de ballet. These girls from poverty-stricken families became known as "les petits rats" because of their reputation for living backstage and nibbling on the scenery. Lynn Garafola in her essay "The travesty dancer in nineteenth-century ballet" demonstrates how the new marketing of the ballet as an art form was inextricably linked to the commodity value of its female corps of dancers. This process of bourgeois commercialization effectively removed the male dancer from the romantic heroic roles and replaced him with the *danseuse en travesti*. Cross-dressed women began dancing the roles of the cavalier, toreador, and sailor roles once assigned to male dancers. Garafola describes how the changing social climate in France and England in the 1820s resulted in a "new kind of gendering." Prior to this period spectators at the ballet witnessed the etherealized ideal ballerina partnered with the male *danseur noble*, a picture of elegant, aristocratic masculinity. With the banishment of the male from the dance stage, however, the binary aesthetic logic of male/female was dramatically shifted to two contrasting types of femininity. The female role – chaste, graceful, embodying romanticism's quest for the ideal –

was opposed to the travesty role, in which the female dancer dressed in skin-tight trousers that displayed legs, hips, thighs and buttocks, an advertisement for sexuality and provocation.

Just as women replaced men in the romantic ballet so did women and young girls replace boys on both the legitimate stage and the pantomime and music hall stage in mid-Victorian England. Ellen Terry, as Nina Auerbach points out, was an adept boy by the time she was 13, playing serious Shakespeare as well as pantomime (Auerbach 1987: 50). The significance of these boy roles for the actress is that they provided an avenue to a range of active, cheeky, boisterous parts in addition to pathetic waifs and criminal heroes. An exciting variety and versatility of acting style was accessible to women through these boy roles unavailable to women elsewhere on the stage. Auerbach describes how Ellen Terry, as an adult consigned to the traditional female roles, longed for the mobility and stimulation of her younger cross-dressed self. The Victorian convention relied on the cultural belief that only females could express the range of emotions – from innocent pathos to exuberant truancy – necessary to the roles of young males. Zeitlin's thesis of a feminized stage which haunts much of the cross-dressing debate seems fully realized in ballets' travesty roles and the Victorian penchant for cross-dressed girls.

Like the English Renaissance, the Victorian era had a fascination with Ovid and with the metamorphic themes prevalent in his work. From androgynous perfection to Pygmalion-like transformations, both the stage and the artistic iconography of the period played out various forms of visual representation of the female form.[6] Laurence Senelick's essay, "Boys and girls together: subcultural origins of glamour drag and male impersonation on the nineteenth-century stage," exemplifies the Victorian interest in metamorphosis as he traces the beginnings of drag performance as we know it today. Senelick describes how, beginning in 1860, the interest in verisimilitude combined with a new cohesive homosexual subculture to create a new genre of men dressing as women. With this new genre men impersonated lively, young women as opposed to the traditional pantomimic Dame. Likewise, Senelick suggests an origin for male impersonation, contrasting this with the more orthodox breeches roles and principal boy parts of pantomime.

Marybeth Hamilton in her essay " 'I'm the Queen of the Bitches': female impersonation and Mae West's *Pleasure Man*" continues Senelick's discussion of a homosexual subculture by analyzing Mae West's play which she produced in New York City in 1928. Hamilton presents new material on West's pre-filmic career while providing a fascinating glimpse of the social and cultural shift in perceptions of female impersonation. Hamilton charts the shift from male cross-dressing, seen as an acceptable form of family entertainment, to its total ban by city ordinances.

Continuing the argument put forth by Hamilton, Elizabeth Drorbaugh looks at the response to cross-dressing in the mid-twentieth century. Drorbaugh's focus, however, like that of Alisa Solomon already discussed, is on the phenomenon of women cross-dressers. Her essay interweaves feminist theory with historical psychological material on Havelock Ellis's concept of the invert to examine the specific perform-ance history of Stormé DeLarverié.[7] Stormé worked with the Jewel Box Revue, a uniquely multiracial company, from 1955 to 1969. During that time she was the single cross-dressed woman complementing twenty-five cross-dressed men. Drorbaugh's account charts the ideological battle waged between the revue's producers (who claimed their production was wholesome, family entertainment) and various city councils (who insisted on reading the revue as homosexual perversity). Against this fractious background of unstable meanings and longings for fixed iden-tities, Drorbaugh provides a fascinating reading of Stormé's refusal of self-identity. As a woman and as an African-American, her performance shatters any of the conventional answers we may expect.

Notions of identity are pursued by Peggy Phelan in her essay "Criss-crossing cultures" which concludes the collection. Counterposed to Stormé's refusal to identify herself is the longing for identity and self-naming that Phelan finds in the performances of African-American and Latino gay males at the competitive balls staged in Harlem. Phelan's essay connects an earlier analysis of the gotipua dancer – an Indian boy who dances the female role – with an examination of voguing as pre-sented in Jennie Livingston's film *Paris is Burning*. Phelan forcefully articulates the interconnectedness of race, gender, and class as she probes the yearning for mimetic perfection, the notion of "the real" that propels much of what defines this performance mode.

But "realness," as Phelan so articulately reasons, is neither the simple nor the settled characteristic one might take it to be. The authors of the last three essays here – Drorbaugh, Solomon, and Phelan – all ask, in their own way, a similar question: does cross-dressing undermine con-ventional masculine and feminine behavior or does it reinscribe the binary, the "truth" of masculinity and femininity? As this introduction was going to press, Samuel French, the world's largest play publisher and leasing agent, has included a rider in its licensing contracts that insists that directors cast all roles "in the gender as written by the author(s); as performed in the original production; and as listed in the published acting edition" (quoted in Corathers 1992: 6). One hardly needs a more telling reminder of the topicality and ideological heat underlying the issues explored in this collection.

NOTES

1 Homer Dickens's *What a Drag*, Anthony Slide's *Great Pretenders*, Kris Kirk and Ed Heath's *Men in Frocks*, and Peter Ackroyd's *Dressing Up* are all works with a decided focus on men cross-dressing as women. Of course, women's absence from the stage has been an important source of this bias. What I question, however, is the way in which the bias extends to trivialization or straight-forward dismissal of women's cross-dressing such as Roger Baker's comment in his book *Drag*: "male impersonation is an excuse for women to display herself" (Baker 1968: 148).

2 This idea of the male as universal finds a parallel in Thomas Laqueur's fascinating work which in many ways connects with the thematics of this collection. Laqueur has demonstrated that the one-sex model – the belief that women had the same genitalia as men only theirs were inside out – dominated biological thinking for over two millenia. As Laqueur has stated, "In a public world that was overwhelm-ingly male, the one-sex model displayed what was already massively evident in culture more generally: *man* is the measure of all things, and woman does not exist as an ontologically distinct category" (Laqueur 1990: 24).

3 See the bibiliography for various essays on cross-dressing in the Renaissance which include those by Laura Levine, Phyllis Rackin, Stephen Greenblatt, Katherine E. Kelly, and Stephen Orgel. Most recently Ursula K. Heise has extended the debate to Spain (Heise 1992).

4 An example of Laqueur's one-sex model can be found among the castrati. Balani, a popular singer in the eighteenth century, was considered a true-born castrato because his testicles were missing at birth. At one performance, however, he exerted himself so much in trying to reach a high note that "those parts which had so long been concealed by nature dropped into their proper place." Instantly, he lost his voice (Heriot 1956: 47).

5 A point I find disturbing in much that has been written about the castrati is that the sound of the voice forgives all. Goethe, in his essay in this collection, says that "the beautiful and beguiling voices of the *castrati* . . . reconcile one to whatever may appear inappropriate in that disguise." More recently Enid and Richard Peschel have written in praise of the castrati's "supreme legacy" despite the "mutilated bodies, their frequently distorted physical appearance, and their neutered sexual condition" (Peschel 1986: 37).

6 J. S. Bratton, in her article "Irrational dress," describes the play *Is She a Woman?* by William Collier performed at the Queen's Theatre in 1835 in which a brother and sister have changed gender roles: the sister hunts and shoots, the brother paints and dresses lavishly in women's clothes. Both are content with their unorthodox behavior (Bratton 1992: 83–4). This nineteenth-century piece which seems to challenge conventional gender roles finds a Renaissance precedent in Beaumont and Fletcher's play *Love's Cure; or, The Martial Maid* (1625?). The plot outline is virtually the same as the Collier play with the exception that both siblings in the earlier version fall in love with a member of the "proper" sex at the end of the play and this cures them as they revert back to their "natural" gender.

7 Stormé, as a woman who cross-dressed both on and off the stage, follows a precedent set by at least two other women discussed in the collection. Mary Frith, known as Moll Cutpurse, and Charlotte Charke were both "notorious" cross-dressers on and off stage. (See Howard and Campbell in this volume; see my chapter "The power of women on stage: the gender enigma in Renaissance England" (in Ferris 1990) for a discussion of Mary Frith's onstage performance.)

2

CROSS-DRESSING, THE THEATER, AND GENDER STRUGGLE IN EARLY MODERN ENGLAND

Jean E. Howard

How many people cross-dressed in Renaissance England? There is probably no way empirically to answer such a question. Given biblical prohibitions against the practice and their frequent repetition from the pulpit and in the prescriptive literature of the period, one would guess that the number of people who dared walk the streets of London in the clothes of the other sex was limited. None the less, there *are* records of women, in particular, who did so, and who were punished for their audacity; and from at least 1580 to 1620 preachers and polemicists kept up a steady attack on the practice. I am going to argue that the polemics signal a sex–gender system under pressure and that cross-dressing, as fact and as idea, threatened a normative social order based upon strict principles of hierarchy and subordination, of which women's subordination to man was a chief instance, trumpeted from pulpit, instantiated in law, and acted upon by monarch and commoner alike.[1] I will also argue, however, that the subversive or transgressive potential of this practice could be and was recuperated in a number of ways. As with any social practice, its meaning varied with the circumstances of its occurrence, with the particulars of the institutional or cultural sites of its enactment, and with the class position of the transgressor. As part of a stage action, for example, the ideological import of cross-dressing was mediated by all the conventions of dramatic narrative and Renaissance dramatic production. It cannot simply be conflated with cross-dressing on the London streets or as part of a disciplining ritual such as a charivari or skimmington. In what follows I want to pay attention to the differences among various manifestations of cross-dressing in Renaissance culture but at the same time to suggest the ways they form an interlocking grid through which we can read aspects of class and gender struggle in the period, struggles in which the theater – as I hope to show – played a highly contradictory role.

Inevitably, such readings of the past as I am about to undertake are motivated by present concerns and involve taking a position within present critical debates.[2] Recently, discussions of cross-dressing on the Renaissance stage have become an important site for talking about the Renaissance sex–gender system in general and about the possibilities of transgressing or subverting that system.[3] Several questions are at issue. First, was cross-dressing by male actors merely an unremarkable convention within Renaissance dramatic practice; was it a scandal, a source of homoerotic attraction, or an inevitable extension of a sex–gender system in which there was only one sex and that one sex male? Second, were women who cross-dressed – in life or in dramatic fables – successfully challenging patriarchal domination, or were they serving its ends? In this chapter I will enter these debates in part by arguing against those readings of the Renaissance sex–gender system that erase signs of gender struggle, in part by arguing that one should not concede in advance the power of patriarchal structures to contain or recuperate threats to their authority. Positioning myself within materialist feminism, I suggest that contradictions within the social formation enabled opposition to and modification of certain forms of patriarchal domination, and that struggle, resistance, and subversive masquerade are terms as important as recuperation and containment in analyzing Renaissance gender relations and female cross-dressing in particular.[4]

It is clear that cross-dressing in the Elizabethan and Jacobean periods caused controversy. At the far end of the era I am going to examine – that is, around 1620 – James I ordered the preachers of London to inveigh from the pulpit against the practice of women dressing mannishly in the streets of London. That year also saw the publication of the two polemical tracts, *Hic Mulier* and *Haec-Vir*, which respectively attack and defend cross-dressing and which suggest that it had become a practice taken up with special enthusiasm by the fashion-mongering wives of the City who are accused of transgressing both class and gender boundaries (*Hic Mulier* 1620: esp. B4v–C). By wearing ever more ornate clothing, they encroached on the privileges of aristocratic women; by wearing men's clothing, they encroached on the privileges of the advantaged sex. Much earlier, during the reign of Elizabeth, the anti-theatrical tracts had attacked cross-dressing by boy actors, and often these attacks spilled over, as I will discuss, into attacks on women who dressed mannishly. Social commentators such as William Harrison in his *The Description of England* regularly railed against the decline of modesty and decorum in dress, and Harrison ends his diatribe against improperly dressed women by remarking that "I have met with some of these trulls in London so disguised that it hath passed my skill to discern whether they were men or women" (Harrison 1587: 147). The word "trull" is important. The *OED* defines "trull" as "a low prostitute, or concubine; a drab, strumpet, trollop." Harrison's diction links the mannish woman with prostitution, and there were strong discursive linkages throughout the period between female cross-dressing and the threat of female sexual incontinence.

By examining records from Bridewell and the Aldermen's Court between about 1565 and 1605, R. Mark Benbow has indeed found that many of the women apprehended in men's clothing during the period were accused of prostitution.[5] For example, on July 3, 1575, the Aldermen's Court records report that one Dorothy Clayton, spinster, "contrary to all honesty and womanhood commonly goes about the City apparelled in man's atire. She has abused her body with sundry persons and lived an incontinent life. On Friday she is to stand on the pillory for two hours in men's apparell and then to be sent to Bridewell until further order" (Repertory of the Aldermen's Court, no. 19, p. 93). Of Margaret Wakeley in 1601, the Bridewell records read: "[She] had a bastard child and went in man's apparell" (Bridewell Court Minute Book 4, p. 207). Of other women it was simply said that they were apprehended dressed as men, though clearly the suspicion was that any woman so apprehended probably led a loose life. One woman, Johanna Goodman, was whipped and sent to Bridewell in 1569 simply for dressing as a male servant so that she could accompany her soldier husband to war (Aldermen's Court, no. 16, p. 522). It is impossible to tell the "class" position of many of these women.[6] Most appear to be unmarried women of the serving class eking out a precarious living in London. Some are recorded as being "in service" to various London tavern-keepers and tradesmen; some may have worn male clothing for protection in traveling about in the city; some may have been driven to prostitution by economic necessity, with their cross-dressed apparel becoming a demonized "sign" of their enforced sexual availability. It is tempting to speculate that if citizen wives of the Jacobean period assumed men's clothes as a sign of their wealth and independence, lower-class women may well have assumed them from a sense of vulnerability, with an eventual turn to prostitution merely marking the extent of that vulnerability.

That actual women of several social classes did cross-dress in Renaissance England is an important fact, but equally important is how their behavior was ideologically processed or rendered intelligible in the discourses of the time. Specifically, what made adopting the dress of the other sex so transgressive that lower-class women were pilloried and whipped and merchant wives were harangued from the pulpit for doing it? For the most general answer, one can begin by stating that cross-dressing, like other disruptions of the Renaissance semiotics of dress, opened a gap between the supposed reality of one's social station and sexual kind and the clothes that were to display that reality to the world. As is well known, the state regulated dress in early modern England, especially in urban settings, precisely to keep people in the social "places" to which they were born. Elizabethan sumptuary proclamations list those who could wear certain colors (such as purple), certain fabrics (such as silk), and certain adornments (such as spurs, daggers, jewels) (Hooper 1915). In myriad ways clothes distinguished one social group from those both above and below; they were precise indicators of status and degree. To transgress the codes governing dress was to disrupt an official view of the social order in which one's identity was largely determined by one's station or degree – and where that station was, in theory, providentially determined and immutable.

Of course, as social historians such as Lawrence Stone, Keith Wrightson, Barry Reay, and David Underdown have argued, this view of the social order was under enormous pressure (see note 6). Social mobility was a fact, its effects strikingly clear in an urban center such as London, and economic and cultural changes were creating tensions between a social order based on hierarchy and deference and one increasingly based on entrepreneurship and the social relations attendant upon the emergence of early capitalism. In general, official social ideologies did not acknowledge such changes. Rather, enormous energy was devoted to revealing the "monstrous" nature of those who moved out of their places (Barker 1984: 31–3).

Dress, as a highly regulated semiotic system, became a primary site where a struggle over the mutability of the social order was conducted. Thus, Phillip Stubbes begins his *Anatomie of Abuses* of 1583 with an analysis of apparel. For Stubbes transgressions of the dress code don't just *signal* social disruption; they constitute such disruption. That is, when common subjects wear the gold, silk, and diamonds that properly signify an aristocratic birth and calling (as apparently a number did), they demean the social place they have usurped and erase necessary social distinctions. As Stubbes writes in his famous attack on social climbers: "there is such a confuse mingle mangle of apparell in Ailgna, and such preposterous excesse therof, as every one is permitted to flaunt it out, in what apparell he lust himselfe, or can get by anie kind of meanes. So that it is verie hard to knowe, who is noble, who is worshipfull, who is a gentleman, who is not" (Stubbes 1583: C2v). In short, when rules of apparel are violated, class distinctions break down.

Crucially for my argument, Stubbes also says that when women dress as men and when men dress effeminately, distinctions between sexual "kinds" are also obliterated. The stability of the social order depends on maintaining absolute distinctions as much between male and female as between aristocrat and yeoman. Stubbes says: "Our Apparell was given us as a signe distinctive to discern betwixt sex and sex, & therefore one to weare the Apparel of another sex, is to participate with the same, and to adulterate the veritie of his owne kinde" (F5v). In *Hic Mulier* the cross-dressed woman is enjoined to "Remember how your Maker made for our first Parents coates, not one coat, but a coat for the man, and a coat for the woman; coates of seuerall fashions, seuerall formes, and for seuerall uses; the mans coat fit for his labour, the womans fit for her modestie" (B2v–B3). To switch coats is to undo the work of heaven.

Stephen Greenblatt has recently argued that modern notions of sexual difference originate later than the Renaissance and that in at least some Renaissance discourses there appears to be only one sex, women being but imperfectly formed or incomplete men. Greenblatt then goes on to argue that a transvestite theater was a natural, indeed, almost an inevitable, product of such a culture (Greenblatt 1988: 88). In contrast, the writings of Stubbes and the other anti-theatrical polemicists suggest that a transvestite theater could also be read, in the Renaissance, as *un*natural, as a transgression of a divinely sanctioned social order. What are we to make of this seeming contradiction? First, it suggests the need to recognize the plurality of discourses about gender in the Renaissance. If dominant medical discourses such as those cited by Greenblatt saw only male genitalia in both men and women and so, in some sense, authorized the view that there was only one sex, the Bible provided authority, seized by Stubbes, for a two-sex gender system: "Male and female created He them" (Genesis 1:27). In some discourses masculine and feminine identity were seen as points on a continuum, not separate essences, but in works such as the anti-theatrical tracts the language of two kinds predominates, and the injunction from Deuteronomy against wearing the clothes of the other sex is repeated with tiresome frequency.

I think the real point is that the Renaissance needed the idea of two genders, one subordinate to the other, to provide a key element in its hierarchical view of the social order and to buttress its gendered division of labor. The interesting possibility raised by Greenblatt's work is that, in the Renaissance, gender differences may not always or necessarily have been built upon a self-evident notion of biological sexual difference as was to be true in the nineteenth century.[7] This simply means that gender difference and hierarchy had to be produced and secured – through ideological interpellation when possible, through force when necessary – on other grounds. If women were not invariably depicted as anatomically different from men in an essential way, they could still be seen as different merely by virtue of their lack of masculine perfection (softer, weaker, less hot), and their subordination could be justified on those grounds. Then, as now, gender relations, however eroticized, were relations of power, produced and held in place through enormous cultural labor in the interests of the dominant gender. In the early modern period the regulation of dress was part of this apparatus for producing and marking gender difference, though cultural shifts were occurring. As I will suggest later in this chapter, with the emergence of the bourgeois subject, whose essence is defined by her or his interiority, less emphasis was to fall on inscribing gender difference solely on the outside of the body through apparel; rather, the marks of gender difference were to be worn inwardly and made manifest through a properly gendered subjectivity.

Catherine MacKinnon has argued that modern emphasis on sexual difference – as used to justify separate and unequal spheres of work and experience – has obscured the political realities of domination and exploitation that have continued to regulate relations between the genders (MacKinnon 1987). By contrast, writers and speakers in the Renaissance were forthright about man's proper domination of women. Discourses of gender in the Renaissance were overwhelmingly hierarchical, with men and women first and foremost described, respectively, as dominant and subservient, perfect and less perfect, fit for rule and unfit for rule. Behind general assertions of man's proper lordship over woman lay standard appeals to differences between men's and women's capacities to reason, to control passion, etc. In short, languages of difference – though not necessarily biological, anatomical difference – were useful for underpinning sexual hierarchy. Keeping that hierarchy in place was an ongoing struggle, and, as with conflicts over social mobility, gender struggles were in part played out on the terrain of dress.

Disruptions of the semiotics of dress by men and by women were not, however, read in the same way. For a man, wearing women's dress undermined the authority inherently belonging to the superior sex and placed him in a position of shame. At the simplest level, wearing effeminately ornate clothes would, in Stubbes's words, make men "weake, tender and infirme, not able to abide such sharp conflicts and blustering stormes" as their forefathers had endured (Stubbes 1583: E).[8] At a more serious level, men actually wearing women's clothes, and not just ornate apparel, are so thoroughly "out of place" that they become monstrous. And in the anti-theatrical tracts, as in the polemical attacks on effeminate Catholic priests, whose vestments were seen as a kind of female clothing, this monstrosity is figured as sexual perversion.[9] Sodomy haunts the fringes of Stubbes's text (Levine 1986: 134–5). A man, and especially a boy, who theatricalizes the self as female, invites playing the woman's part in sexual congress. For a man this is shameful, as is the carrying of the distaff and the wearing of female dress by defeated or women-mastered warriors from Artegal to Antony. In comic form we see this in *The Merry Wives of Windsor* when Falstaff assumes the clothes of the Wise Woman of Brainford and is roundly beaten by the misogynist Ford.

For women the significance of cross-dressing is different. In the polemical literature women who cross-dressed were less often accused of sexual perversion than of sexual incontinence, of being whores. This was in part because the discursive construction of woman in the Renaissance involved seeing her as a creature of strong sexual appetites needing strict regulation. Her sexual desire was both a mark of her inferiority and a justification for her control by men. As Peter Stallybrass has argued, discipline and control of woman's body were central patriarchal preoccupations (Stallybrass 1986). The orifices of that body were to be policed, the body's actions circumscribed. Women who gadded about outside the home or who talked too much (by male standards) were suspected of being whores – both the open door and the open mouth signifying sexual incontinence. The good woman was closed off: silent, chaste, and immured within the home. As Edmund Tilney asserted in a piece of advice that quickly became a Renaissance commonplace, the best way for a woman to keep a good name was for her never to leave her house (Tilney 1587:E2v–E3). When women took men's clothes, they symbolically left their subordinate positions. They became masterless women, and this threatened overthrow of hierarchy was discursively read as the eruption of uncontrolled sexuality.

The *Hic Mulier* tract of 1620 presents most clearly this particular construction of the cross-dressed woman and the kinds of repression it elicited. Predictably, cross-dressed women are accused in the tract of excessive sexual appetite. With their short waists and French doublets "all unbutton'd to entice," they "give a most easie way to every luxurious action" (A4v). Along with giving over their long hair and their sewing needles, they have given over modesty, silence, and chastity. Moreover, such women signal the breakdown not only of the hierarchical gender system, but of the class system as well. The author calls them "but ragges of Gentry," "the adulterate branches of rich Stocks," "all base, all barbarous" (B). The mannish woman not only produces bastards but is one herself, and she threatens the collapse of the entire class system. The very state is represented as threatened by her behavior. The author writes: "If this [cross-dressing] bee not barbarous, make the rude *Scithian*, the untamed *Moore*, the naked *Indian*, or the wilde *Irish*, Lords and Rulers of well gouerned Cities" (Bv). In a stunning revelation of a racial and national chauvinism, the aspiration of women beyond their place is associated with the monstrous notion of the black in rulership over the white, the Irish over the English. Such consequences – though imagined only – invite reprisal. Predictably, what is evoked at the end is the power of the state and of the patriarch within the family to quell woman's unruliness. The author wants the "powerfull Statute of apparell [to] lift vp his Battle-Axe, and crush the offenders in pieces, so as euery one may bee knowne by the true badge of their bloud, or Fortune" (Cv). For when women "catch the bridle in their teeth, and runne away with their Rulers, they care not into what dangers they plunge either their fortunes or Reputations" (C2); consequently, those who are "Fathers, Husbands, or Sustainers of these new *Hermaphrodites*"

(C2v) must keep them in order, forbid the buying of such outrageous apparel, and instruct them in the virtues which are women's best ornaments. It is important to remember that for the lower-class woman who found herself in the Aldermen's court, it was not just a husband's chastisement but the whip, pillory, and prisons of the state's repressive apparatuses that constituted her as a guilty subject and effected her punishment.

I suggest that these worries about the unruly cross-dressed woman, as well as the various means of control devised to contain the threat she constituted, are signs – as Karen Newman, Catherine Belsey, and others have indicated – that early modern England was permeated not only by well-documented social mobility and unsettling economic change, but by considerable instability in the gender system as well (Newman 1986: esp. 91–2 and Belsey 1985a: 129–221). Social historians have found that in some areas, particularly where economic change was most rapid and changes in family form most pronounced, the disciplining and restraint of women increased during this period, sometimes taking the form of an increased regulation of women's sexuality. Martin Ingram has argued, for example, that the period 1580–1620 witnessed an increase in the prosecution of prenuptial pregnancies and an increasing preoccupation with the strains that bastards placed on the commonweal (Ingram 1985a: esp. 148). By 1620 it was common, as it had not been before, for a woman who produced a bastard to be jailed for up to a year (ibid.: 155).

But not all the disciplining of women went on through the ecclesiastical or civil courts. Charivaris, skimmingtons, or rough ridings were communal rituals through which unruly women were disciplined and insufficiently dominating husbands reproved.[10] The charivari specifically punished a woman's violation of her place in the gender hierarchy. Sometimes she had merely "worn the breeches" in the sense of ordering her husband about; sometimes she was accused of beating her spouse, sometimes of having made him a cuckold. In the punishment of those guilty of female dominance, the couple's inversion of gender hierarchy was mirrored by having the husband ride backward on a horse through the town while the neighbors played cacophonous music. Husband-beating was specifically punished by having the husband or his substitute hold a distaff while riding backward on a horse, while a woman figure, a Lady Skimmington (often a man dressed as a woman), beat him with the ladle used for making butter and cheese. These ritual punishments were all ways of registering the fact that important cultural boundaries had been erased, important social hierarchies disrupted, by the offending parties. Similarly, women who talked too much, who were "scolds," were put upon a cucking stool and dunked in water to stop the incontinence of the mouth.

David Underdown has argued that there was a marked increase in the years immediately after 1600 in charivaris and uses of the cucking stool, especially in communities where traditional modes of ordering society along vertical lines of hierarchy, deference, and paternalism were being disrupted and displaced by what we associate with the more modern horizontal alignment of people within classes and with the rise of proto-capitalist economic practices.[11] For example, the upland wood and pasture areas of the west counties, where there was a strong influx of migrant labor, where families were dispersed and where capitalism had penetrated in terms of the heavy reliance on the putting-out system of cloth manufacture, evidenced more occurrences of charivaris, etc., than did the more centralized village communities of the grain-growing valleys where the population was more stable, families less isolated, and the pace of social change less rapid. Cities were another site of gender tension, in part because they uprooted people from traditional social structures. As many have noted, in times of general social dislocation, fears about change are often displaced onto women.[12] Cities also created new and unsettling positions for women (middle-class women, in particular) to occupy: positions as consumers of urban pleasures such as theatergoing and of the commodities produced by English trade and manufacture; positions of economic power as widows of merchants or as visible workers in their husbands' shops (see Thirsk 1978). A foreign visitor to London, Thomas Platter, noted in 1599 how much freedom English women had *vis-à-vis* their continental counterparts (quoted in Harbage 1941: 76–7). But this freedom, I have been arguing, was unsettling to the patriarchal order. The calls at the end of *Hic Mulier* for the reining-in of women's freedom are but one sign of just how unsettling change in the sex–gender system had become.

Ironically, and this seems to me a chief point to remember, if the vast social changes of the period led to intensified pressures on women and a strengthening of patriarchal authority in the family and the state, these changes also produced sites of resistance and possibilities of new powers for women. I do not mean to contest the view, which I believe is essentially correct, that the English Renaissance was no real Renaissance for women – i.e., it was not for most women a time of increased freedom from patriarchal oppression and exploitation.[13] Yet I want to argue that a dialectical view of history may enable us to attend not only to the success of dominant groups in controlling the social field but also to their failures and to the myriad ways in which subaltern and marginal groups contest hegemonic impositions.[14] If every cultural site is a site of social struggle, attention to the specifics of that struggle may reveal the lapses and contradictions of power that produce social change. Thus, even if, as has been argued, the invention of printing and the admittedly slow increase in women's literacy in the early modern period in part simply increased the ways in which women could be controlled and interpellated as good subjects of a patriarchal order (witness the outpouring of books on housewifery and female piety after the 1580s as documented by Suzanne Hull 1982), none the less skills in reading and writing allowed some women access to some authorities (such as scripture) and to some technologies (such as print), which allowed them to begin to rewrite their inscription within patriarchy. Many scholars, following on the work of William and Malleville Haller (1942), have noted the contradictions in Protestant marriage theory. Chiefly a means for making the home the center of patriarchal control and for instantiating the wife within the domestic sphere, this theory none the less stresses the wife's importance within that sphere and her spiritual equality with her husband. This calls into question the inevitability of starkly hierarchical theories of gender and opens a space for ideas of negotiation, mutuality, and contract between husband and wife, some of which mutuality we may sense being worked out in Shakespeare's romantic comedies.[15]

All of this, I think, bears on how we are to evaluate the various forms of cross-dressing detailed earlier in this chapter. In a period of social dislocation in which the sex–gender system was one of the major sites of anxiety and change, female cross-dressing in any context had the *potential* to raise fears about women wearing the breeches and undermining the hierarchical social order. In the *Haec-Vir* tract the mannish woman declares that not nature but custom dictates women's dress and women's subservient place in society and that, moreover, "*Custome* is an idiot" (*Haec-Vir* 1620: B2v). No matter that the tract changes direction and ends up with the familiar plea that if men would be more mannish, women would return to their accustomed role; the fact remains that through the discussion of women's dress has come an attack on the naturalness of the whole gender-system.

The subversive potential of women dressed as men was self-consciously exploited in other cultural contexts as well. Natalie Davis (1978: 54–5 and 176–83) has documented that cross-dressed figures were prominent both in carnival – where gender and class boundaries were simultaneously tested and confirmed – and in food riots, demonstrations against enclosures, and other forms of lower-class protest. Sometimes in such activities men performed as Lady Skimmingtons, appropriating the powerful iconography of the unruly woman to protest the unequal distribution of power and material goods within the social order (Sharp 1980: 5). Clearly, cross-dressing had enormous symbolic significance, and the state had an interest in controlling it. Witness James I's injunction to the preachers of London that they preach against the practice. The question I want to address in the remainder of this chapter concerns the role of the theater in gender definition. Did the theater, for example, with its many fables of cross-dressing, also form part of the cultural apparatus for policing gender boundaries, or did it serve as a site for their further disturbance? If women off the stage seized the language of dress to act out transgressions of the sex–gender system, did the theater effectively co-opt this transgression by transforming it into fictions that depoliticized the practice? Or was the theater in some sense an agent of cultural transformation, helping to create new subject positions and gender relations for men and women in a period of rapid social change? And how did the all-male mode of dramatic production – the fact of cross-dressing as a daily part of dramatic practice – effect the ideological import of these fictions of cross-dressing?

I will start by stating the obvious: that most Renaissance plays that depict cross-dressing, with the exception of a few works such as *The Roaring Girl* (Plate 7), do not in any direct way constitute "comments" on the cross-dressing debates. The plays are not topical in that way, and in employing cross-dressing motifs they are using a staple of comic tradition with a long dramatic lineage. None the less I contend that many of the cross-dressing plays I have examined are intensely preoccupied with threats to, disruptions of, the sex–gender system. Collectively they play a role in producing and managing anxieties about women on top, women who are not "in their places," but are gadding, gossiping, and engaging – it is assumed – in extramarital sex, and in managing anxieties about the fragility of male authority. Moreover, while the thrust of many of these plays is toward containing threats to the traditional sex-gender system, this is not uniformly so. The plays are themselves sites of social struggle conducted through discourse, and they were produced in a cultural institution that was itself controversial and ideologically volatile. Not surprisingly, the ideological implications of plays that feature cross-dressing vary markedly.

At one extreme, consider Jonson's *Epicoene*. This is a play saturated with the fear of women who have moved or might move from their proper place of subordination, and it points to some of the changing social conditions that made such movement a possibility and a threat. Specifically, the play, set in contemporary London and produced in 1608 for the boy company at Whitefriars, shows how the emerging metropolis offers new opportunities for women to be other than chaste, silent, and obedient. At the center of the play is the cross-dressed Epicoene, but prominent are the Collegians, a coterie of "masculine" women who live away from their husbands, gad about London, and spend money on the consumer goods (such as coaches) and commercial pastimes (such as theater) increasingly available in the city. Money, mobility, and the presence of other women in similar circumstances allow the Collegians to form a society in which female tastes prevail and the authority of men, specifically husbands, is flouted. Masculine authority is further undermined by Mistress Otter, a woman who brought a sizable fortune to her marriage with the sea captain Tom Otter, and who through a favorable marriage contract has retained control of much of that money and consequently of her spouse. As she reminds him, he agreed that she "would be princess and reign in mine own house, and you would be my subject and obey me" (III.i.29–30).[16] The unnaturalness of her relation to the henpecked Tom Otter is a major part of the play's misogynist humor. Though not literally cross-dressed, all of these women symbolically presume to masculine rule and, predictably, display the devouring appetites (for food, drink, things, sex) associated with women who have taken the bit in their teeth and run from their masters.

The play's misogyny finds its most complex expression in the figure of Morose, who, hating everything about the bustling world of London (upon which, ironically, he depends for his wealth), especially hates the thought of marrying a bossy, noisy London wife. Morose, however, needs a wife to produce an heir and thus prevent the passage of his wealth to his nephew, Dauphine. He wants to exploit woman's power of reproduction without having to deal with her demands, desires, and noise. Cleverly, Dauphine uses male cross-dressing to defeat his uncle – presenting a man dressed as a woman to be Morose's wife. The disguised man pretends almost to lack voice, and is presented as one who will spend Morose's wealth not to fulfill her own desires, as the Collegians do, but to display *his* tastes and *his* position. Even her tailors (as is true of the tailor in Petruchio's country house in *The Taming of the Shrew*) will take their directions from Morose, the control of female dress being singled out again as crucial terrain on which masculine authority will be affirmed (II.v.66–82).

We should notice that Dauphine uses the cross-dressed figure of Epicoene to present a masculine construction of female perfection, and then, after the marriage, uses the same figure to embody a demonized version of female misrule, as Epicoene joins the Collegians and outdoes them in filling Morose's house with noise, food, and luxuries. In resolving his power struggle with his uncle, then, Dauphine does not cure his uncle of misanthropy and misogyny but exploits these traits and exacerbates them. He outwits his uncle not with the help of women but at their expense, as the man playing Epicoene usurps woman's person and place to act out degrading masculine constructions of her. In the end, the problem of the complexities of right rule in marriage – in the urban setting of London – is sidestepped. The "wife" turns into a man; neither Dauphine nor Morose marries; and property conveniently passes to the next generation without the disruptive agency of woman having anywhere to be openly acknowledged. In this instance, male cross-dressing becomes a way to appropriate and then erase the troubling figure of wife.

Dramas in which women dress as men, however, are my chief concern, and the question is: do they present constructions of woman that challenge her subordinate place in the Renaissance sex–gender system and so, perhaps, lead to the transformation of that system? Or do they recuperate, countervail, the threat the figure posed in the streets of London and in the symbolic economy of the period? Often plays of female cross-dressing do the latter. They contain, they vitiate, challenges posed to masculine authority and the traditional gender hierarchy by wealthy women, by unmarried women, by women with voices, desires, and, though not a room, a coach of their own.

But that is not all – or the only thing – they do. Some also, through their fables, made possible changes in the way gender identities and gender relations were discursively constructed in the period, and they allowed for challenges to the most repressive aspects of patriarchal ideology.

As a way of placing dramas of female cross-dressing within larger gender struggles, I am going to look briefly at three Shakespearean comedies, beginning with what I consider to be the most recuperative: *Twelfth Night*. Undoubtedly, the cross-dressed Viola, the woman who can sing both high and low and who is loved by a woman *and* by a man, is a figure who can be read as putting in question the notion of fixed sexual difference. For Catherine Belsey (1985b) that blurring of sexual difference opens the liberating possibility of undoing all the structures of domination and exploitation premised on binary sexual oppositions. The play therefore seems susceptible to a radical reading. For Stephen Greenblatt (1988: 92–3), by contrast, Viola's sexual indeterminacy simply signifies the play's projection onto the cross-dressed woman of the process of *male* individuation, a stage in "the male trajectory of identity." For Greenblatt the play thus echoes those Renaissance medical discourses of gender that largely erased the question of female subjectivity and rooted masculine privilege in the natural "fact" "that within differentiated individuals is a single structure, identifiably male" (ibid.: 93).

I wish to question both readings, first by probing just how thoroughly Viola's gender identity is ever made indeterminate and thereby made threatening *to the theater audience* (the subjects being addressed by the play's fictions), second by calling attention to the degree to which the political threat of female insurgency enters the text not through Viola, the cross-dressed woman, but through Olivia, a figure whose sexual and economic independence is ironically reined in *by means* of the cross-dressed Viola. The play seems to me to embody a fairly oppressive fable of the containment of gender and class insurgency and the valorization of the "good woman" as the one who has interiorized – whatever her clothing – her essential difference from, and subordinate relations to, the male.[17] Put another way, the play seems to me to applaud a cross-dressed woman who does not aspire to the positions of power assigned men, and to discipline a non-cross-dressed woman who does.

Discussion of androgyny, or of the erasure of sexual determinacy, always centers with regard to this play on the figure of Viola. Yet the first thing to say about her cross-dressing is that it is in no way adopted to protest gender inequities or to prove that "*Custome* is an idiot." Viola adopts male dress as a practical means of survival in an alien environment and, perhaps, as a magical means of keeping alive a brother believed drowned, and of delaying her own entry into the heterosexual arena until that brother returns. In short, for her, cross-dressing is not so much a political act as a psychological haven, a holding place. Moreover, and this is a key point, from the time Viola meets Orsino in I.iv there is no doubt in the audience's mind of her heterosexual sexual orientation or her properly "feminine" subjectivity. As she says when she undertakes to be Orsino's messenger to Olivia, "Whoe'er I woo, myself would be his wife" (I.iv.42).[18] She never wavers in that resolve even while carrying out the task of wooing Olivia in Orsino's name. The audience always knows that underneath the page's clothes is a "real" woman, one who expresses dislike of her own disguise ("Disguise, I see thou art a wickedness" (II.ii.27)), and one who freely admits that she has neither the desire nor the aptitude to play the man's part in phallic swordplay. The whole thrust of the dramatic narrative is to release this woman from the prison of her masculine attire and return her to her proper and natural position as wife. Part of the larger ideological consequence of her portrayal, moreover, is to shift the markers of sexual difference inward, from the surface of the body and the apparel which clothes that body to the interior being of the gendered subject. The play shows that while cross-dressing can cause semiotic and sexual confusion, and therefore is to be shunned, it is not truly a problem for the social order if "the heart" is untouched, or, put another way, if not accompanied by the political desire for a redefinition of female rights and powers and a dismantling of a hierarchical gender system. Despite her masculine attire and the confusion it causes in Illyria, Viola's is a properly feminine subjectivity; and this fact countervails the threat posed by her clothes and removes any possibility that she might permanently aspire to masculine privilege and prerogatives. It is fair to say, I think, that Viola's portrayal, along with that of certain other of Shakespeare's cross-dressed heroines, marks one of the points of emergence of the feminine subject of the bourgeois era: a woman whose limited freedom is premised on the interiorization of gender difference and the "willing" acceptance of differential access to power and to cultural and economic assets.

Just as clearly, however, the play records the traditional comic disciplining of a woman who lacks such a properly gendered subjectivity. I am referring, of course, to Olivia, whom I regard as the real threat to the

33

hierarchical gender system in this text, Viola being but an *apparent* threat. As Stephen Greenblatt points out, Olivia is a woman of property, headstrong and initially intractable, and she lacks any discernible male relative, except the disreputable Toby, to control her or her fortune (Greenblatt 1988: 69). At the beginning of the play she has decided to do without the world of men, and especially to do without Orsino. These are classic marks of unruliness. And in this play she is punished, comically but unmistakably, by being made to fall in love with the cross-dressed Viola. The good woman, Viola, thus becomes the vehicle for humiliating the unruly woman in the eyes of the audience, much as Titania is humiliated in *A Midsummer Night's Dream* by her union with an ass. Not only is the figure of the male-attired woman thus used to enforce a gender system that is challenged in other contexts by that figure, but also, by a bit of theatrical handy-dandy, the oft-repeated fear that the phenomenon of boy actors dressed as women leads to sodomy is displaced here upon a woman dressed as a man. It is Viola who provokes the love of Olivia, the same-sex love between women thus functioning as the marker of the "unnatural" in the play and a chief focus of its comedy.

The treatment of Orsino, by contrast, is much less satirical. He, too, initially poses a threat to the Renaissance sex–gender system by languidly abnegating his active role as masculine wooer and drowning in narcissistic self-love. Yet Orsino, while being roundly mocked *within* the play, especially by Feste, is ridiculed only lightly by the play itself, by the punishments meted out to him. His narcissism and potential effeminacy are displaced, respectively, onto Malvolio and Andrew Aguecheek, who suffer fairly severe humiliations for their follies. In contrast, Orsino, the highest-ranking male figure in the play, simply emerges from his claustrophobic house in Act V and assumes his "rightful" position as governor of Illyria and future husband of Viola. Moreover, Orsino, in contrast to Olivia, shows no overt sexual interest in the cross-dressed Viola until her biological identity is revealed, though his language often betrays an unacknowledged desire for the Diana within the male disguise. The point, however, is that the text makes his attraction to Cesario neither overt nor the object of ridicule.

If, as I have been arguing, this text treats gender relations conservatively, the same is true of its treatment of class. If unruly women and unmanly men are sources of anxiety needing correction, so are upstart crows. The class-jumper Malvolio, who dresses himself up in yellow stockings and cross garters, is savagely punished and humiliated, echoing the more comically managed humiliation of Olivia, the woman who at the beginning of the play jumped gender boundaries to assume control of her house and person and refused her "natural" role in the patriarchal marriage market. The play disciplines independent women like Olivia and upstart crows such as Malvolio and rewards the self-abnegation of a Viola. In the process, female cross-dressing is stripped of nearly all of its subversive resonances present in the culture at large. There is no doubt that the play flirts with "dangerous matter": wearing clothes of the opposite sex invites every kind of sexual confusion and "mistaking." But the greatest threat to the sex–gender system is not, I would argue, the potential collapse of biological difference through the figure of Viola but the failure of other characters – namely, Orsino and Olivia – to assume culturally sanctioned positions of dominance and subordination assigned the two genders. As I noted earlier, it is ironic that it is through the cross-dressed Viola, with her properly "feminine" subjectivity, that these real threats are removed and both difference and gender hierarchy reinscribed.

Not all the comedies are so recuperative. Portia's cross-dressing, in *The Merchant of Venice* for example, is more disruptive than Viola's precisely because Portia's is not so stereotypically a feminine subjectivity. We first see her chafing at the power of a dead father's control over her. And when she adopts male dress, she proves herself more than competent to enter the masculine arena of the courtroom and to hold her own as an advocate in that arena. Her man's disguise is not a psychological refuge but a vehicle for assuming power. Unlike those cross-dressed heroines who faint at the sight of blood or who cannot wield a sword, Portia seems able to play the man's part with conviction. Her actions hardly dismantle the sex-gender system; but they do reveal that masculine prerogatives are based on custom, not nature, since a woman can indeed successfully assume masculine positions of authority.[19] Portia's actions are aimed not at letting her occupy man's place indefinitely, however, but at making her own place in a patriarchy more bearable. She uses her disguise as Balthazar not only to rescue Antonio from death but also to intervene in the male/male friendship of her husband and Antonio and to gain control over her sexuality while setting the terms for its use in marriage. By the ring trick she gains the right to sleep not with her husband but by and with herself. In a play that insists on the patriarchal authority of fathers to dispose of daughters and that of husbands to govern wives, Portia's ability – through her impersonation of a man – to remain a married virgin and to set the terms for the loss of her virginity is a remarkable feat, as is her ability to guide Bassanio's choice of the correct casket without violating the letter of her father's will.

The incipient subversiveness of this representation – a subversiveness registered still in those modern critical readings of her that stress her manipulative, castrating qualities (Berger 1981) – is not unrelated to the fact that this is the most mercantile of Shakespeare's comedies in its preoccupations. At one level its ideological project is the reconciliation of landed and commercial wealth, a mediation between feudal and proto-capitalist economic systems.[20] But the mediation of class conflict through the trope of marriage in this instance cuts against the patriarchal gender system. By feminizing the gracious world of landed wealth and masculinizing the commercial world of Venice, and by making the latter ill and unable to cure itself, Shakespeare created a fictional structure in which the ideology of male dominance breaks down. The woman is the only source of secure wealth, the only person in the courtroom capable of successfully playing the man's part and ousting the alien intruder. Portia may be "merely" an exception to her culture's patriarchal assumptions, but she, like Elizabeth I, is an exception that has continued to provoke uneasiness.

More complex still is *As You Like It*, which explicitly invites, through its epilogue, a consideration of how secure even the most recuperative representations of cross-dressing could be in a theater in which male actors regularly played women's roles. Rosalind's cross-dressing, of course, occurs in the holiday context of the pastoral forest, and, as Natalie Davis (1978: esp. 153–4) has argued, holiday inversions of order can spur social change or, in other instances, can merely reconfirm the existing order. The representation of Rosalind's holiday humor has the primary effect, I think, of confirming the gender system and perfecting rather than dismantling it by making a space for mutuality within relations of dominance.[21] Temporarily lording it over Orlando, teaching him how to woo and appointing the times of his coming and going, she could be a threatening figure if she did not constantly, contrapuntally, reveal herself to the audience as the not-man, as in actuality a lovesick maid whose love "hath an unknown bottom, like the bay of Portugal" (IV.ii.208) and who faints at the sight of blood. Crucially, like Viola, Rosalind retains a properly feminine subjectivity: "dost thou think, though I am caparison'd like a man, I have a doublet and hose in my disposition?" (III.ii.194–6). As Annette Kuhn (1985: esp. 55–7) has argued, in certain circumstances cross-dressing intensifies, rather than blurs, sexual difference, sometimes by calling attention to the woman's failure to perform the masculine role signified by her dress. Rosalind's fainting constitutes such a reminder, endearing her to earlier generations of readers and audiences for her true "womanliness." And, as in *Twelfth Night*, the thrust of the narrative is toward that long-delayed moment of disclosure, orchestrated so elaborately in Act V, when the heroine will doff her masculine attire along with the saucy games of youth and accept the position of wife, when her biological identity, her gender identity, and the semiotics of dress will coincide.

Where this account of the consequences of Rosalind's cross-dressing becomes too simple, however, is in a close consideration of the particular way in which Rosalind plays with her disguise. Somewhat like Portia, Rosalind uses her disguise to redefine (albeit in a limited way) the position of woman in a patriarchal society. The most unusual aspect of her behavior is that, while dressed as a man, Rosalind impersonates a woman, and that woman is herself – or, rather, a self that is the logical conclusion of Orlando's romantic, Petrarchan construction of her. Saucy, imperious, and fickle by turns, Rosalind plays out masculine constructions of femininity, in the process showing Orlando their limitations. Marianne Doane (1982) has argued that "masquerade," the self-conscious staging, parody, exaggeration of cultural constructions of self, offers women a choice between simple identification with male selves – which is how she reads the meaning of cross-dressing – or simple inscription within patriarchal constructions of the feminine. In my view, the figure of Rosalind dressed as a boy engages in playful masquerade as, in playing Rosalind for Orlando, she acts out the parts scripted for women by her culture. Doing so does not release Rosalind from patriarchy but reveals the constructed nature of patriarchy's representations of the feminine and shows a woman manipulating those representations in her own interest, theatricalizing for her own purposes what is assumed to be innate, teaching her future mate how to get beyond certain ideologies of gender to more enabling ones.

Moreover, this play, more than other Shakespearean comedies, deliberately calls attention to the destabilizing fact that it is boy actors playing the roles of all the women in the play, including Rosalind. There is a permanent gap on the stage between the incipiently masculine identity of the boy actors and their appropriation of the "grace,/ Voice, gait, and action of a gentlewoman" – to borrow a definition of the actor's task from the job assigned the Page in the Induction to *The Taming of the Shrew* (Ind., ll.131–2). I agree with Kathleen McLuskie (1987: esp. 121) that at some level boy actors playing women must simply have been accepted in performance as a convention. Otherwise, audience involvement with dramatic narratives premised on heterosexual love and masculine/feminine difference would have been minimal. It is also true, as McLuskie and others suggest, that the convention of the boy actor playing a girl can, at any moment, be unmasked as a convention and the reality (that the fictional woman is played by a boy) can be revealed. One of those moments occurs at the end of *As You Like It*. The play has achieved closure in part by reinscribing everyone into her or his "proper" social position. The duke is now again a duke and not a forest outlaw, Rosalind is now Rosalind and not Ganymede, and so forth. But when in the Epilogue the character playing Rosalind reminds us that she is played by a boy, the neat convergence of biological sex and culturally constructed gender is once more severed. If a boy can so successfully personate the voice, gait, and manner of a woman, how stable are those boundaries separating one sexual kind from another, and thus how secure are those powers and privileges assigned to the hierarchically superior sex, which depends upon notions of difference to justify its dominance?[22] The Epilogue playfully invites this question. That it does so suggests something about the contradictory nature of the theater as a site of ideological production, an institution that can circulate recuperative fables of cross-dressing, reinscribing sexual difference and gender hierarchy, and at the same time can make visible on the level of theatrical practice the contamination of sexual kinds.

I would argue that a play like *Epicoene* comes much closer than a play like *As You Like It* to making clear what is at stake in maintaining a hierarchical two-gender system. Money is at stake – who will control the spending of wealth and the passage of property. Control of other assets is at stake – such as woman's reproductive capabilities and her time and labor. Morose wants a legitimate heir and a wife who will not gad and gossip and spend money but will manage his house and display his wealth as he dictates. Only *The Merchant of Venice*, of Shakespeare's romantic comedies, because of its emphasis on the control of wealth and of woman's sexuality comes as close as *Epicoene* to revealing the material consequences of patriarchy's gender ideology. At best these other comedies reveal the constructed nature of gender definitions and distinctions even as they return women, at play's end, to their admittedly somewhat ameliorated places within the dominant patriarchal order. Such revelations of the human, rather than the divine, origins of the gender system are not negligible. They are part of that process of demystification that Thomas Sorge (1987) and others have seen as one of the chief social functions of the Renaissance stage, one of the ways it participated in the historical process eventuating in the English Revolution.

In a few cases, however, plays of female cross-dressing were more than sites where creative accommodations to a demystified patriarchy were enacted. Instead they protested the hierarchical sex–gender system and the material injustices that, in conjunction with other social practices, it spawned. The obvious case in point is Middleton and Dekker's *The Roaring Girl*, a work based on an actual London woman's life and a work traversed by discourses of social protest not found in most of the plays I have so far examined. First, as Mary Beth Rose (1984) has argued, this play is unusual in presenting us with a woman who does not use male dress *as a disguise*. She does not don male apparel to escape from danger or to pursue a husband. In this she differs from Mary, the hero's love interest in the drama, who in the first act puts on the clothes of a seamstress to approach her lover secretly and later dresses as a boy. Her disguises give Mary a certain freedom, but their sole purpose is to enable her, ultimately, to become a wife, though even she defies patriarchal authority by taking a husband of her own choosing. By contrast, Moll adopts male dress deliberately and publicly; and she uses it to signal

38

her freedom from the traditional positions assigned a woman in her culture. As she says to the young hero:

> I have no humour to marry, I love to lie o' both sides o'th'bed myself, and again o'th'other side; a wife you know ought to be obedient, but I fear me I am too headstrong to obey, therefore I'll ne'er go about it. I love you so well, sir, for your good will I'd be loath you should repent your bargain after, and therefore we'll ne'er come together at first. I have the head now of myself, and am man enough for a woman; marriage is but a chopping and changing, where a maiden loses one head and has a worse i'th'place.[23]
>
> (II.ii.36–44)

The issue is control. Refusing a male head, Moll asserts a freedom extraordinary for a woman. Dressed as a woman she enters the merchants' shops; dressed as a man she fights with Laxton at Gray's Inn Fields; and at the end of the play she moves easily among the rogues and "canters" of the London underworld.

Of course, a woman who thus contravenes the accepted conventions governing female dress – who smokes a pipe, carries a sword, bobs her hair, and dons French slops (see the frontispiece of the play for an illustration of such a subversive and disorderly woman (Plate 7)) – invites being read as a whore, as a woman at the mercy of an ungovernable sexual appetite. Importantly, the play insists on Moll Frith's chastity. This insistence can be read as a way of containing the subversiveness of her representation, of showing her accepting the central fact of the good woman's lot – i.e., that she not use her sexuality except in lawful marriage. Another way to read the insistence on chastity is to see it as an interruption of that discourse about women which equates a mannish independence with sexual promiscuity. In the play Moll is constantly read by the men around her as a potential bedmate, a sexual prize. Even Trapdoor, the servant hired to spy on Moll, assumes he can master her sexually, that, when "her breeches are off, she shall follow me" (I.ii.223). Laxton, the gentleman rake, makes the same mistake, finding her mannish clothes sexually provocative, the gap between the semiotic signals of her dress and her well-known biological identity making her hidden body the more alluring. Tellingly, Moll both refuses Laxton's sexual advances and offers him a reading of some women's sexual promiscuity that is refreshingly economic in orientation. If the master narrative of the *Hic Mulier* tracts is that women's sexual looseness stems from their unnatural aspiration beyond their assigned place, that is, beyond the control of the male, Moll argues that women are unchaste because they are poor. She may give us the best gloss on those women, dressed as men, who were hauled before the Aldermen's Court and accused of "lewd" behavior. To Laxton, Moll says:

In thee I defy all men, their worst hates,
And their best flatteries, all their golden witchcrafts,
With which they entangle the poor spirits of fools.
Distressed needlewomen and trade-fallen wives,
Fish that must needs bite or themselves be bitten,
Such hungry things as these may soon be took
With a worm fastened on a golden hook:
Those are the lecher's food, his prey, he watches
For quarrelling wedlocks, and poor shifting sisters,
'Tis the best fish he takes: but why, good fisherman,
Am I thought meat for you, that never yet
Had angling rod cast towards me?' cause, you'll say,
I'm given to sport, I'm often merry, jest:
Had mirth no kindred in the world but lust?

(III.i.90–103)

Rather than agreeing that it is women's nature that is to be endlessly debated and her person disciplined, Moll turns attention to the social realities that create conditions for the sale of sex and to the assumptions made by men about women.

More than the other cross-dressed women we have so far examined, Moll is also associated with various sorts of protest against social injustice. At the beginning of Act V she is explicitly associated with Long Meg of Westminster, another colorful character described in Renaissance ballads and in a lost play, who embodied lower-class resistance to established authority and for much of her life protested against the injustices of patriarchal marriages.[24] For the last two acts of *The Roaring Girl*, Moll, like Meg of Westminster and a bit like a Lady Skimmington, protests against and remedies various social injustices. It is she who, for example, rescues Jack Dapper from the law when his father would have him unjustly incarcerated, proclaiming "If any gentleman be in scrivener's bands/Send but for Moll, she'll bail him by these hands" (III.iii.216–17). She is also instrumental in interrupting the tyrannous plans of Sebastian's father to keep his son, for economic reasons, from marrying Mary Fitz-Allard. And she is the one who unmasks the knavery of the two lowlife characters, Tearcat and Trapdoor, who are impersonating wounded soldiers and in that guise fleecing people for alms money. Further, she makes a thief promise to return a purse he had filched from one of her friends. In short, Moll is heavily involved in righting wrongs, though it is not always perfectly clear that she embodies a consistent social philosophy or class–gender position. For example, seeing marriage as a straitjacket for herself, she none the less promotes it for Mary Fitz-Allard and other women. No thief, she none the less knows all the lowlife types of London and knows their canting jargon, their thieving tricks.

40

Middleton and Dekker have attempted to decriminalize Moll, to present her as neither thief nor whore, to make her an exception to society's rules concerning women's behavior but not a fundamental threat to the sex–gender system. But her portrayal is not entirely innocuous and sanitized. It partakes of discursive traditions of social protest, including protest against Renaissance patriarchal marriage and women's position within such marriages, that contradict the tendency simply to construct her as an eccentric "exception." In the final moment of the play, asked when she will marry, Moll replies:

> . . . I'll tell you when i'faith:
> When you shall hear
> Gallants void from sergeants' fear.
> Honesty and truth unslandered,
> Woman manned but never pandered,
> Cheaters booted but not coached,
> Vessels older ere they're broached.
> If my mind be then not varied,
> Next day following I'll be married.
>
> (V.ii.216–24)

Enigmatic, like the fool's prophecy in *Lear*, Moll's prophecy is clear in its utopian aspirations, clear in making the ending of women's oppression a central part of a more encompassing utopian vision of social reform. Unlike the other plays I have discussed, *The Roaring Girl* uses the image of the cross-dressed woman to defy expectations about woman's nature and to protest the injustices caused by the sex–gender system.[25] And if comedy demands a marriage, it gets the marriage of Mary Fitz-Allard and Sebastian, but not the marriage of Moll.

What then can we say, in conclusion, about female cross-dressing on the Renaissance stage? I think that, often, female cross-dressing on the stage is not a strong site of resistance to the period's patriarchal sex–gender system. Ironically, rather than blurring gender difference or challenging male domination and exploitation of women, female cross-dressing often strengthens notions of difference by stressing what the disguised woman *cannot* do, or by stressing those feelings held to constitute a "true" female subjectivity. While some plots do reveal women successfully wielding male power and male authority, they nearly invariably end with the female's willing doffing of male clothes and, presumably, male prerogatives. It is hard to avoid concluding that many cross-dressing comedies have as their social function the recuperation of threats to the sex–gender system, sometimes by ameliorating the worst aspects of that system and opening a greater space for woman's speech and action. Yet this recuperation is never perfectly achieved. In a few plays, such as *The Roaring Girl*, the resistance to patriarchy and its

41

marriage customs is clear and sweeping; in others, such as *The Merchant of Venice*, the heroine achieves a significant rewriting of her position within patriarchy even as she takes up the role of wife. Others, simply by having women successfully play male roles, however temporarily, or by making women's roles the objects of self-conscious masquerade, put in question the naturalness, the inevitability, of dominant constructions of men's and women's natures and positions in the gender hierarchy.

Moreover, I think it is a mistake to restrict our considerations of the ideological import of Renaissance theater to any analysis of the scripts, even an analysis of the scripts in relation to extradramatic practices and texts. Ideology is enacted through all the theater's practices, from its pricing structure for admission to the times of its performances. As we have seen, the fact of an all-male company complicates the ideological import of these cross-dressing plays in ways that simply don't obtain when, as is generally true today, women play women's parts on the stage. Moreover, whatever the conservative import of certain cross-dressing fables, the very fact that women went to the theatre to see them attests to the contradictions surrounding this social institution. Women at the public theater were doing many of the very things that the polemicists who attacked cross-dressing railed against. They were gadding about outside the walls of their own houses, spending money on a new consumer pleasure, allowing themselves to become a spectacle to the male gaze.

Andrew Gurr (1987: esp. 61–4) has concluded in his exhaustive study of Shakespeare's audience that women were indeed at the public theaters, and that many of them were probably citizens' wives – wives of the shopkeepers and merchants increasingly playing a leading part in the life of urban London. These were the very women whose enhanced freedoms made them threats to the patriarchal order, and who were heavily recruited to the banner of chastity, silence, obedience, and domesticity. This is, in fact, the group – the gentlewomen citizens of London – to whom, as early as 1579, Stephen Gosson (1579: Fv–F4v) spoke in his warnings against the pollutions of the playhouse, enjoining them to "Keep home and shun all occasions of ill speech." His argument was that women who went to the theater made themselves spectacles and therefore vulnerable to the suspicion of being whores. "Thought is free; you can forbidd no man, that vieweth you, to noute you and that noateth you, to judge you, for entring to places of suspition" (F2). It might be all right for court ladies to put themselves on public display, to occupy a box at the private theaters, for example, but not middle-class wives. Massinger (1964: 100) ends *The City Madam* by warning city dames "to move/In their spheres, and willingly to confess/In their habits, manners, and their highest port,/A distance, twixt the city and court" (V.iii.153–6). One of the most transgressive acts the real Moll Frith performed was to sit, in her masculine attire, on the stage of the Fortune and to sing a song upon the lute. She did what only court ladies and gallants were allowed to do: she made a spectacle of herself.

Of course, the average woman playgoer did not claim the clothes of the male gallant or his place upon the stage; none the less, to be at the theater, especially without a male companion, was to transgress the physical and symbolic boundaries of the middle-class woman's domestic containment. Perhaps unwittingly, these women were altering gender relations. The public theater was not a ritual space, but a commercial venture. Citizens' wives who went to this theater might, at one extreme, be invited by its fictions to take up positions of chastity, silence, and obedience, but at another extreme by its commercial practices they were positioned as consumers, critics, spectators, and spectacles. The theater as a social institution signified change. It blurred the boundaries between degrees and genders by having men of low estate wear the clothes of noblemen and of women, and by having one's money, not one's blood or title, decide how high and how well one sat, or whether, indeed, one stood. To go to the theater was, in short, to be positioned at the crossroads of cultural change and contradiction – and this seems to be especially true for the middle-class female playgoer who by her practices was calling into question the "place" of woman, perhaps more radically than did Shakespeare's fictions of cross-dressing.

NOTES

1 For the idea of the sex–gender system, see Rubin (1975: 157–210).
2 As Louis Montrose argues, speaking of new forms of historical inquiry: "Integral to this new project of historical criticism is . . . a recognition of the agency of criticism in constructing and delimiting the subject of study, and of the historical positioning of the critic vis-à-vis that subject" (Montrose 1986: 5–12 esp. 7). Clearly, my investments in contemporary feminism have shaped the focus of the present essay, which is an attempt to contribute to the collective project of making intelligible a gender system in many ways quite different from our own and yet one in large measure having the similar political effect of women's subordination and exploitation.
3 In regard to boys playing women's roles, see Levine (1986), who argues that this practice brought to the surface deep-seated fears that the self was not stable and fixed but unstable and monstrous and infinitely malleable unless strictly controlled. Behind the repeated protestations that the boy actors will be made effeminate by wearing women's clothing, she argues, lies the fear they will found to have no essential being. By contrast, Greenblatt (1988: esp. 88) argues that an all-male acting troupe was the natural and unremarkable product of a culture whose conception of gender was "teleologically male." Jardine (1983: 9–36) sees the Renaissance public theater as in large measure designed for the gratification of male spectators and argues that in many cases it was homoerotic passion that the boy actors aroused in their male audience. McLuskie (1987) in effect critiques this position by arguing that it collapses theatrical practice with real life and that in performance the sex of

the actor is irrelevant and, on the Renaissance stage, conventional. A similar divergence of opinion characterizes scholarship on the presence of cross-dressing in dramatic works of the period. Dusinberre (1975: 231–71), for example, argues that plays of cross-dressing were sites where the freedom of women to play with gender identity was explored; while Park (1980: 100–16) suggests that women who cross-dress in these scripts doff their disguises willingly, providing the – to men – gratifying spectacle of spunky women who voluntarily tame themselves to suit male expectation. Rackin (1987) and Belsey (1985b) both argue that at least in some instances cross-dressing on the stage opens up the possibility of revealing the plurality and fluidity and cultural-constructedness of gender, thus toppling the essentialist binarism that was used to hold women in an inferior place.

4 Materialist or socialist feminism, better known in Britain than in the United States, assumes that gender differences are culturally constructed and histor-ically specific, rather than innate, and that the hierarchical gender systems based on these differences can therefore be changed. Material feminists also recognize the plural nature of woman, i.e., that factors such as class and race forbid women sharing an easy "sisterhood." This suggests the undesirability of analyzing the gender system in isolation from other systematic modalities of oppression. For a brief introduction to materialist feminism, see Newton and Rosenfelt (1985: xv–xxxix). For an indication of the usefulness of meterialist feminism to the analysis of drama, see Case (1988). For a more complicated account of the history of materialist feminism, its relation to other feminisms, and the conceptual problems it presently faces see Omvedt (1986).

5 I am extremely grateful to Professor Benbow for sharing his research with me. The following material is taken from his transcription of records from the Repertories of the Aldermen's Court in the London City Record Office and from the Bridewell Court Minute Books between approximately 1565 and 1605.

6 As Leonard Tennenhouse pointed out in an astute critique of this paper, class categories derived from nineteenth-century culture are in some degree anachronistically imposed on the Renaissance social formation, which was, in part, simply a two-class culture with a tiny but powerful privileged group composed of gentry and aristocracy poised above an undifferentiated mass of laboring "others." Yet social historians of the period increasingly speak of the clash in the late sixteenth and early seventeenth centuries between emergent capitalistic social relations and older modes of social organization based on status or degree. Especially in London, the emergence of an entrepreneurial middle class, "the middling sort," seems an established fact by 1600, and to some degree enclosure movements, the putting-out system of cloth manufacture, and changes in agricultural practice were creating a rural proletariat dependent on wage labor for subsistence and creating that pool of "vagabonds and masterless men" so feared by the Elizabethan authorities. For discussions of class and status structures in this period, see Underdown (1985a), Stone (1966), Wrightson (1982), Reay (1985), and Sacks (1988).

7 Behind Greenblatt's essay stands the work of Thomas Laqueur, particularly his important essay (1986).

8 As Norbert Elias and others have noted, here we witness the highly mediated repercussions of the transition from a feudal culture, in which military prowess was required of the ruling orders, to a courtier culture, in which the arts of civility and social negotiation are more urgent(Elias 1939).

9 For a venomous attack on the theatricality of the Catholic Mass and the

sexual perversions encouraged by the wearing of ornate vestments by lewd priests see Becon (1637: esp. 733–75).

10 For discussion of these disciplining rituals, see Ingram (1985b), Underdown (1985b), and Davis (1978).

11 See Underdown (1985b: esp. 125–35); for an expanded version of his argument, see Underdown(1985a).

12 For a general statement of this argument in regard to the Renaissance, see Jardine (1983: esp. 162).

13 I think it is as yet impossible to give a definitive answer to Joan Kelly's famous question "Did women have a Renaissance?" (Kelly 1984). If Dusinberre's (1975) account of the freedoms opening up for middle-class women in the Renaissance seems to take too little account of the recuperative powers of patriarchal systems, Stone's (1977) more sober account of the intensification of patriarchy toward the end of the sixteenth century, especially among the upper classes, tends simply to assign to patriarchy the absolute power it claimed for itself and to ignore the possibilities for women's resistance, which it has been the work of feminist scholars such as Belsey (1985a) and others to explore. We know that the gender system *changed* in the Renaissance as new family structures emerged, as patterns of work and production changed, etc.; but change does not necessarily mean progress or the amelioration of oppression. Feminist scholarship is in the process of discovering where these changes made possible instances of resistance and female empowerment, as well as the many ways in which change simply meant the old oppression in new guises.

14 In the wake of Althusser's writings on ideology (see, for example, Althusser 1971) much emphasis in cultural analysis fell on the success of various apparatuses in interpellating subjects within dominant ideologies. Such an emphasis allowed little latitude for theorizing change or resistance. As a corrective, it is important to emphasize what Althusser states but does not develop: namely, that "ideological state apparatuses" are not only the stake but the site of class struggle (p. 147) and that resistance occurs within them; and to make use of Gramsci's (1971) work on the way subaltern groups contest hegemonic ideological practices. For a useful overview of contemporary views of ideology, see Boswell *et al.* (1986).

15 For an important study of the juxtaposition of patriarchal absolutism and contractual theories of state and family relations, see Schochet (1975). For a fascinating examination of how Restoration drama embodies these changing ideologies of marriage and authority see Staves (1979).

16 Jonson (1966). All further references to *Epicoene* are to this edition of the text.

17 For a much less political reading of the play see my own essay (Howard 1984). In that essay, while accurately mapping the actual and metaphorical disguises in the play, I did not explore the political implications of the text's insistence on the return to an "undisguised" state – what that meant for aspiring servants, independent women, etc. In short, I accepted the play's dominant ideologies as a mimesis of the true and natural order of things.

18 Shakespeare (1974: 416). All further references to *Twelfth Night* and other Shakespearean texts are taken from this edition of the plays.

19 Here I am agreeing with Newman (1987), that Portia is an unruly woman who challenges masculine rhetorical hegemony and intervenes in the traffic in women upon which Renaissance patriarchal authority depended.

20 For a complex argument concerning the play's relationship to changing economic practices in the Renaissance see Cohen (1985: 195–211).

21 For the view that the romantic comedies champion mutuality between the sexes, see Novy (1984: esp. 21–44).

22 For good discussions of the disruptive effects of the Epilogue, see Belsey (1985b), and Rackin (1987).

23 Middleton and Dekker (1976: 47). All other quotations from the play refer to this edition.

24 For a good discussion of both Moll Frith and Long Meg of Westminster, see Shepherd (1981: esp. 67–92).

25 After finishing my own essay, I was delighted to come upon Dollimore (1987), in which he argues that female cross-dressing can, in some circumstances, be a mode of transgression and not an exemplification of false consciousness. I found particularly useful his critique of the essentialist theories of subjectivity underlying the assumption, in many discussions of female cross-dressing, that it is a social practice that distorts or erases authentic female identity.

1 Neil Bartlett directed the Goodman Theater's 1992 production of *Twelfth Night*. Top: Viola Cleft (played by Nikkieli Lewis) is reunited with her twin brother Sebastian (played by William Jones). Bottom: Sir Toby Belch (played by Lola Pashalinski) conspires with Maria (Robin Baber). (Photos: Eric Y. Exit.)

2 Kelly Maurer as Hamlet and Susan Hightower as Ophelia in Eric Hill's Stage West production (Springfield, MA, 1991).

3 Herculine Barbin, the nineteenth-century hermaphrodite, from Caryl Churchill's and David Lan's *Mouthful of Birds* at the Birmingham Repertory Theatre, and the Royal Court, 1986. (Photo: Phil Cutts.)

4 Charles Ludlam as Marguerite Gautier in The Ridiculous Theatrical Company's 1973 production of *Camille* with Bill Vehr as Armand. (Photo: John Stern.)

5 Bette Bourne, François Testory, and Beverly Klein in Gloria's production of *Sarrasine* by Neil Bartlett and Nicolas Bloomfield. (Photo: Sean Hudson.)

6 Split Britches/Bloolips 1991 production of *Belle Reprieve* at La Mama, with Lois Weaver as Stella and Peggy Shaw as Stanley. (Photo: Sheila Burnett.)

The Roaring Girle.

OR
Moll Cut-Purse.

As it hath lately beene Acted on the Fortune-stage by
the Prince his Players.

Written by *T. Middleton* and *T. Dekkar.*

My case is alter'd, I must worke for my living.

Printed at *London* for *Thomas Archer*, and are to be fold at his
fhop in Popes head-pallace, neere the Royall
Exchange. 1611.

7 Frontispiece to Middleton and Dekker's play *The Roaring Girl; or, Moll Cut-Purse*, 1611. The character of Moll Cutpurse was based on the real life of Mary Frith, who cross-dressed in daily life.

8 Pen drawing of the castrato Farinelli in gala dress attributed to Antonio Maria Zanetti. The drawing displays the oversized legs and arms attributed to castration. (© British Museum.)

3

GOETHE'S "WOMEN'S PARTS PLAYED BY MEN IN THE ROMAN THEATER"

Translated by Isa Ragusa

TRANSLATOR'S FOREWORD

The following essay is an eyewitness report by a modern man of letters of one of the last all-male performances that could still be considered the product of an unbroken theatrical tradition. On January 3, 1787, in Rome Johann Wolfgang von Goethe, whose lifelong interest in the theater both as a dramatist and as a director is well known, saw a performance of Carlo Goldoni's *La Locandiera*. Ten years later the invading French armies declared a Roman Republic to succeed the defeated papal states and the laws banishing women from the stage were repealed.

Goldoni's play was first presented in Venice – where women were permitted to perform – in 1753, with a woman playing the title role of Mirandolina, the innkeeper. Goethe knew the play well, having produced it in Weimar in 1777. In Rome he meets this new experience – of seeing a man in the title role of Mirandolina.

This essay is not part of Goethe's *Italienische Reise* and has therefore not been much publicized. It was written for Wieland's *Der Teutsche Merkur*, the influential journal of the literati of the period, in which it appeared anonymously in 1788 as "Auszüge aus einem Reise-Journal."[1] It has not been translated into English as far as I know and does not appear in the usual excerpted versions of Goethe's works or in his thoughts on the theater. However, it was found by the young Benedetto Croce when he researched the subject of the Roman theater for an introduction to Alessandro Ademollo's *I teatri di Roma nel secolo decimosettimo* in 1888, and he provided a translation into Italian for this work.[2]

WOMEN'S PARTS PLAYED BY MEN IN THE ROMAN THEATER

Johann Wolfgang von Goethe

Nowhere in the world does the past speak to the observer so directly and with so many voices as in Rome. Thus it is that one among many customs has by chance survived there which bit by bit has almost completely disappeared everywhere else.

The ancients, at least in the best periods for art and morality, did not permit women on the stage. Their plays were organized in such a way that either women could be more or less dispensed with, or else female roles were played by an actor who had prepared himself especially for them. This is still the case in modern Rome and in the rest of the papal states, except for Bologna, which among other privileges also enjoys the freedom of being able to admire women on its stages.

This Roman tradition has been the object of so much criticism that it may be permitted to say a word in its favor, or at the very least (in order to avoid seeming altogether paradoxical) call attention to it as an anti-quarian survival.

Opera is not at issue here, inasmuch as the beautiful and beguiling voices of the *castrati* – who moreover seem more suitably dressed in women's clothes than in men's – reconcile one to whatever may appear inappropriate in that disguise. What we must establish is to what extent the Roman tradition can offer pleasure in tragedy and comedy.

I take for granted what must be taken for granted in any perform-ance, that the plays are suited to the characters and abilities of the players: a prerequisite without which no theater and hardly the greatest, most versatile actor could survive.

Modern Romans have first of all a special inclination to the inter-changing of the dress of the two sexes at masquerades. At Carnival many young men walk about dressed as women of the lower classes and seem very much pleased with themselves in that guise. Coachmen and ser-vants often look extremely handsome when dressed as women, and if they are young and well-built they look graceful and charming. Similarly, there are women of the middle class dressed very well and successfully as Pulcinellas, and women of the upper classes in officers' uniforms. Everyone appears to enjoy these games – which once enter-tained us all as children – with renewed youthful folly. It is quite noticeable how both sexes take pleasure in the appearance of this transformation, seeking as much as possible to usurp the privilege of Tiresias.

In addition, the young men who devote themselves to female roles have a special passion for showing that they are masters of their art. They observe the facial expressions, the movements, the behavior of women with the utmost care; they try to imitate them and to give their voices suppleness and sweetness, even though they cannot change their deeper timbre. In short, they try to estrange themselves as much as possible from their own sex. They are as keen about new fashions as women are, have themselves decked out by the most able milliners, and the leading lady of the theater is usually fortunate enough to achieve her goal.

As far as the supporting roles are concerned, they are not as a rule well cast; and one cannot deny that sometimes Columbine fails to hide her blue beard completely. But supporting roles are a difficult matter in most theaters; and bitter complaints are often heard from the capital cities of other states (where much greater care is taken in the staging of plays than in Rome) about the awkwardness of third and fourth actors and consequently the complete destruction of illusion.

I did not attend these Roman comedies without preconceived notions; but without giving it much thought I soon found myself won over. I felt a pleasure I had not felt before and noticed that many others shared it. Wondering about the reason for this, I think that I have found the answer in the fact that in these performances the idea of imitation, the thought of art, remained keen throughout and that by means of skillful play only a kind of self-conscious illusion was produced.

We Germans can remember seeing a talented young man create the most perfect illusion when he played old men, and we can also remember the double pleasure that actor gave us.[3] A double attraction arises likewise from the fact that these actors are not women but portray women. The young man has studied the characteristics of the female sex in its essence and bearing; he has learned to know them and to give them life as an artist; he does not portray himself but a third nature actually foreign to him. We come to know this nature even better because someone else has observed it, reflected on it, and presents us not with the thing itself but with the result of the thing.

Since all art is distinguished from simple imitation primarily in this respect, it follows naturally that we feel a special pleasure in such a representation and can overlook a number of imperfections that can arise in the execution of the whole.

It goes without saying, as we have already indicated earlier, that the plays chosen for this kind of performance must lend themselves to it.

These are the reasons why the audience of *La Locandiera* could not fail to respond with full appreciation to its performance.

The young man who played the part of the innkeeper was excellent at expressing the various nuances which this role entails. The cool calmness of a young woman who attends to her work, is polite, friendly, and obliging to everyone, but neither loves nor desires to be loved, and is even less inclined to listen to the passions of her aristocratic lodgers; the gentle, secret flirtations through which she nevertheless succeeds in captivating her male guests; the offended pride, when one of these is hard and unfriendly to her; the many delicate flatteries by which she succeeds in baiting this one too; and finally the triumph of having conquered him!

I am convinced and have myself been a witness to it, that a clever and understanding actress can earn much praise in this role; but the last scenes, if they are played by a woman, will always be offensive. The expression of that invincible coldness, of that sweet feeling of revenge, of malicious joy in the discomfiture of others, shock us in their unmitigated truthfulness. And when she finally gives her hand in marriage to her servant only so that she may have a manservant about the house, the trivial ending of the play hardly satisfies us. But on the Roman stage we found no cold absence of love, no female wantonness – the performance merely reminded us of them. We were comforted by the fact that this time at least it was not true. We applauded the young man lightheartedly and were delighted that he was so well acquainted with the ensnaring wiles of the fair sex that through his successful imitation of feminine behavior he had avenged us for every such offense women had made us suffer.

I repeat what I said already: what we found here was the enjoyment of seeing not the thing itself but its imitation, to be entertained not through nature but through art, to contemplate not an individuality but a result.

To this must be added that the actor's figure was well-suited to portraying a person of the middle class.

And so, though imperfectly, Rome preserved this old tradition among many other survivals from the past. And if not everyone should find pleasure in it, it still makes it possible to think oneself back, to some extent to that distant time and to be more inclined to believe the evidence of ancient writers when they repeatedly assure us that male actors in female dress often succeeded in the highest degree to delight nations discriminating in taste.

NOTES

1 The most recent publications of the complete works of Goethe in which the essay appears are: *Gedenkausgabe der Werke, Briefe und Gespräche. Schriften zur Literatur* 14, ed. Ernst Beutler, Zurich: Artemis Verlag, August 28, 1949: 11–13; *Schriften zur Literatur*, ed. Horst Mahler, Historisch-kritische Ausgabe, Berlin: Akademie Verlag, 3 (Text: 1973): 11–14; 6 (Notes: 1978): 21–3.

2 Croce was 22 when Ademollo's work was published. His translation reappeared in 1983 in an edition of the *Locandiera* by Guido Davico Bonino (Milan, Mondadori), 121–5.

3 Goethe refers to a young German actor he has seen playing old men with remarkable ability. This is the most famous actor of his day, August Wilhelm

Iffland (1759–1814), whom Goethe saw in Mannheim in 1779 playing such roles, when the actor was only 20.

THE LEGACY OF GOETHE'S MIMETIC STANCE
Lesley Ferris

Goethe's basic premise – that in performance men make better women – is one of the enduring theatrical prejudices against women acting. In order to fully understand the impact of Goethe's essay, I want to briefly situate this essay in its historical context and to discuss the connections between Goldoni's play *La Locandiera* and Goethe's written response to this play. Finally I want to show twentieth-century instances in which versions of Goethe's view on male mimesis still maintains an uncomfortable grip on the way the cultural practice of acting impacts on its female participants.

Goldoni's play was first produced in Venice in 1753, and later by Goethe himself in Weimar in 1777. In both these productions actresses played the leading female role of Mirandolina. During his visit to Italy in 1787, Goethe, a theater professional himself as a playwright, director and producer, saw the all-male Roman performance of Goldoni's play. The practical reason for this all-male production is that the papal ban on actresses was still in force.

The Catholic Church had launched an offensive against actresses with Pope Sextus V's edict in 1588 which banned the appearance of women on the stages of Rome and the surrounding papal states (Duchartre 1966: 262). This influential prohibition, lasting over two hundred years, accounts for the rise in numbers of castrati, as female singers in opera were denied access to the stage until the late eighteenth century (Neuls-Bates 1982: xii).

Significantly, the narrative theme of Goldoni's play centers on misogyny. Mirandolina, the leading female character of the play and the eponymous innkeeper of the play's title, is an unmarried, independent working woman who with great forthrightness and efficiency runs an inn. Two of her guests at the inn, a wealthy Count and an impoverished Marquis, declare love for her and their readiness to marry her. Mirandolina is impressed neither by the money of the former nor by the title of the latter, and effectively and humorously keeps them at bay. A third patron of the inn, the Baron, is a self-professed, vociferous woman-hater, who finds it utterly ludicrous that the Count and the Marquis should argue over a woman:

Was there anything ever less worth arguing about! To argue over a woman! To upset yourselves over a woman! A woman? I can't believe it. Over a woman? Well, one thing's certain: that's something I'll never be in danger of arguing over. Women are by nature stupid, selfish, and dogmatic. The great tragedy of life is that they've made themselves indispensable. To put it plainly women bore me utterly, absolutely, and completely.

(Goldoni 1982: 196)

Although both the Count and the Marquis try to convince the Baron that Mirandolina has qualities far superior to any ordinary woman, the Baron maintains his role as a stage misogynist with his implacable rebuffs: "Women? They're all the same" (Goldoni 1982: 197).

Because of the Baron's uncompromising and relentless position in relation to the topic of women, Mirandolina decides to trick him into falling in love with her against his will. Her primary ruse to fool the Baron is to agree with everything he says, especially his damning views of women. When the Baron, for example, says he has no need of women, Mirandolina responds by saying "Wonderful! Don't ever change! If you only knew signore . . . but I shouldn't speak badly of my own sex" (Goldoni 1982: 210). By the end of the play the Baron has fallen madly in love with the innkeeper and rages so jealously that Mirandolina has to admit to herself that her scheming has ventured too far. In the presence of the Baron, the Marquis and the Count, the men of social status in the play, she chooses as her husband-to-be the working-class servant in her employ. The Baron, outraged by Mirandolina's maneuver, leaves the inn cursing all womankind, comfortably and vehemently returned to his misogynistic stance:

You wretched woman, a dagger is what you deserve. And your heart cut out and shown as a warning to all women like you. Let me get out of your sight. I scorn and curse your female tricks, your tears, your lies. One thing you taught me, to my bitter cost. It's not enough to despise women. No! One should flee from the very sight of them. As I do now. From you!

(Goldoni 1982: 251)

The avenging tone of this final speech of the Baron's resonates in the concluding paragraphs of Goethe's essay. Goethe applauds the talents of the male actor who plays the role of Mirandolina; through the actor's excellent portrayal of the "ensnaring wiles of the fair sex," "his successful imitation of feminine behavior [has] *avenged us* for every such offense women had made us suffer" (italics mine). In watching this all-male performance of *La Locandiera* Goethe is not confronted with the "reality" of an insincere, flirtatious, fickle woman in the title role. As the fictional Baron flees the mendacious Mirandolina with his violent final words, Goethe likewise flees from women actors who, from his point of view, cannot be separated from generic "woman." Goethe's essay denies the actress access to mimesis, a male-only artistic prerogative. In the Roman production, with Mirandolina played by a man, Goethe enjoyed "not the thing itself but its imitation"; he was entertained "not through nature but through art."[1]

Goethe's view of the cross-dressed actor as the epitome of male artistry is not limited to the late eighteenth century. In the early part of the twentieth century, for example, Jean Cocteau espoused a similar sentiment after his first viewing of Barbette, a male trapeze artist who dressed as a woman for his performances.[2] Cocteau worked hard to promote Barbette both to the art community of Paris and to his friends elsewhere in Europe. Writing to the Belgian music critic Paul Collaer in 1923 to alert him to Barbette's upcoming Brussels debut, Cocteau wrote:

> Next week in Brussels, you'll see a music-hall act called "Barbette" that has been keeping me enthralled for a fortnight. The young American who does this wire and trapeze act is a great actor, an angel, and he has become the friend of us all. Go and see him, be nice to him, as he deserves, and tell everybody that he is no mere acrobat in women's clothes, nor just a graceful daredevil, but one of the most beautiful things in the theatre.
>
> (quoted in Steegmuller 1969: 134)

Cocteau had found "a real masterpiece of pantomime, summing up in parody all the women he has ever studied, becoming himself *the* woman – so much so as to eclipse the prettiest girls who precede and follow him on the program." Cocteau's enthusiasm for Barbette is captured in an essay he wrote which celebrated the artifice of theater entitled "Le Numéro Barbette." Sounding much like the opening of Goethe's essay, Cocteau celebrated Barbette's mimetic artistry by likening his performance to the theatrical past with the conclusion "that it was not merely for reasons of 'decency' that great nations and great civilizations gave women's roles to men" (quoted in Steegmuller 1970: 366). In other words, if not for "decency," then it was for *art*; and according to Goethe the "best periods" for art are also those times when art was moral, i.e. without women treading the boards.[3]

Another theatrical figure who espoused this sentiment was Alfred Jarry, *enfant terrible* and author of the controversial *Ubu Roi* (1898). Jarry advocated the superiority of theater during the English Renaissance and the classical Greek periods because in them "one would have never dared give a role to a woman." Attacking the commonplace nineteenth-century practice of women or girls playing the roles of young boys (further discussed in Laurence Senelick's essay in this collection), Jarry argued against this convention. The practice was partially condoned because of the belief that women had more acting experience than

young boys. Jarry is vociferous in his condemnation because this experience "is small compensation for the ridiculous profile and unaesthetic
walk of women, or for the way the outline of their muscles is blurred by
fatty tissue, odious because it has a function – it makes *milk*." Jarry
believed, like Goethe, that women only brought themselves to the roles
they played. In Jarry's view, the actor must "depersonalize" himself, lose
his own personality, a metamorphosis that the male actor is singularly
suited to (quoted in La Belle 1980: 58).

Another example which supports Goethe's thesis on the superiority of
male mimesis from the viewpoint of educational theater can be found in
Guy Boas's book *Shakespeare and the Young Actor*. Boas, who was head-
master at the all-boy Sloane School in Chelsea, London, wrote this book
as a practical guide to Shakespearean productions in a school situation,
such as his own. The book was published in 1955, reprinted in 1961
andintended by its author/headmaster to be an "objective," educated
guide to producing Shakespeare's plays; it is also an argued defense for
the appropriateness and preference for boy actors in Shakespeare's
women's roles. Boas begins his first chapter with a focus on characters:

> Most writers on Shakespeare have noted the original playing of his
> female characters by boys as an historical fact and have left it at
> that. But the significance of the fact, its influence on the plays, and
> the problems set for producers, who ever since the Restoration *have*
> *had to make do with actresses*, are aspects which have largely escaped
> notice. The reason, as so often, is that few writers on Shakespeare
> have produced the plays on the stage – the purpose for which the
> plays were written.
>
> (Boas 1955: 1, italics mine)

As demonstrated from his opening paragraph, actresses are second best
in Boas's theatrical world. Much like Goethe, Cocteau, and Jarry before
him, he reiterates the theme that the best period for theatrical art was
that time without actresses. Poetic drama's zenith, according to Boas, was
the Elizabethan period despite various attempts at reviving it by Dryden,
Tennyson, Browning, Fry, and Eliot. The poetic drama of Shakespeare
is inextricably linked to the boy actor and this combination –
Shakespeare's creative genius and the boy actors' presence – created the
greatest women's roles in drama: "Poetic drama and the boy actor
disappeared together. Was it a coincidence? I do not think it was" (Boas
1955: 16).

What is it that the boy actor brings to the female roles of Shakespeare
that sets him apart from the actress? Boas claims it is his "simple
objectivity," his "impersonal quality," or perhaps, in the words of Alisa
Solomon, found later in this book, it is his "universal maleness." Boas
believes that the poetry of Shakespeare is paramount in any production

and that the actor must do the poetry justice. "But how can they [the actors] hope to accomplish this enormous task . . . if in the portrayal of his female rôles the *subjective qualities of the actress* take the place of the simple objectivity of boys?" (Boas 1955: 9, italics mine).

In Boas's second chapter – "The boy actor as Shakespeare's women" – he argues that the boy actor can comprehend the female roles because Shakespeare's women have a simplicity to them that is readily understandable to young males. Desdemona, for example, has a "childlike ignorance and childlike purity, and the boy actor has to interpret nothing beyond his ken." Boas argues for the "same simplicity" in the roles of Ophelia, Cordelia, Perdita, and Miranda, concluding that "again and again the young Shakespearean heroine is more like a flower – beautiful, pure, aspiring – than a woman of exacting flesh and blood" (Boas 1955: 9–10). And what about the more mature female roles such as Cleopatra? Even Cleopatra, perhaps the most difficult role for a boy, still provides the young male actor with experiential material well within his realm. Her death, for example, is a quiet affair that requires "no passionate treading of the stage, no preliminary fainting-fits, no flood of tears, no tearing of the bosom, beating of the breast, such as would give scope to a prima donna, but is foreign to a boy's temperament" (Boas 1955: 14). In his final defense of a boy-Cleopatra, Boas returns to one of his anti-actress themes: that the real, flesh and blood actress prevents the audience from seeing Shakespeare's creation in its fullest:

> Are we more likely to appreciate Shakespeare if a gifted actress delivers Cleopatra's death-speech, giving her particular interpretation of the part, impressing the personal qualities of her voice and enunciation on the ear, and her individual beauty on the eye, or if a boy utters the lines clearly, sincerely, quietly, and leaves us to ourselves to experience the impression which the words produce? I, for one, would unhesitatingly choose the boy.
>
> (Boas 1955: 15)

This focus on the individuality of the actress versus the simple neutrality of the boy actor underscores a way of seeing women in performance. Boas, like Goethe, can see only the "real" woman, who unfortunately always brings her "personal qualities" to the role. Both are blind to her creativity as an actress while simultaneously celebrating the creative powers of men whose universality as "man" gives them a prodigious, prolific inventiveness.

Both Peggy Phelan in her essay in this collection and Erika Munk (1986) describe a similar problem in a much more recent performance event. In September, 1985, ISTA (International School of Theatre Anthropology), run by Eugenio Barba, presented an international conference on The Female Roles as Represented on the Stage in Various

Cultures. Munk and Phelan, as well as a range of theater critics and scholars, attended the conference expecting a range of debates, reflections, and analyses centering on the performances and work-shops. Instead, what the conference participants found was a focus on performance technique and style with a refusal to think about cross-dressing in a social or cultural context. Barba, in the confer-ence program, stated:

To concentrate on psychological questions . . . the vicissitudes of repression and emancipation, historical and social problems, all this is useful, but not in order to confront an elementary pro-fessional problem: the double-edged nature of the actor's energy, the existence of an Anima-energy and an Animus-energy . . . which have nothing to do with the distinction between masculine and feminine.

(quoted in Munk 1986: 37)

Centuries removed from Goethe, and still an insistence on the import-ance of the actor's technical ability – "an elementary professional prob-lem." And as Munk observes, Barba promotes a technical focus, down-playing the significance of the "historical and social problems" while relying on gender-laden words – animus and anima – to describe an actor's energy.

Munk points out that Jan Kott's often reprinted commentary on cross-dressing (which sounds much like crib notes from Goethe: "Femininity can only be acted by a man.") was used by Barba as an ISTA program note to support Barba's own position on male mimesis (Kott 1984: 124). (See also Alisa Solomon's essay here which discusses Kott's remarks.) Barba, without ever asking the question – *why* is the enactment of a female role by a man more inspiring than when performed by a woman? – continues the centuries-old assumptions.

And such assumptions are not merely theoretical flag-waving. In the early 1980s a new wave of female impersonators flooded the Italian performance market. Leopoldo Mastelloni, who sounds like a cross between Charles Ludlam and Ethyl Eichenberger, performed pieces from *Mother Courage* as well as sketches of Cleopatra, Lucretia Borgia, and Maria Callas. Renato Zero, a cross-dressed pop star, whose pheno-menal popularity has lead to film-making, ownership of a record com-pany and a large traveling tent theater that seats five thousand, is described by many as "super-drag." And returning to Rome, where we began this commentary, Erio Masina, a former cabaret performer now known for his female roles, starred in the role of Mirandolina in a revival of Goldoni's *La Locandiera* in 1982 (Davis 1982: 5).

NOTES

1 See my chapter "Goethe, Goldoni and woman-hating" in Ferris (1990) for a development of this idea as well as the suggestion that Goethe, blinded by his limited and stereotyped notions of "woman," does not really understand the character of Mirandolina.
2 See Senelick's essay in this collection for a look at the phenomenon of cross-dressing in the circus.
3 See Elizabeth Drorbaugh's essay later in this collection which points out a parallel example found in the promotion material for the Jewel Box Revue. The producers of this revue make a similar claim for artistic superiority and historical valorization of men playing women to promote the integrity of their female impersonators.

4

"WHEN MEN WOMEN TURN"
Gender reversals in Fielding's plays
Jill Campbell

I

Having earned royal favor and the stature of a hero by preserving King Arthur's kingdom from the giants, Fielding's little Tom Thumb asks not for political power or monetary reward but for domestic bliss: "I ask but this, / To Sun my self in *Huncamunca's* Eyes." The King grants Thumb the Princess Huncamunca, but Queen Dollalolla objects, since she is in love with Thumb herself. When Arthur remains firm, Dollalolla threatens violence, but Arthur refuses, on principle, to "truckle to her Will":

> For when by Force
> Or Art the Wife her Husband over-reaches,
> Give him the Peticoat, and her the Breeches.
> (Fielding 1918: 98–100)

For *Tom Thumb*'s original audience in 1730, King Arthur's blustering defense against "petticoat government" must have called to mind a specific scenario of female domination: England's own queen, Caroline, was widely rumored to govern the country indirectly through her control of King George (Quennell 1940: 124–8). At the same time, for the audience at many of the play's early performances, the dramatic scenario before them itself provided satiric commentary on this passage: the Thumb King Arthur here addresses was himself most often a "her" in breeches – a female actor typically filled Thumb's singularly heroic trousers – and in some cases the Princess Huncamunca Thumb is to wed was a "him" in petticoats – a male actor occasionally took this role.[1] In *Tom Thumb*, Fielding burlesques political and literary notions of public heroism or "greatness" not only by mixing inflated with deflated diction and by shrinking his hero to a "Lilliputian" scale, but by casting a woman as masculine hero.

King Arthur's principled defense of patriarchy confirms that the theatrical device of cross-gender casting signifies as more than farce in this play. In the widely varied body of the twenty-six plays Fielding wrote in the first decade of his literary career, interest in problems of gender identity recurs again and again, and Fielding repeatedly links the significance of gender, particularly as revealed at the moment of gender inversion, to matters of "government," both political and literary. He often uses gender as a means of representing other issues, but also as a vexed issue with political and literary consequences itself. Of course, it is the historical meaning of "masculine" and "feminine" that he draws on when he makes a female Tom Thumb serve to comment on the nature of that hero, and much of his satiric use of gender works to protect or enforce certain historical notions of masculine authority. But his plays also explore the costs of that system. While his career as a playwright and stage manager lasted, the genre of drama and its forum, the theater, provided Fielding with a particularly powerful – though ultimately restrictive – means of imagining and representing issues of gender identity and reversal, and all they might imply.

In his plays, as elsewhere, Fielding often uses ridicule of a character's compromised masculinity to associate that character with the compromising of traditional political, cultural, or social standards. He uses familiar figures from the standard repertoire of contemporary topical satire to make the association. The figure of Lord Hervey, agent of Walpole and bisexual – Pope's "Sporus" and "Lord Fanny," Pulteney's "pretty, little *Master-Miss*" (Pulteney 1731: 6), and an inexhaustible ideological crux for many Opposition satirists – serves to link political with sexual corruption in the role of Miss Stitch in *Pasquin*. Fielding repeatedly uses the ambiguous gender as well as the foreign birth of the Italian castrato singers so popular in London at this time to represent the decline of the values of native theater. That signature of Restoration comedy, the fop or beau, marks Fielding's comedies as well, but with a difference: most often, this familiar comic type is reduced by Fielding to its disruptive signification in a system of gender oppositions. "I have known a beau with everything of a woman but the sex," observes Wisemore in *Love in Several Masques*, "and nothing of a man besides it" (Fielding 1902: I.ii).

The stock jokes about gender in Fielding's plays show not only a satiric interest in men who abdicate their masculinity and all it is imagined to entail – the corrupt courtier, the castrato singer, the beau – but an apocalyptic vision of women's appropriation of that masculine power. "And if the Breed ben't quickly mended," warns the poet's muse at the end of a passage satirizing beaux in Fielding's first published work, *The Masquerade*,

> Your Empire shortly will be ended:
> Breeches our brawny Thighs shall grace,
> (Another *Amazonian* Race.)

For when Men Women turn – why then
May Women not be changed to Men?[2]

Women's appropriations of male "empire," the threat of "petticoat government," is the most general and persistent topic of sexual satire in Fielding's plays. "We are all under petticoat government," Trapwit announces as the Cibberian "moral" to the second act of his comedy within *Pasquin* (II.i). In *The Grub-Street Opera*, which presents the English royal family as a Welsh family of henpecked husband, domineering wife, and "puny" son, Puzzletext the parson comforts Sir Owen with the company his misery keeps: "Petticoat-government is a very lamentable thing indeed. – But it is the fate of many an honest gentleman" (I.i). And Fielding extends the problem even into the afterlife and the underworld: when a critic asks the author of the rehearsal play within *Eurydice*, "Why have you made the devil hen-pecked?" the author replies, "How could hell be better represented than by supposing the people under petticoat government?" King Arthur himself is described in the Dramatis Personae of *The Tragedy of Tragedies* as a "passionate sort of King, Husband to Queen *Dollalolla*, of whom he stands a little in Fear."

Most of these scenarios of the "misrule" of female domination involve the government of a public realm as well as of a household, superimposing a domestic onto a political hierarchy of power: the henpecked husband is also the dubious ruler of the English people of King Arthur's or King George's reign, or of hell's ghostly "people." Domestic and political satire are, for Fielding, closely linked. Often the content of his political satire might be said to consist of linking it with domestic material – the intrusion of the domestic realm into the realm of public action and rule, or the domination of political by domestic or sexual power, is repeatedly the source both of Fielding's humor and of his serious critique. When Fielding presents inverted masculine and feminine power relations, he often seems to be representing through them an inversion in the priority of public over private concerns assumed to be the respective domains of men and women.[3] As we can see in the conjunction of a female Tom Thumb with Arthur's remarks on "petticoat government," gender reversals or impersonations signify analogously to express more than the disruption of sexual roles. In a period that saw itself as fallen hopelessly below past standards of public heroism, the gender inversion of a female hero functions as one species of mock-epic. The diminishment or corruption of the public world of heroism and power appears in its collapse into the female world of mere domestic squabble.

Many of Fielding's uses of gender inversion, however, employ a sense of the feminine domain not simply as the negation of the masculine public world but as a domain of other kinds of values and powers that can itself be betrayed by a collapse into its opposite. Fielding often employs the association of women with internal life – both the moral life of virtue and the psychological one of feeling. He counts on women to preserve that province apart from the public and commercial world of the male, but he frequently suspects them of merely using their association with virtue and feeling to serve their own purposes of power and acquisition. "Virtue" becomes "vartue" in Fielding's *Shamela*, a high-blown word deflated by vulgar usage, reduced to a means for getting her man; and, once married, Shamela overreaches her husband through an artful use of feminine feeling – feeling that is calculated and constituted for the effect of its representation. The rupture of gender categories involved in "petticoat government" implies for Fielding, then, not only the intrusion of domestic concerns into political or public ones, but the betrayal of the space of interior feeling associated with femininity by a counterfeit or "sham" exterior version of it, fabricated for its effects in the public world of the male.

When Fielding discusses affectation as the central problematic of character in "An Essay on the knowledge of the characters of men," printed in his *Miscellanies* in 1743, he explicitly renders the problem in the terms of dramatic acting: "the generality of mankind mistake the affectation for the reality; for, as Affectation always overacts her part, it fares with her as with a farcical actor on the stage, whose monstrous overdone grimaces are sure to catch the applause of an insensible audience" (Fielding 1903: IX.414). Fielding immediately identifies Affectation as both female and hyper-theatrical, and the mixed sexuality of cross-dressing may be what evokes the strong term "monstrous" in the description of Affectation's grimaces, for the image of "a farcical actor on the stage" raises the idea of both male players in female roles and female players in male roles that were an important element of English farce tradition. The arguments of the anti-theatricalists – which extended 150 years before Fielding and which contributed to the Stage Licensing Act that ended his career – had used cross-dressing as a paradigm for the moral dangers of the theater, making gender the ultimate preserve of natural identity to be broached, in its most scandalous extremity, by theatrical impersonation, and setting up the theater as the forum in which the boundaries of gender might be tested (Barish 1981; Ackroyd 1979: 92–4). Problems of gender and problems of affectation or impersonation were historically linked, then, in the controversial institution of the English theater within which Fielding began his literary career.

As we saw in the scene from *Tom Thumb* with which we began, Fielding explores issues of gender identity and inversion in his plays not only by treating them thematically, or by recurring to topics of social satire involving gender, but also by actually staging the situation of gender

impersonation. As the manager of the Haymarket Theatre, he capitalized upon the dramatic possibilities of the theatrical device of cross-
gender casting objected to by the anti-theatricalists. With this device,
Fielding made the institutional and representational space of the theater
a vivid embodiment of larger cultural and ideological structures.
Stephen Orgel's work on Renaissance theater has allowed us to conceive
this function of the stage (see Orgel 1975). More broadly, Stephen
Greenblatt has suggested strategies of reading Renaissance literary texts
in conjunction with the documents and experiences of social life which
we will bring to the problem of gender in Fielding's dramas and to the
new institutions and cultural forces of eighteenth-century England (see,
for example, Greenblatt 1983 and 1985). These methods of reading,
designed to tease out the complicated underpinnings of cultural forms,
will not provide us with a single feminist, political, or sociological summary of Fielding's dramatic production, but they will open up the
constellation of interrelated problems – sexual, political, and social – that
that production repeatedly stages. Using Fielding's *Historical Register* as a
touchstone and a guide through the complex and ambivalent commentary on gender in Fielding's plays, we will focus in what follows on
Fielding's employment of cross-gender casting as a usefully bald and
explicit rendering of his interest in the abstract systems of oppositions
associated with gender, dramatically disrupted by these parts.

II

Fielding's *Historical Register for the Year 1736*, performed at the Little
Theatre in the Haymarket in May, 1737, places us and a small onstage
audience of author, critic, and lord at a rehearsal of Medley's new play.
This new play consists of a series of brief satiric scenes that are to provide
an "historical register" of the events – political, social, and theatrical – of
the preceding year. Medley's first scene is spare: a thinly veiled political
satire of Sir Robert Walpole and his cohorts. The second scene is more
complex. At its center is the stage enactment of an auction, which Medley
calls the best scene in the whole performance, for it is "writ in allegory"
(Fielding 1967: II.i. 70 and 80). The casting of Medley's auctioneer – a
satiric portrait of London's popular auctioneer of the time, Mr
Christopher Cock, here called Mr Hen – contributes to the allegory of the
scene: the role of Mr Cock/Hen was filled by the noted male impersonator
and eccentric, Colley Cibber's daughter, Mrs Charlotte Charke.
Fielding's cross-gender casting of Mr Hen creates a dramatic context for
the selling of goods that interprets both that selling and sexual inversions
in a particular way. But before the auction has even begun, the terms of
such an interpretation have been established in a short dramatic prologue, a conversation among the ladies who will attend.

"Now you shall have a council of ladies" or "female politicians," Medley promises as his second scene opens, but the "affairs of great importance" they are discussing when the curtain is drawn replace the politics of Medley's first scene with matters of social and sexual fashion – an interchangeability characteristic of Fielding's satiric humor.

	The LADIES all speak together.
ALL LADIES.	Was you at the opera, Madam, last night?
2d LADY.	Who can miss an opera while Farinello stays?
3d LADY.	Sure he is the charmingest creature!
4th LADY.	He's everything in the world one could wish!
1st LADY.	Almost everything one could wish!
2d LADY.	They say there's a lady in the city has a child by him.
ALL LADIES.	Ha, ha, ha!
1st LADY.	Well, it must be charming to have a child by him.
3d LADY.	Madam, I met a lady in a visit the other day with three . . . All Farinellos, all in wax.
1st LADY.	O Gemini! Who makes them? I'll send and bespeak half a dozen tomorrow morning.

(II.i.6–18)

The stage direction and first line open the scene with a caricature of the univocal control fashion exerts over the ladies' words: the same voice, the voice of fashionable society, speaks through all of them. They all seem to have attended the opera the night before, but they discuss not the music or performance but its lead singer. And they discuss Farinelli (that is, Carlo Broschi, the great Italian singer in Porpora's opera between 1734 and 1737)[4] not as a musical performer but as an object of desire: "He's everything in the world one could wish!" (Plate 8). When the First Lady qualifies this statement with an "almost," she acknowledges the irony of female society's selection of Farinelli as popular sex symbol or romantic idol: the sweet extraordinary voice of Farinelli that is said to have ravished the heart of every woman in his audience manifested precisely his inability to ravish a woman physically, his victimization and election to that strange foreign elite of castrato singers. But it is the same First Lady who complicates the view of Farinelli's disabled phallus as simply a qualification to his desirability when she declares, "it must be charming to have a child by him." The ladies laugh at the rumor that Farinelli has fathered a child, yet the First Lady's comment and their universal willingness to resume discussion of the rumor as if it were truth express some simultaneous wish for this contradiction.

Fielding's "female politicians" weren't alone in their titillated interest: the Italian castrato singers who began to perform in London in 1707 (see White 1983) served widely as a cultural occasion through which the ambivalences and pressures of the period's sexual ideology could be played out, in the form both of a tremendous popular vogue and of a tireless satiric abuse. Even without children, the castrati presented their audiences with a contradiction in terms; and their treatment elsewhere, both by Fielding and by other satirists of the 1730s, helps us understand all that is at stake in the simple jokes of this prologue, and how it prepares us for the auction scene to follow.[5]

The satiric reactions to the disruption a castrato creates along the boundary between masculine and feminine identity reveal some of the larger systems of oppositions normally stabilized by alignment with gender terms. Because the castrato's exception to masculine identity consists ultimately in the facts about his genitals, the castrati provided an occasion to isolate, and to literalize, to make explicit, the cultural significances of the phallus itself: in considering the nature of the castrato's loss, the satirists at times assume the phallus to be the guarantor of everything from moral discourse to English currency to English-ness. And in the real or imagined responses of women to them, the castrati provided a rare opening in the normally monolithic entity of masculinity in which to explore – whether with wishfulness, fear, or denunciation – complexities or contradictions in women's relation to the phallus. While some of the satiric material concentrated its ridicule on the castrati themselves, much of it, like this scene from the *Historical Register*, turned its satiric attention on the women interested in them, competing to articulate what it would mean for a woman to prefer a man without the use of his penis.

By the time Fielding presented the ladies' discussion of Farinelli in *The Historical Register* in 1737, two pamphlets, appearing in London in 1735 and 1736, had humorously argued for the greater desirability of a castrated man. In the first, Teresia Constantia Phillips, the notorious courtesan who appears in the shadowy background of *Shamela* (see Rothstein 1968), had rejected the male fantasy (present in *Pamela, Fanny Hill*, and many other novels) that a woman's sexual desire is necessarily adjoined to dread, pain, and awe, and with it she at least playfully rejected the phallic ideal of a lover in favor of Farinelli:

> Man, like his Brother Brute, the shaggy Bear,
> Where he attempts to stroke, is sure to tear . . . .
> Discord and Thunder, mingle when he speaks,
> And stunning Noise the Ears thin Membrane breaks.
>   How fit for Dalliance and for soft Embrace,
> Is Man, that carries Terror in his Face? . . .
> Can we with Pleasure, what we dread enjoy,
> That very Dread does Love itself destroy.
>   How much do those display their want of Sense,
> Who scoff at Eunuchs, and dislike a Thing,

For being but disburthen'd of its Sting?

(Phillips 1735: 3 & 7)

In the first stanza, masculine "Discord" and "Noise" stand in for the phallus, deflowering the female ear, and in the last, the sweet-voiced and "sting"-less Eunuch emerges as the ideal object of a feminine desire unmixed with terror or pain. Fielding had used a similar set of images in 1733 in his epilogue to *The Intriguing Chambermaid*, where he complains that the popularity of "Italian warblers" has brought about the decline of native theater. He ironically approves his female audience's choice:

> – But though our angry poets rail in spite,
> Ladies, I own, I think your judgments right:
> Satire, perhaps, may wound some pretty thing;
> Those soft Italian warblers have no sting.
>
> . . .
>
> 'Tis hard to pay them who our faults reveal,
> As boys are forced to buy the rods they feel.
> No, let 'em starve, who dare to lash the age,
> And, as you've left the pulpit, leave the stage.

(26–9, 34–7)

Fielding, like Con Phillips, compares the uncastrated phallus to a wounding sting and a violent rod, but his irony attempts to recuperate the masculine discord and noise that Phillips rejects as the harsh but moral voice of satire: phallic satire "gives the wounded hearer pain" (33) but only in order to reveal our faults; the rod "lashes" us that we may learn. Thus Fielding presents the rejection of phallic masculinity as a moral "softness" or degeneracy, and at the same time he renders a man's penis violent, alienating, an inhuman tool. Fielding associates this degeneracy particularly with the reduction of moral discourse to a consumer transaction: satire's instruction is passed over in favor of "tuneful charms" (30) because "'Tis hard to pay them who our faults reveal."

When, in *The Author's Farce* (1730), Fielding recreated Pope's vision of the reign of Mother Dullness on the stage, he characteristically combined Pope's satire of a court's misrule and the inverted literary and social values it promotes with his own insistent satire of inverted sexual identity and nonsensical female desire. In the play within this play, not only does the Goddess of Nonsense choose Signior Opera as the dunce-laureat of her underworld realm, but she has fallen in love with him, and plans to marry him until Mrs Novel arrives and claims him as her own. When the Goddess of Nonsense chooses the castrato singer over the other competitors for her hand, he bursts into a passionate aria – not one, however, that frames his gratitude or love, but one that sets to music his belief that "In riches is centered all human delight" (Fielding

65

1966: III, Air VIII). The Goddess repeats the last line of his tribute to riches "in an ecstasy" and cries "Bravissimo! I long to be your wife": like the ladies' choice in Fielding's epilogue, Nonsense's choice of Signior Opera, rejecting together the phallus and moral "sense," reduces both cultural value and personal desire to a highly-charged monetary worth. The enormous salaries and extravagant gifts commanded by several of the castrato singers performing in London at this time figured repeatedly in the satire against them (see Ralph 1728 and Highfill *et al.* 1982: V.148–50), serving to link fashion's inflation of prices and destabilizing of value with that intrusion of foreign influence and disruption of gender categories represented by the castrato. Mrs Novel objects to Nonsense's choice, claiming Signior Opera as her own with the surprising announcement that "he knows I died for love; for I died in childbed" with his child (III.i. 390). The important subjects of female desire, reproduction, and value intersect repeatedly in the figure of the castrato – who stands for trouble within each of them – and satire's variations on the simple joke of a castrato reproducing, with which we began, show that joke working through complex relations between the three subjects.

When Fielding included this joke in the scene of the "female politicians" in *The Historical Register*, it had already been spun out at some length in the second of the two pamphlets about Farinelli published in the years preceding the original performance of the play. In Fielding's *Pasquin*, performed one year before *The Historical Register*, the country mayor's daughter shows off her taste and her knowledge of London by describing what she expects to see in town: ". . . and then we shall see Faribelly, the strange man-woman that they say is with child; and the fine pictures of Merlin's cave at the play-houses; and the rope-dancing and the tumbling" (II.i). Miss Mayoress only reveals, of course, her appetite for low entertainments, and she garbles Farinelli's name, but she does so in a way coherent with her version of the miracle of a castrato parenting a child. In giving her the story that Farinelli himself is pregnant, Fielding probably refers to a pamphlet that appeared the same year as *Pasquin*: "An Epistle to *John James H–dd–g–r, Esq.*; On the Report of *Signior F-r-n-lli's* being with Child."[6] This pamphlet reiterates the theme of female sexual desire for a eunuch, but it also imagines the revelation that Farinelli's ambiguous gender actually disguises his true identity as a woman, exposed by the disgrace of his pregnancy:

> What may we think? the Doubt has made me wild;
> Is the soft Warbler then a Wench with Child?
> . . .
>
> WHAT Words can speak the chaste CLARINDA'S Woe!
> Who now must all her hop'd-for Bliss forgoe?
> Her lovely *Eunuch* to a Woman turn'd,

> For whose secure Embrace so long she's burn'd!
> She who's refus'd a thousand filthy Men,
> Must she still hug her beastly Lap-dog then?

(pp. 3–4)

The pamphlet's exclamation, "Her lovely *Eunuch* to a Woman turn'd," recalls *The Masquerade*'s apocalyptic vision of gender instability: "For when Men Women turn – why then / May Women not be changed to Men?" At the same time, the pamphlet, by turning the castrato into a woman, explicitly reveals the threat of a woman's sexual preference for another woman beneath the threatening oddity of a woman's sexual preference for a eunuch. Con Phillips's pamphlet had linked Farinelli, with his ambiguous gender, to interruptions of the class system ("Your glitt'ring Equipage the Ring shall grace, / And to no Man of Quality's give place"), to disruptions of others' gender identities ("And he that would not start at Death, or Fire, / Shall like a Girl at thy soft Trill expire"), and even to confusions of the categories of animate and inanimate beings ("Your Voice shall cast all Mortals in a Trance, / Ev'n Things inanimate to that shall Dance") (Phillips 1735: 13). This second pamphlet ends by implying that the stability of currency's value rests on the stability of gender categories: as long as a castrato stays at least "half a Man," his value insures the value of his subscriber's investment, and only the proof of his possession of a phallus, even a castrated one, can provide that insurance. The pamphlet presents the abstract principle of the masculine basis of monetary value in crude and material form: the author recommends to opera subscribers that in the future they "serve your Eunuchs as they serve the Pope / Before they sign, let every Member grope." Each member of a jury of "good Matrons" is to swear

> That she has seen and felt how Matters stand,
> With her own naked Eye and naked Hand.
> Unless you take this Method for the future,
> Your Silver Tickets may as well be Pewter.

(pp. 6–7)

The penis here submits to examination by palpation to sustain a system of monetary values, just as it submits to use as a lashing rod to sustain a system of moral values in Fielding's vision of satire, or as the Pope's penis must be grasped, according to the pamphleteer, before he can head a system of religious authority. Of course the phallus to be witnessed by the opera subscribers is a specifically diminished one. Ironically, by focusing on the "half" of masculine identity the castrato maintains rather the half he lacks, the pamphlet deepens the castrato's association with instability of value; by taking a castrated penis as its guarantor that silver will not turn to pewter, the pamphlet comments on the already deteriorated standard of its society; and by reenacting the replacement of the phallic man by the prized eunuch with the turning of that eunuch to a woman, it implies that once ambiguity has been introduced, value is open always to further deterioration. In an economy undergoing a financial revolution, newly dependent on the impalpable worth of paper credit and the invisible transactions of "stock-jobbing" and national debt (see Dickson 1967), the author warns investors to see and feel themselves the object of value, here embodied in a penis, and figures the collapse of value as the disastrous interruption of the opera season by the pregnancy of its supposed castrato lead singer – actually a male impersonator.

This pamphlet imaginatively links the significance of the figure of the castrato to the significance of the figure of a male impersonator, and I think that this interpretation of the fertile castrato informs Medley's scene in *The Historical Register*, even though the ladies go on to imagine the miracle of a castrato's reproduction in a different way, as the miracle of mechanical reproduction and market distribution. The children they imagine for Farinelli are the wax figures, sold at the New Exchange, that were the fashionable purchase of the moment.[7] When the First Lady says she'll "bespeak half a dozen tomorrow morning," the Second out-does her, planning to order "as many as I can cram into a coach with me." The women who have "all spoken together" in favor of Farinelli, substituting fashion's influence for sexual desire, blur together sexual reproduction and consumer transaction; their idol Farinelli fathers fashionable commodities that present multiple, identical images of life. One lady suspects that her husband will resent her acquisition of the "children" – "I'm afraid my husband won't let me keep them, for he hates I should be fond of anything but himself" – but another asserts the autonomy from male authority that the ladies' new-found power of purchasing can give them, and treats her devotion to commodities as a replacement for her maternal role within the family: "If my husband was to make any objection to my having 'em, I'd run away from him and take the dear babies [i.e., dolls] with me" (II.i.19–36). The lady extends the refusal of phallic moral enforcement implied by women's choice of "tuneful charms" over satire to a threatened desertion of masculine authority and masculine lineage altogether.

In this scene, Fielding links the figure of the woman as a powerful consumer in a newly commodified society with the figure of the castrato performer, and he implicates the two of them in the issue of ambiguous gender and gender impersonation, the notion of inanimate objects representing or even impersonating life, the spectacle of prices being attached to what should be living things, and the spectre of value's instability in such a scene – all of which concerns will carry over into the onstage auction.

III

The public space the auction occupies is coextensive with the theatrical space of the play within *The Historical Register*. When Lord Dapper, one of the onstage viewers of Medley's work, finds himself carried away by the action and begins to bid on the lots offered (II.i.239), crossing from audience of a play to participant in an auction, we are reminded of the ways in which an auction is itself a kind of theatrical event. The fashionable pastime that Fielding chose to succeed the ladies' discussion of the opera is at once the scene of theatrical, social, and economic activity: it is a performance with material consequences, a theatrical event that sets prices and establishes values through the dramatics of the auctioneer's presentation of objects and the dynamics of audience reaction. Fielding's frequent references to auctions in his work show his interest in this process of dramatic value-setting.[8] The value finally assigned to a lot at an auction marks the strength of the mediated desire it provokes in the audience, arrived at through the interplay of imitation and competition in the crowd. This method of price-setting does not register either the labor value or the use value of an object; the auction attaches value in some sense not to the object but to its dramatic shell, to the representation of the object the auctioneer offers. The auction did not emerge in England as a method of price-setting until the end of the seventeenth century, and it was in the eighteenth century that it first became institutionalized with the founding of the earliest auction house, Sotheby's, in 1744, followed by Christie's in 1766 (Cassady 1967: 29–30). Christopher Cock has been called "the first auctioneer" (Ash 1958: 33–7), and the events he presided over provided a new form of social occasion for the fashionable set in London: Cock's auctions made *buying* a social event, and the crowds that gathered at an auction for entertainment acted out the movement of price-setting through demand that was crucial to their emerging "consumer society," as well as the spectatorship to consumption upon which that society depends (see McKendrick *et al.* 1982).

When the ladies of the introductory conversation turn their attention from the opera to the auction they will attend, the First Lady links Mr Hen, the auctioneer, to Farinelli, the castrato, when she exclaims, "Oh, dear Mr Hen! . . . I never miss him," recalling the Second Lady's rhetorical question, "Who can miss an opera while Farinello stays?" In the play's original productions, the auctioneer's entrance enforced and rendered more substantial this association of the two men: Charlotte Charke enters, in male dress, as "*Mr Hen*, auctioneer, bowing," another figure of ambiguous gender. The castrato singer and the auctioneer are similarly public characters and objects of fashion's hyperbolic and platitudinous desire ("I never miss him"), and Fielding's alteration of the name of the real auctioneer he satirizes – Hen for Cock – deepens the relation between them. The simple alteration involves not only changing gender but also taking the penis out of the slang denotations of the auctioneer's name,[9] and instead evoking connotations of "hen-pecking," the term of "petticoat government" derived from henhouse politics. When the auction begins, we see that, as Medley has promised, the curiosities Hen offers are all allegorical objects, abstract personal qualities represented as pieces of clothing, cosmetics, liquid in a bottle, massive books. Hen takes bids not only on the public virtues of political honesty and patriotism but on modesty, courage, wit, a clear conscience, interest at court, the cardinal virtues, and Common Sense. Fielding here renders comically literal the externalizing of personal virtue with which Shamela makes her bid for profit. To the extent that personified inner virtues are identified as the cultural realm of the feminine, those ideally female qualities here take the form most often of outer garments, to which the public affixes a price.

Although the humor of the scene depends on this nonsensical notion of auctioning off abstract personal qualities in the form of concrete objects, in his advertisements for many of the lots Hen acknowledges that what he offers for sale are not those qualities themselves but the profitable appearance of them. When he argues to raise the bids offered for patriotism, for example, Hen emphasizes that it is something that can be taken off or put on when its appearance is advantageous ". . . sir, I don't propose this for a town suit. This is only proper for the country. Consider, gentlemen, what a figure this will make at an election." He promises his inquiring audience that the "valuable commodity" of modesty which he offers in the form of "a beautiful powder" will "not change the color of the skin" but "serves mighty well to blush behind a fan with, or to wear under a lady's mask at a masquerade" (II.i.157–77). Thus Fielding implies that Hen's farcical reduction of political honesty to the visible, palpable cloak sold in his auction is only an extension or literalization of the way in which the impalpable virtue of political honesty, like other virtues, has been reduced by the times to the advantageous appearance of such. This reduction leads, Fielding implies, to a confusion of the feminine and masculine realms of inner life and public action, to a kind of cross-dressing of one as the other – to Shamela's (profitable and powerful) affected sufferings and affected "vartue," the "cloak" of honesty, or the impersonations of a Mr Hen.

Fielding would satirize Christopher Cock again by supplying Cock's name in place of a general reference to auctions in his translation of Juvenal's Sixth Satire as "modernised in Burlesque Verse" (revised and published in the *Miscellanies*, 1743). The context of the reference in Juvenal's satire allows Fielding to associate Cock and his auction directly with the transgression of gender categories. The misogynist satire turns its attention for the moment from adultery and female willfulness to "fighting females, / Whom you would rather think to be males." As translated by Fielding, the poem asks, "Will they their sex entirely quit?" and warns:

> . . . should your wife by auction sell,
> (You know the modern fashion well)
> Should Cock aloft his pulpit mount,
> And all her furniture recount,
> Sure you would scarce abstain from oaths,
> To hear, among your lady's clothes,
> Of those superb fine horseman's suits,
> And those magnificent jack-boots.
>   And yet, as often as they please,
> Nothing is tenderer than these.
> A coach! – O gad! they cannot bear
> Such jolting! – John, go fetch a chair.
> Yet see through Hyde Park how they ride!
> How masculine! almost astride![10]

While Cock remains Cock in this passage, what he sells from his pulpit are the cast-offs of women dressing as men. Fielding expands Juvenal's reference to an auction into a description of the "modern fashion" and its primo auctioneer, and this description leads to his free rendering of Juvenal's complaint in the terms of "masculine" women riding in Hyde Park. But, following Juvenal, he complicates his portrait of the masculine woman by saying she, contradictorily, can at times assert the special claims of high femininity: when not riding astride, she may insist on her need for a more delicate conveyance than a coach. The woman's demand for a chair in this passage repeats an association of women with extravagant consumerism throughout the satire, and Fielding's use of Juvenal to comment on modern women makes clearer a complication in the cross-dressing of *The Historical Register*'s auction of virtues.

While in many contexts women are consigned to the idealized or at least etherealized realm of inner virtues, in the context of the classical tradition of misogynist satire they are implicated in the material realm of the commodity more deeply than men. As Pope does in "To a lady," Fielding uses Juvenal's satire to turn his attack on modern luxuries and commodification against women (Brown 1985: 103). Tellingly, Fielding chooses to close his translation of the satire – he breaks off less than half-way through Juvenal's poem – at the point at which Juvenal makes his denunciation of women a denunciation of luxury, consumption, and money. Juvenal goes on to consider women's crimes of lust and violence, but Fielding stops here to conclude his version of the satire:

> Whence come these prodigies? . . . I' th' mountain

71

> The British dames were chaste, no crimes
> The cottage stain'd in elder times;
> When the laborious wife slept little,
> Spun wool, and boil'd her husband's kettle . . . .
> Money's the source of all our woes;
> Money! whence luxury o'erflows
> And in a torrent, like the Nile,
> Bears off the virtues of this isle.
>
> (pp. 341–3)

Fielding locates the virtue of chastity in the past economy of a "laborious wife" with her cottage industry, and, in associating the luxury and expenditure of the new economy with the women Juvenal's satire abuses, he acknowledges that England's developing capitalism has made women generally consumers rather than producers, and so figures for commodification itself.[11]

If we look back to Hen's auction of virtues now, we can see how it uses the contradiction between two simultaneously maintained cultural realms of the feminine. Its reverse allegory of abstract qualities offered for sale as concrete objects ironically conjoins, in those objects, the sentimental association of women with inner life and the satiric association of them with material commodities. The auction shows one passed off as the other, and so makes women the brunt of its commentary on a society in which luxury has borne off virtues and the public world of action has been converted to a theater of goods. Mr Hen, the cross-dressed auctioneer who calls for bids on items with names from one feminine realm and shapes from the other, stands as a figure for the way money and purchasing have entered into, and disrupted, the division of male and female roles. The influence of fashion upon women is one way both Fielding's translation of Juvenal and his auction scene in *The Historical Register* describe women's betrayal of the realm of virtues for that of commodities. Mr Hen receives no bids on the "valuable commodity" of modesty, for his audience informs him that it is "out of fashion" (II.i.163–5).

As Neil McKendrick has demonstrated, the first half of the eighteenth century saw the emergence in England of a commercialized society that made rapidly changing fashion for the first time more influential than tradition (see McKendrick *et al.* 1982: 34–99). And Fielding often locates his account in his historical moment, making it a satiric commentary on what the world has come to. At the same time, the implications of his commentary are often philosophical: he uses England's consumer revolution as a means of raising, and negotiating, the most basic questions about gender and identity.

IV

By offering virtues and other personal qualities for sale by bidding, Mr Hen's auction caricatures the possibility that aspects of personal identity may be mere acquisitions. The last lot Hen offers receives no bids because, as Medley explains, "everyone thinks he has it" already: Lot 10 consists of "a little Common Sense." Medleys's satire, however, depends on the implication that in passing over the "very valuable commodity" of Common Sense, the crowd doesn't realize its own lack, and Fielding's original audiences would be especially ready to catch this implication if they knew of Fielding's extremely popular play of the year before, *Pasquin*. Lot 10 is the first of Hen's lots that appears in capital letters as a personified entity, and the figure Common Sense had appeared, not only personified but dramatized and enthroned, as Queen Common-sense in Fustian's tragedy within *Pasquin*. Indeed, Fielding's presentation of Common Sense there had been memorialized just a month and a half before *The Historical Register*'s first performance when Chesterfield and Lyttleton named their new Opposition newspaper after her, commenting in their first leader that they took the name from "an ingenious Dramatick Author [who] has consider'd Common Sense as so extraordinary a thing, that he has lately, with great wit and humour, not only personified it, but dignified it too with the title of a Queen" (quoted in Cross 1918: I.218–19). In *Pasquin*'s final scene Queen Common-sense, with only one follower, battles against Queen Ignorance, who lands with a "foreign force."

Fielding often imagines fashion as a force from outside native English society, responsible for its increasing decadence. And this foreign force, as we might expect, is deeply implicated in gender confusions and inversions. It includes opera singers and welcomes "Squeekaronelly" to its fold; it sponsors Lord Hervey's play *The Modish Couple* (V.i; see Woods 1933), and it extends its sponsorship of impersonation beyond gender to species when it welcomes "Two dogs that walk on their hind legs only, and personate human creatures so well, they might be mistaken for them" and "A human creature that personates a dog" (V.i). Gender impersonation remains the central paradigm for Ignorance's inversions: played by Mr Strensham in *Pasquin*'s original productions, the role of Queen Ignorance is one of Fielding's most obviously significant cross-gender casting choices. Common-sense is a feminine personification, and she lacks any attendant, active force in the masculine military world. Ignorance, with all her followers, is a man masquerading as a queen.

A poet who approaches Queen Common-sense in the last stages of her battle identifies Ignorance as an impersonator by nature. He threatens Common-sense:

> . . . I'll dedicate my play
> To Ignorance, and call her Common-sense:
> Yes, I will dress her in your pomp, and swear
> That Ignorance knows more than all the world.
>
> (V.i)

The force of Ignorance has dressed itself, according to this play, in feminine pomp in order to impose upon the England it seeks to conquer. The danger Fielding sees in his equation of virtues with clothing in the auction scene of *The Historical Register* is that clothing and pomp, inherently transferable, immediately introduce the possibility of appropriation: any ways in which virtue manifests itself externally allow for its impersonation. We are left to choose between the invisible authenticity of Virtue and the dramatically visible but monstrous impersonations of Affectation.

Defeated, Common-sense is murdered at the end of *Pasquin*, though she returns as a ghost to pronounce the moral:

> My ghost, at least, they cannot banish hence.
> And all henceforth, who murder Common-sense,
> Learn from these scenes that though success you boast,
> You shall at last be haunted with her ghost.
>
> (V.i)

The triumph of Common-sense here is equivocal at best; she loses her life but retains some form of voice, gaining the special authority of ghostly speech. Under the humor of this surprise second ending to Fielding's version of the *Dunciad* lies, I think, some kind of serious attempt to imagine a way out of the dilemma posed in his writing by the separation of inward virtue and outward authority: Common-sense escapes the hopeless alternatives of invisible truth and visible impersonation by returning as an after-effect, a lost presence, a haunting. To ward off any possibility of impersonation, apparently, she must be deprived not only of clothing and pomp but of her body. Woman bears the representational burden for Fielding of his disappointment about the relation between internal and external selves, as, culturally, she must sustain the realm of private life, interior feeling, and personal identity apart from the public and commercial word of the male; inevitably, then, she must fail Fielding through her reliance on the "harlotry" of pomp, ostentation, or the drama of self-display if she is to be a part of this world. Becoming a ghost is her only alternative. And yet Fielding fears this alternative fate as well, though he may seem to wish it on her.

In taking on a cultural understanding of gender and identity that divorces the private, inner life from the physical and public self, and grants to women that shadowy inner realm, Fielding finds himself with a mixed legacy, which he represents with all the intelligent subtleties of his own ambivalence. Women are rendered by this system of thought both conveniently powerless in public terms and conveniently receptive to all the values men abdicate, values perhaps in conflict with the demands of public life, and yet ones which they have some stake in preserving, even as ghost-presences. Yet Fielding seems to suspect that by using gender to divorce these realms, he has rendered both sexes sexless, inhuman in some way: a ghost's spirit or a mechanically animated body. In insisting that Virtue remain invisible and not seize the raiments of outward authority or drama, Fielding exiles spirit to the underworld of ghostly abstraction – and also exiles outward authority to the lifeless materiality of puppetry or costume. Fielding's interest in puppets and other mechanical impersonations of life is as insistent as his interest in ghosts.

V

We can conclude our inspection of Fielding's exploration of gender and impersonation by moving outside the theater – though not far from Cock and Hen – and considering his account of the career of one male impersonator, who came to represent for Fielding the failure of the phallus to guarantee a masculine authority based on the possession of an inalienable natural part. The specter of a constructed or acquired phallus – so shocking an object as to remain unnameable for Fielding – figures large in his most direct, extended, and violently defensive representation of gender impersonation, the pamphlet account of *The Female Husband* (1746).

Based very loosely on an actual case tried before Fielding's first cousin, *The Female Husband* recounts the adventures of "Mrs. Mary, alias Mr. George Hamilton," a lesbian and male impersonator who courts and actually marries several women in the guise of a man.[12] Fielding fabricates most of his account of Mary's life (see Baker 1959 and Castle 1982), and one possible source for much of his fabrication seems to me revealing. The fictional life he gives Mary Hamilton shares much with the real life story of another male impersonator, Charlotte Charke, whom we have met already in the role of Mr Hen in *The Historical Register*.[13] Fielding's treatment of her life, as conflated with Mary Hamilton's, can provide us, then, with a view into a final level of reference for the figure of Mr Hen as he presides over the auction of virtues within the "allegory" of this scene.

Within the theater, Fielding played with and capitalized upon the dramatic possibilities gender impersonation offers, but Charlotte Charke's acting career carried over into her offstage life – she lived as a male impersonator outside the theater as well – and her life, superimposed onto Mary Hamilton's, seems to have raised for Fielding the

75

difficulty of containing impersonation within the theater, the frightening extension of impersonation onto the whole "stage of life," where appropriation comes to stand in for identity and donning the breeches makes one as good as male. In this pamphlet Fielding tells us that, for all intents and purposes, it matters not to the female husband's wives what her penis is made of, whether it is artificial and "affected" or real. After the consummation of Mary's first marriage, "the bride expressed herself so well satisfied with her choice, that being in company with another old lady, she exulted so much in her happiness, that her friend began to envy her" (38). When Mary's second wife is questioned as to whether "she imagined [her husband] had behaved to her as a husband ought to his wife? Her modesty confounded her a little at this question; but she at last answered she did imagine so" and that she had harbored no suspicion of "being imposed upon" (50). In fact, this wife too had aroused suspicious envy in other women by "the extraordinary accounts which she had formerly given of her husband" (49).

At the same time, not everyone he meets is thoroughly impressed with "George" Hamilton's masculinity. A widow he courts early in his adventures sends him a sarcastic letter of rejection that describes her astonishment at receiving a written proposal from him: "I thought, when I took it, it might have been an Opera song, and which for certain reasons I should think, when your cold is gone, you might sing as well as *Farinelli*, from the great resemblance there is between your persons" (36). Like the dramatic satires of the 1730s, the letter Fielding writes for the widow makes explicit for us the male counterpart to the female husband, appearing beside her within the same halo of anxiety she inhabits for Fielding: the detachability of masculine identity and power implied by the castrato prepares us for the appropriation of phallic identity represented by that "something of too vile, wicked and scandalous a nature, which was found in [Hamilton's] trunk," the artificial phallus which forms the basis of her conviction and the final and unspeakable outrage in Fielding's account of her (49). Of course, this appropriated phallus has its shortcomings, its inconvenient absences, but, as Fielding himself points out, so does a natural phallus – Fielding glosses a story of George's near discovery through the unexpected amorous advances of his wife with an analogy to the failures of unimpersonated masculinity:

One of our English Poets remarks in the case of a more able husband than Mrs *Hamilton* was, when his wife grew amorous in an unseasonable time.

> *The Doctor understood the call,*
> *But had not always wherewithal.*

So it happened to our poor bridegroom, who having not at that

time *the wherewithal* about her, was obliged to remain meerly passive, under all this torrent of kindness of his wife. (39)

That phallus which was to safeguard normative masculinity from the
disruptive implications of the figure of the castrato – that phallus which
was to insure moral and rhetorical, financial and political order – we
here find reduced to an erratic and undignified means, a *"wherewithal"*
which flickers in and out of the possession even of "a more able husband
than Mrs *Hamilton."* And *"wherewithal"* in this passage serves to describe
both the original and the constructed phallus: they are bracketed
together here under one demeaning term, and belittled, together, in the
face of the demands of female desire.

The Female Husband plays out the concerns that pervade Fielding's
early plays, literalizing in an unpleasant but often revealing way one
valence of those concerns. An implication of Mary's story that Fielding
refers to but does not emphasize hints at other valences. As an effective
female husband, she may disrupt systems of distributing not only sexual
but financial power by gender. The scandalous motivation for her first
marriage, Fielding tells us, is not lesbian love but "the conveniency which
the old gentlewoman's fortune would produce in her present situation"
(36–7) – as nominal husband Mary would legally control the fortune she
wedded in her impersonated role (see Stone 1979: 221–2 and Watt
1957: 141–2). In some sense, it is all the authority of every kind with
which the masculine phallus has been entrusted in Fielding's works that
makes it hard to distinguish from its "vile, wicked and scandalous"
counterfeit: vested with so much authority, the phallus threatens detach-
ment and dispossession, the possibility of appropriation. Other repositories of authority and power, other fetishized parts of sexual or political
bodies, undergo a similar process. A *Champion* essay printed at the end
of 1739 discusses the "strange *Lignifaction*" that spreads from the staffs
of authority to the men that wield them, turning living flesh to wood and
puppetry.[14]

As personal identity merges with social, political, or professional role
in the exclusive masculine realm of public life, an acquired phallus
comes to serve as well as a natural one. While the women who attend
Hen's auction represent the collapse of the disembodied feminine realm
of virtue into the alternative, negative realm of the material commodity,
the male impersonator who presides over the auction reminds us of the
susceptibility to impersonation of masculine identity as conceived in
relation to those realms. The notorious offstage life of the woman who
played Mr Hen provided another layer to the figure of Mr Hen onstage,
deepening the audience's awareness of that susceptibility. *The Female
Husband* shows Fielding at once at his most violently defensive about the
scandal of female appropriation of male identity and at his most explicit

about the thorough appropriability of a masculine identity constituted by clothing and the force of the phallus. When the phallus, counted on to insure so much, becomes indistinguishable from an inanimate impersonation of life, like virtue's treacherous "pomp," it becomes transferable – then the castrato appears too typical, and the male impersonator emerges as too powerful, too capable of convincingly wearing the breeches which the man, after all, only filled with something not really his own. Fielding holds an ambivalent relation to patriarchal power: he wants to clothe phallic identity in the outward authority of political, financial, and moral power, but he is not blind to the ways in which, put to such uses, the phallus becomes a part of the impersonal trappings of power, leaving the domain of personal identity and desire void and the trappings in precarious possession of their wearer. Though in the satire of his plays he cannot seem to move beyond imagining separate domains of masculine and feminine power, Fielding anxiously observes that such a geography of gender populates its world with ghosts and puppets.

NOTES

1 See the casting information for original productions of both *Tom Thumb* and *The Tragedy of Tragedies* in Scouten (1961). The 1730 edition of *Tom Thumb* lists Miss Jones as the hero, and she seems to have appeared in this role from the play's opening night on April 24, 1730, at the Haymarket through its long run into March, 1731. When the play reopened as *The Tragedy of Tragedies* on March 24, 1731, the role of Tom Thumb seems to have been taken for a while by a young male actor, billed as "Young Verhuyck," but the role reverted to female actors such as "Miss S. Rogers, the Lilliputian Lucy," Miss Jones Jr, Miss Brett, and Mrs Turner in subsequent productions in the early 1730s. Princess Huncamunca was played by the comic actor Harper at Drury Lane in 1732 and 1733, and by Pearce at Goodman's Fields in 1731. Though some cross-gender casting was part of the English farce tradition, *Tom Thumb* is highly atypical of eighteenth-century plays in the amount of cross-gender casting its productions included, particularly in the role of hero. See Nicoll (1925: 49–50); Ackroyd (1979: 90–8); and Rogers (1982: 244–58).

2 Fielding (1728: 5–6). Copy in Yale's Beinecke Library. I am indebted to Terry Castle (1983).

3 On masculine and feminine domains and the disruption of those distinctions, I am indebted to John Guillory (1986).

4 For a brief account of Farinelli's career in London, see the entry under his name in Highfill *et al.* (1982: V.145–52). Hogarth records Farinelli's wild popularity in fashionable London society at this time in plate two of "The Rake's Progress," where he incorporates the famous expression of one lady's hyperbolic devotion to him: she cried out from the audience at one performance, "One God, one Farinelli!"

5 Fielding includes satire of the castrati in *The Author's Farce, Pasquin, Eurydice*, and *Miss Lucy in Town*, as well as in *The Historical Register*. When I treat the castrato as representative, for Fielding and other satirists, of the absence of phallic power, I refer not to the absence of the penis – for castration removes the testicles, leaving the penis impotent and developmentally infantile – but to the absence of the phallus as a sexually potent penis, with all its figurative implications. Recent research confirms that satires from this period concerning individual castrato singers actually impreg-

nating women are unfounded. See Peschel and Peschel (1986).

6 I have used the copy of this anonymous pamphlet held at Yale's Beinecke Library.

7 As noted by Appleton in his footnote to these lines (Fielding 1967: no. 16: 25). See also Reilly (1953: 71–80), and Early (1955).

8 The references to auctions occur in Fielding's *The Temple Beau* (II.xiii), *The Coffee-House Politician* (II.iii), *The Modern Husband* (II.x), *The Universal Gallant* (I.i), *Joseph Andrews* (III.iii), and *Amelia* (VIII.ix). See Agnew (1986) for an extended discussion of the relations between the market and the theater in this period.

9 Partridge (1961: 164) confirms that "cock" was used to mean "penis" in slang long before 1737.

10 Henley edition of Fielding's works (1902): XII.337–9.

11 See Brown (1985: 104). As early as Ian Watt's ground-breaking *The Rise of the Novel* (1957), critics have recognized the importance of the new exclusion of women from the means of production for the treatment of women in eighteenth-century literature. Ellen Pollak has explored this subject in depth. See also McKendrick *et al.* (1982), on the special association of women with the period's new consumerism.

12 This pamphlet is available as reprinted in Fielding (1960). I give further citations of *The Female Husband* by page number in this edition, parenthetically in the text.

13 For example, Fielding invents escapades in the assumed identity of a male doctor for Mary Hamilton which seem to have no basis in her life but which do appear among the early adventures of Charlotte Charke. Fielding may have known of Charke's adventures even before the publication of her memoirs from his acquaintance with her at the Haymarket. See Charke (1969).

14 *The Champion* (1743: 12–20–39). This essay may be Ralph's rather than Fielding's.

5

BOYS AND GIRLS TOGETHER

Subcultural origins of glamour drag and male impersonation on the nineteenth-century stage

Laurence Senelick

I

Tapping into the popular culture of the past involves, for the revisionist historian, not only a stretch of the imagination but a wariness in assaying extant evidence. As Dario Fo has warned, such a study must go beyond mere assimilation of "things of the people." "It means taking everything that the masters have taken from that culture and turned upside down, and revealing their origins and developments" (Fo 1979: 16). Fo believes that popular culture is by nature subversive but that its most potent manifestations have been subverted in turn by the dominant culture. The job of the contemporary performer or critic or historian is to strip away these repressive accretions to reveal the original impulse.

Since the eighteenth century at least, sexuality that is socially branded as deviant has comprised a recognizable subculture in the west, but its most characteristic and enduring manifestations have often been coopted by the dominant culture which ignores or refuses to recognize their origins. Only recently have the debts owed to these subcultures begun to be acknowledged: unfortunately the cover-up or neglect has gone on so long that the act of retrieval is not easy. This has certainly been the case with the etiology of two relatively modern versions of cross-dressing – glamour drag and the male impersonator – which came to the fore in the nineteenth-century English-speaking theater.

The glamour drag queen in his sequins and feather boa is a familiar, even homely figure on the modern stage. Audiences accept, with varying degrees of enthusiasm, the ambiguous figure of the adult male decked out in feminine frippery intended to allure. Revues and nightclubs specializing in glamour drag pride themselves on projecting a convincing image of feminine pulchritude, undiluted by last-minute dewiggings or farcical antics. In a different way, the male impersonator has been resuscitated as a kind of totem by feminist theater groups; Edwardian masculinity emblazoning its unquestioned prerogatives is a sitting duck for such a show as Eve Merriam's *The Club.* (See Alisa Solomon's chapter in this collection.)

Glamour drag is, however, much more prevalent than male impersonation. In contrast to the ancient and ritualized sanctions of men portraying women on stage, female adoption of male prerogatives has occurred historically in the theater as a novelty, a salacious turn, a secular Bertie-come-lately. The bacchanalian release triggered by men capering about as women, exposing their "feminine" streak, has been seen as a necessary safety valve, especially if masculine and feminine roles in society are mutually exclusive. When the subservient sex wears the pants, such behavior is condoned only in anodyne modes which contradict the disguise by emphasizing female allure. This was the case in the Restoration when the prime attraction of women in men's clothes was that cited by Pepys: "To the Theatre . . . where a woman . . . came afterwards on the stage in men's clothes, and had the best legs that ever I saw, and I was very well pleased by it" (Pepys 1942: I, 180).

Conversely, by 1700, convincing female impersonation was no longer allowed to be sexually viable. As women replaced boy players as the x factor in the theatrical sexual equation, the *adult* male in woman's clothing remained what he had customarily been – a figure of fun, invariably burlesque or grotesque, the travesty Medea or Polly Peachum and, later, the pantomime Dame personated by a comedian. This tradition was maintained because, as a nineteenth-century observer noted, "a man in female garb is apt to appear awkward and ungainly" and, in a word, "unsexed" (Sage 1889: 284, 286).[1] The principal boy in Christmas pantomime came to be played by a young woman, but sexual transposition was never extended to let a youth play the heroine. Such transpositions were acceptable only when the age represented was transitional and, according to social conventions, the least sexually active: young women might play prepubescent lads – the Peter Pan motif – and men might play post-menopausal matrons – the Charley's Aunt motif – for those conditions offered minimal threat to standard gender identities.

Consequently, the tradition of the breeches role on the English stage avoided a convincing impersonation of a male (Plate 9). When such a thing did occur, it was rare enough to be remarked. Even Madame Vestris, whose fame "arose from the facility with which she could unsex herself, and the confident boldness with which she made her bow to the audience, in breeches," was less mannish than boyish. Macheath in her interpretation, complained one critic, "diminishes into a smart boy, and the voice of the brave man is lost in the half-womanish notes of the stripling" (unidentified newspaper clippings in Mme Vestris file, Harvard Theater Collection). The same held true for a popular portrayal such as Mrs Keeley's Jack Sheppard (Plate 10), praised for its avoidance of vulgarity, where the hero's tender years could excuse whatever effeminacy crept into the characterization.[2] These "hobblede-hoydens", as they might be termed, were thought, in an era of increasing sentimentality, to be better than boys at evoking pathos. More tears might be shed over a waif portrayed by a woman, by definition a victim, than over a gangling youth.

The dame and principal boy traditions permeated the early variety stage as well. Red-nosed comedians carried on as sex-starved harridans and slatterns; while a female serio-comic impersonating a tar or a tommy presented a somewhat amphibious creature, male in coiffure and cos-tume to the waist, but wide-hipped and often encased in tights below. Theatergoers were not confronted with a man playing a desirable woman or a woman playing a he-man.

The glamour drag artist and the male impersonator, who did intend to convey a plausible impression of sexes to which they did not belong, were therefore revolutionaries when they made their entrance in the late 1860s. Where had they sprung from? They were, as I hope to show, outgrowths of a newly conspicuous homosexual subculture, which pro-vided wish-fulfillment for society at large, and, despite English antec-dents, found their earliest opportunities in the New World.

II

Around 1800, Isaac d'Israeli, writing of the Elizabethan practice, spoke for most of his contemporaries when he professed there was "something . . . repulsive in the exhibition of boys, or men, personating female characters" (d'Israeli n.d.: 274). In the mid-Victorian era, however, epicene young men began to appear on the popular stage as attractive young women. The practice became widespread in America, England, and, to a lesser extent, Germany.[3] There the speciality was known as a *Damenimitator*; in America as a "male soprano"; in England as a "female impersonator." The word "impersonator" was itself a neologism in the 1850s, and its usage argues the innovation of a performance that lacks a traditional label. J. Redding Ware, the lexicographer of Victorian neo-terism, considered the term "female personator" as "a misnomer for the performer is a male who impersonates female appearance . . . while the male impersonator is a woman who dresses and acts like a man" (Ware 1909: 129). He would have reversed the terminology, with the adjective clarifying the sex of the performer. In any case, the novelty of the term suggests that the gender impersonator in our sense first took stage in an anglophone culture, originating along with the newest forms of variety entertainment. No more than fifty years after d'Israeli's expression of distaste, the female impersonator was a fixture of the entertainment world, and professional journals displayed such advertising cards as

"Harold Shromburg, world renowned male barmaid, golden-haired beauty, costly dresses. – Wire Mason's Arms, Blackburn" (quoted from *The Magnet* in Gray 1930: 122).

Which factors prepared the way for these performers? The Elizabethan boy player had come out of academe, and there the tradition was revived by the Victorians. At first " 'sex' was not yet recognized" (Motter 1929: 120): pupils at the Merchant Taylor's School in the 1860s made love to "ladies" in tail-coats and white ties, and at Harrow female characters were symbolically represented by a skirt worn over dress trousers.

Such student performances of the standard repertory were already common at public schools when a dramatic club was founded at Cambridge University in 1855, to the dismay of college tutors; the Earl of Lytton was acknowledged "the cleverest and most convincing of [its] 'heroines' " ("Men as stage 'Heroines' " 1909: 567–8). Oxford followed suit in the 1870s. A contemporary witness there says of the Rev. H. D. Astley as the female title character in *Villikins and his Dinah*, "his light, graceful dancing and extraordinary falsetto singing were such that the audience fairly shout with delight at the ingenuity"; and of Lord Montagu of Beaulieu, "in female parts he was quite irresistible, showing himself a close observer of the flirt, the minx, and the hoyden" (ibid.). American undergraduate romps like the Harvard Hasty Pudding, the Princeton Triangle Club, and the Mask and Gown at the University of Pennsylvania, burlesqued feminine behavior, and in these cases the production followed what one commentator called the "healthy rule" which "never permits an audience to draw a conclusion other than that the members of the company are boys and boys alone" (Wiedersheim 1941: 29). But "straight" plays performed at men's schools, Yale among them, which had all-male casts well into the twentieth century did seek to project an illusion of femininity on the part of their impersonators.

With the exception of Shakespeare, the plays selected were those with a minimum of love interest, "where, as an Irishman might say, all the ladies were gentlemen" (*College Theatricals* 1843: 738). Still, it is likely, certainly in the case of boarding schools, that the homoerotic sentiments they fostered could find a sanctioned refuge, without even implied recrimination, in theatrical cross-dressing and spectating. The closed society, on the *qui vive* against overt homosexuality, could relieve its anxieties and experiment with feminine behavior in a way that was neither suspect nor threatening.

A more professional influence came from the circus where feminine disguise was used to enhance the skill of the acrobat and the equestrian. The first male circus performer in female garb may have appeared in Franconi's *Mme Angot* during the Napoleonic period (Hippisley-Cox 1969: 39). Sexual enigma was played to the hilt by Omar Kingsley, better known as Ella Zoyara (1840–79), a trick equestrian from childhood (Plate 11). His billing teased "Is she a boy or a girl?" An Englishwoman who caught a performance at Niblo's Garden, New York, in 1860 said that Zoyara "whether he or she – was about the most astonishing rider I ever saw. Her pirouettes, leaps and attitudes are given with the most graceful ease, *figure* and *feet* were handsome, and dress perfectly modest without being prudish" (Cowell 1934: 25, 28, 127). He inspired a number of imitators, and, as his marriage tottered to divorce, a number of male suitors, usually from the European officer class (Kingsley obituary 1879; Hirschfeld 1910: 451–2).[4]

The acrobat Farini similarly disguised a boy he had adopted and who as "M'lle Lulu", the great female gymnast, made a sensation at the Holborn Amphitheatre in 1870. The confusion was compounded by the pseudo-girl's descending a lofty arrangement of trapezes and ladders to sing a song whose refrain was "Wait till I'm a man!" Shrewd London audiences recognized her as the boy-child who had earlier been one of the Flying Farinis. But the androgyne kept up the deception for seven years, photographed, interviewed and fêted throughout Europe and America. Only after an injury required a doctor's examination did he admit the truth, causing considerable embarrassment to the many men who had sent him love letters (Rendle 1919: 209–12; "Old time circus attractions" 1899; Peacock 1990: 17).

Zoyara and Lulu were not isolated phenomena, and their androgynous guises benefited from a homosexual undercurrent in circus life which has been occasionally noted but not extensively studied, despite Cocteau's celebration of the aerialist Barbette in the 1920s. (See Chapter 3 for a discussion of Cocteau's fascination with Barbette.) Those eminent gymnasts, the Hanlons and Voltas, testified in the 1880s that an admiration for the muscular masculine form and professional reliance on one another's strength and skill made most acrobats and trapezists scornful of women: they sought their sentimental attachments in their own company (Le Roux 1889: 197–202). For them, a female impersonator was preferable to a female as member of their band. Although this trait has been studiously ignored by circus historians, it plays a central role in such well-researched novels as the Goncourts' *Les Frères Zemganno*, Pierre Loti's *Azyadé* and, in our own time, Marion Zimmer Bradley's *The Catch Trap*, one of whose gay trapezist heroes begins his career as a "girl aerialist."

Another innovative variation was the wench role in minstrel shows. Brought to prominence by George Christy in the 1840s, it sought to delineate a young mulatto woman in a refined manner. After the Civil War, the female impersonator emerged, according to Robert Toll, as "minstrelsy's most important new speciality role" (Toll 1974: 139–44). The leading exponents of the genre were Rollin Howard, noted for the "richness, elegance and taste of his costumes" (Rollin Howard obituary 1879), Eugene (d'Amilie, 1836–1907), thought by his German audiences actually to be a woman (Plate 12), and, particularly, Francis Leon (born *c.* 1840).

Leon, whose real name was Patrick Francis Glassey, had sung Mozart as a choirboy at a Jesuit school: apparently his soprano voice never changed for as late as 1900 reviewers commented on it ("Leon, the female impersonator" n.d.; Rice 1911; "Revival of Negro Minstrelsy" 1900). He made his debut as a minstrel at the age of 14, studied ballet for eight years despite a frail physique, and became the star of his own company. The manager M. B. Leavitt noted that Leon's "work was novel and in the nature of a sensation" (Leavitt 1912: 36). What was sensational was the gentility and delicacy with which Leon played women. Billed without joking as "Premiere figurante and danseuse, Prima donna assoluta," he paid close attention to feminine fashions and mannerisms in his act. An elegant display of the latest modes became *de rigueur* for minstrel impersonators; by 1878, the male prima donna of Haverly's troupe was seriously lauded for displaying "one of the most beautiful toilets ever worn in Chicago" (New York *Clipper* April 6, 1878: 15).

Minstrelsy was the most respectable popular entertainment of its time: families that regarded the theater as the devil's chapel had no qualms about entering minstrel halls. Yet the popularity of such impersonators cannot be attributed to the common alienation effect promoted by the mask-like blackface. Minstrel wenches sported a "high-yaller" tinge; Leon's makeup, for instance, was considered by critics a convincing work of art utterly unsuggestive of disguise. Some other factor must be operative here.

School theatrics, circus stunts, and minstrel wenches helped condition the public to accept a new genre in which men frankly portrayed lovely women. But the genre was not so much natural evolution from these models as an offshoot of a thriving transvestite demi-monde impinging on the norms of popular entertainment. The association of cross-dressing and sexual relations between men had become proverbial by the mid-eighteenth century, with the revelations of London's molly-houses. The term "drag" itself, the brake on a coach, had filtered from the cant of thieves and fences into homosexual[5] slang, to connote the drag of a gown with a train. To *go on the drag* or *flash the drag*, i.e., to use female attire to solicit men, is dated by Eric Partridge to around 1850. Just when it entered theatrical parlance is uncertain. Partridge says 1887 (Partridge 1953: 239), but Ware puts it in the late 1860s, defining it first as a "theatrical petticoat or skirt used by actors when playing female parts," and then adding "Also given to feminine clothing to eccentric youths when dressing up in skirts" (Ware 1909: 116). In 1870, we find a young man writing to one such eccentric youth of his acquaintance "even if in town, I would not go to [the Derby] with you in drag . . . I am sorry to hear of your going about in drag so much . . . Of course, I won't pay any drag bills, except the one in Edinburgh" (*The Trial of Boulton and Park* 1871).[6] The recipient of this letter and others like it was a central figure in the popularization of glamour drag, Ernest Boulton.

The Boulton and Park Case of 1871 is usually cited as a forerunner of Oscar Wilde's trials to illustrate the common attitude towards effeminacy fifteen years before the Labouchère amendment imposed prison terms for sexual acts between men whether in public or private, consensual or not. Ernest Boulton, a 22-year-old bank clerk, and Frederick William Park, a 23-year-old law student (Plate 13), had been arrested for wearing women's clothes in public and for soliciting, although it is unclear whether as female or male prostitutes. The Attorney General arraigned them and three others for conspiracy to commit the catch-all crime of "buggery." His case was built primarily on the couple's public appearances in drag and the equivocally affectionate terms found in their circle's correspondence.

Although the defendants had been reviled on their way to the preliminary hearing, sympathy built before the trial when one of the alleged co-conspirators, Lord Arthur Pelham Clinton, MP, died reportedly of "exhaustion resulting from scarlet fever." Since his death occurred the day after he received his subpoena, suicide is a more likely diagnosis. The attorney for the defence, aware that the prosecution had crippled itself by not going for a more demonstrable charge of public indecency, structured its case on two cornerstones: first, the lack of any hard evidence to prove the commission of sodomy; and second and more important, the defendants' use of women's clothes for *theatrical* purposes. Even the opening address for the prosecution had admitted "that to assume a woman's dress for that purpose was no offense whatsoever." Time and again, the defence attorneys elicited from witnesses, including Boulton's doting mother, the facts that he performed widely in amateur theatricals as a woman; that his intimacy with Clinton resulted from a mutual interest in dramatics; that references in letters to their "matrimonial squabbles" referred to the plays they acted in; that the numerous photographs of Boulton in drag were made for distribution to his adoring public; that wearing these "costumes" on the street was a harmless if tasteless lark. As to the defendants' performing female characters openly, Boulton's lawyer apostrophized the jury:

the practice of men performing female characters prevailed at this moment upon the stage, even with the sanction of the Lord Chamberlain . . . No doubt familiarity was bred upon the stage. A greater degree of familiarity necessarily prevailed among actors and actresses than among other and graver classes of society.

As a matter of fact, reporters had observed that at the preliminary hearing, the police court had been packed with theatrical professionals, "such an interest have they taken in the case."

To our more jaded, if not necessarily more tolerant, age, the circumstantial evidence tells a different story. That Boulton called himself Lady Stella Clinton, consort of Sir Arthur, displaying a wedding ring and even ordering crested visiting cards under that name, suggests more than that he and Clinton had played wife and husband in a one-act farce. The passionate terms of devotion in letters from admirers – one of them deeming Boulton "Lais and Antinous in one" – reflects more than what the defence attorneys qualified as theatrical exuberance.

But the fact remains that deviant behaviour which invited prosecution in the street received considerable acclaim on the stage. The simpering and mincing that had Boulton and Park thrown out of the Alhambra Music Hall when in women's clothes, and out of the Burlington Arcade when in men's clothes, won them, behind the footlights, applause and admiration. Again the defence witnesses testify to a remarkable public appetite for female impersonation. Typical is the photographer Oliver Sarony: "There was a great demand for these photographs. They were sold out as fast as they could be printed. The performances were very favourably criticized in the local papers." One Scarborough journal qualified them as "something wonderful." Another, after suggesting that Boulton should have been born a woman, hurried to say "Let it by no means be understood that there is anything of the 'social monster' business connected with him . . . it is really difficult . . . to believe that he is not a really charming girl" (*The Unnatural History* 1871). Four years later, a writer in the *Dublin University Magazine*, attacking stage transvestism in general, excluded Boulton, praising "the utter absence of anything approaching indecorum . . . the genuine histrionic talent displayed . . . We may even go so far as to say, that many real actresses might have taken a lesson in modesty of demeanour from this counterfeit one" ("The London hermit" 1875: 249–50). Such accolades were echoed at the end of the trial, when the defendants were fully acquitted of the charges to loud cheers and cries of "Bravo."

Earlier commentators smugly remark that Boulton and Park then returned to deserved obscurity, but, as I have discovered, this was not the case, for the irrepressible Boulton soon pops up again. It would become common for notorious characters like the Tichborne Claimant and the alleged murderess Mme Steinheil to exhibit themselves on the music-hall stage. Boulton was a pioneer in flaunting his notoriety, for he suddenly turned up in the pottery towns of Burslem and Hanley performing the female role in an evening of duologues. Report has it that they were "fairly patronised" (Almaviva 1871: 14). Three years later he resurfaced in New York under the name Ernest Byne (Plate 13), playing at variety houses like the Theatre Comique and Tony Pastor's, assisted by "his brother Gerald" and under the management of the estimable agent Col. T. Allston Brown. The New York *Clipper* extolled him in doggerel:

> Your airs and graces make us all
> Believe you must be feminine:
> Your arts, though you're no *Harlequin*,
> Do well deserve a *column, Byne*.
>
> (September 30, 1876: 214)[7]

Boulton and Park were probably not unique in transferring their private predilections from the demi-monde to the public sphere. Commenting on the minstrel wench impersonators, Olive Logan remarked that many of them were "marvelously well fitted by nature for it, having well-defined soprano voices, plump shoulders, beardless faces, and tiny hands and feet" (Logan 1875: 698).[8] An interviewer spoke of Francis Leon's "real feminine pride" in showing off his costumes in private ("Leon, the female impersonator"). By transferring taboo behavior to the stage, such gay deceivers did more than find sanctuary for otherwise criminalized behavior. They offered surrogate gender alternatives to the general public. As the genre became commercially attractive, it was taken up by heterosexual – often transvestitic – performers as well. Of fourteen stage female impersonators studied by a German physician at the turn of the century, only six were homosexual, although eight (including three of the married men) wore women's clothes at home (S 1901: 317).

These clothes themselves deserved and got close attention. It is noteworthy that at the Boulton and Park trial, the police inventory of their feminine wardrobes was dilated on *in extenso*, not unlike reporters' tallies of the apparel of minstrel wench performers. The lists run on for long paragraphs, with fetishistic lingering on detail. The female impersonator came to the fore just when a mania for display was prevalent in women's clothing (Parsons 1923: 308–14). The 1870s was, as design historian Geoffrey Squire has pointed out, a period of "dashingly erotic appeal in dress," which, by exaggerating physical characteristics, emphasized the difference between the sexes. With padded bosom, jutting bustle and towering chignon, "woman was a fetchingly animated caricature of voluptuousness" (Squire 1984: 166). The tightly-laced "Grecian bend" with its corresponding high boots and facial enamelling created a look that was doll-like and artificial (Banner 1983: 119–20). The male of the species had, on the other hand, adopted as his uniform sober, baggily cut black broadcloth, the customary suit of woe for what Alfred de Musset called "a century in mourning for itself" (Hollander 1978: 380). What more natural than that man should covet the elaborate plumage of his mate?

The extremes of these fashions were worn by a newly conspicuous class of courtesans, "the pretty horse-breakers," made familiar by cheap photography, and by professional beauties on the stage. Public censure embraced courtesans and actresses indiscriminately, condemning the expenditure and lavishness of their toilettes; but this censure did not extend to the actors who flaunted such modes. An actor could hardly be accused of using pretty dresses to lure clientele: males were not expected to be attracted to men nor women to transvestites. When Boulton and Park dressed as men, their tight trousers and open-throated shirts, their powdered necks and rouged cheeks, were more disturbing and offensive to passers-by than their drag, which seemed the proper uniform for effeminacy. On stage, however, they were extolled for a becoming display of the latest modes.

III

Women might long for the convenience and lack of constriction in male garb, but those who sought to pass as men in Europe ran up against the same municipal strictures as did their cross-dressing brothers. Despite clandestine "drag balls," most European cities had civil statutes prohibiting public cross-dressing.[9] Even the bearded lady Clémentine Delait needed mayoral approval to wear masculine clothes when travelling (Nohain and Caradec 1969). America offered more receptive scope for the growth of male impersonation because, traditionally, women were more welcome in active professions, especially with their men at war, and the frontier provided a chance of upward mobility by means of transvestism. The gold rush and western expansion prompted so great an influx of cross-dressers that advertisements in mining regions had to specify "No young woman in disguise need apply," and one memoirist recalled droves of prostitutes crossing the plains in masculine apparel in search of a new line (Richardson 1867: 200). During the Civil War, the vivandières and even middle-class matrons serving in the Sanitary Commission adopted an "army costume" of loose trousers covered by a sashed kilt and kirtle. Encomiasts were swift to emphasize that the trappings of masculinity in no way detracted from a fundamentally tender and "womanly" nature, so long as their manly exteriors were confined to the field and the camp. It became cause for remonstrance, however, when Dr Mary Walker continued to wear her kilts and pantaloons in the post-bellum period (Moore 1866: opp. 54, 112; Ellington 1870: 30).[10]

Reformers in the early 1870s, animadverting on the institution of the "fast man," a gambling, tippling lounge-lizard who proliferated in the get-rich-quick atmosphere of the Grant Administration, also noted the advent of the "fast woman".

These women possess very much the same characteristics. They indulge in all the "manly sports" which it is possible for women to indulge in, and their philosophy or belief . . . is to eat, drink and be merry . . . They are young widows of gay proclivities; they are wives who are tired of the married relation and who crave for excitement; they are young girls who are more or less addicted to reading sporting novels and the flash papers of the day, and who possess a large amount of masculinity in their natures; they are women of every and any age, who have a large amount of vital and physical energy, and who in their early youth were known as being "wild," and whose wildness has not been tamed or curbed by the advance of years or the varied experiences of life.

(Ellington 1870: 385–7)

As papers like the *Illustrated Police Gazette* graphically pointed out, the fast woman often chose to dress as a young man-about-town and to attend primarily stag resorts, the concert saloon and the variety hall. These theaters burgeoned in the wake of the "leg shows," ballet extravaganzas like *The Black Crook* and English burlesque as introduced by Lydia Thompson and her British Blondes. When the leg shows closed, their coryphées and back-row beauties sought employment as turns in the new variety houses. The result, moralists would bemoan, was fast women on the stage and, to a lesser degree, fast women in the audience. When Ernest Boulton/Byne appeared in New York, he found himself on the same variety bills as a woman who may be said to have done as much for lesbian cross-dressing as he had for glamour drag. Annie Hindle, an early star of the concert saloon, may deserve the title of Mother (Father?) of Male Impersonation.

Although many aspects of Annie Hindle's life remain obscure,[11] journalistic accounts of her early life offer these data as fact. Born in England around 1847, she was adopted at the age of 5 by a woman who bestowed her own name on her and put her on stage in the pottery district of Staffordshire to sing love songs. The child was a favorite of the working-class audience, and in London adopted male costume as a joke, when singing a rollicking refrain about wine, women, and racing. A shrewd manager suggested that she make it her speciality, which won her immediate notoriety. There had been earlier female singers who had included male types in their music-hall repertoires.[12] Annie Hindle, however, appears to be the first woman both to specialize in male impersonation in the music-hall, and to do so not as a sailor or wagoner or schoolboy but as a flash young spark, clad in natty male streetwear.

In 1867 Hindle was brought to New York by an American manager, as the "first out-and-out male impersonator New York's stage had ever seen" ("Stranger than fiction" 1891); and her triumph and financial rewards were considerable. At this time, she was a plump blonde, about five foot six, with small well-shaped feet and closely-cropped hair which she parted on one side, man-like. Her voice was said to be deeper than alto, but sweet and tuneful.

The next year she was courted by Charles Vivian, an English comic singer of the *bon vivant* ilk, the life of stage parties and smokers; he had just co-founded the Benevolent and Protective Order of Elks. After a brief courtship, he and Hindle were married on September 16, 1868, and set out for the West Coast. A few months later they separated at Denver, never to meet again. Vivian's story was that the honeymoon lasted but one night; Hindle bitterly reported her variant, "He lived with me several months – long enough to black both eyes and otherwise mark me, yet I was a good and true wife to him" ("Stranger than fiction" 1891). There is corroborative evidence of Vivian's brutality in other situations,[13] and it may be that his masculine pride was wounded by the sizable salary his wife commanded. They never filed for divorce.

We may speculate that Hindle's unfortunate experience of heterosexual romance may have confirmed latent lesbian tendencies (or the latent lesbianism may have undermined the marriage's chances). In any case, Hindle's male impersonations became more veristic from this point on: her physique thickened, her voice deepened, and she took to shaving regularly, so that the down on her upper lip blossomed into a moustache and her chin sprouted the stubble of a beard. In her popular act, she wore fashionable men's wear and portrayed the standard *lion comique*, the bluff, high-living sport, a devil with the ladies but a decent chap at heart (Plate 14). Her repertory included such undistinguished but characteristic numbers as "Do not put your foot on a man when he's down," "Racketty Jack" and "Have you seen my Nellie?," in which the second and fourth verses contradict one another in their protestations of fickleness and domesticity:

> I'm a regular dashing swell, to ev'ry dodge I'm down,
> I'm admired by all the Boston sports and all the girls in town,
> They call me their dear Charlie, and they vow they love me true,
> To gain my young affections but, that caper doesn't do . . .
> I'm tired of single life and wish that I could find,
> One to make a loving wife so gentle and so kind,
> She'd always find love beaming in every smile and glance,
> I'm sure that many a lady here, should jump at such a chance.
> (Boston: Oliver Ditson, 1869; sheet music in the
> Harvard Theater Collection)

Although ladies in the audience may not have leapt on stage in response, their attraction to this equivocal appeal was attested by the number of "mash notes" Hindle received. She once compared billets-doux with Henry J. Montague, the matinee idol of Wallack's Theater, and her admirers, all women, far outnumbered his. She was quite indifferent to whether her correspondents addressed her as "Sir" or "Madam." Her closest attachments were to her dressers, of whom she had half a dozen over a fifteen-year period, and one night in June, 1886, she and her current dresser, a demure brunette named Annie Ryan, left the theater in Grand Rapids, Michigan, to be married in Room 19 of the Barnard House. The groom wore a dress suit, the bride a travelling ensemble, and the best man was, appropriately, the female impersonator Gilbert Sarony. When news leaked out the next day, there was a scandal but the minister insisted,

> I know all the circumstances. The groom gave me her – I mean his – name as Charles Hindle and he assured me that he was a man. The bride is a sensible girl, and she was of age. I had no other course to pursue. I believe they love each other and that they will be happy.
>
> ("Stranger than fiction" 1891)

This statement led many to conclude, erroneously, that Hindle was indeed a man who had passed as a woman for twenty years.

As the clergyman predicted, the marriage was a happy one, and with her savings Hindle retired and built a cottage in Jersey City, where husband and wife both dressed as women. Annie Ryan died in December, 1891, and her funeral, sparsely attended by a dozen figures from the variety stage, was the occasion for reporters to descend on Hindle and review her curious career. She herself declared that "the best of her life is gone" ("Stranger than fiction" 1891). I have been unable to establish a date for her death.[14]

Annie Hindle's example spawned a number of stage imitators, whom she did not begrudge. The first and most influential of these was Ella Wesner (1841–1917) who had started as a ballet girl, performing *pas de deux* with her sister in the late 1860s; she was Hindle's dresser for a while and, having learnt the tricks of the trade at first hand, was hired by Tony Pastor as a trial turn in the male impersonator line. She received $30 for a week's engagement, but, as her popularity grew, she earned as much as $200 a week. Wesner, like Hindle, recycled English music-hall material, her theme song the *lion comique* standby "Captain Cuff", and she even imitated Charles Vivian's hit numbers; but she was best remembered for her portrayal of a tipsy dude getting a shave. San Francisco went wild over her in 1871, reviewers regretting that "ladies can't go to the Bella Union, they would all fall in love with Ella Wesner" (San Francisco *Figaro* August 9, 1871).[15] Wesner's ersatz masculinity seems to be validated by a sapphic private life. She never married and her only intimated romance was with Jim Fisk's notorious mistress Josie Mansfield; after Fisk was shot by another of Josie's lovers, the two women went abroad and presided over a *louche* salon at the Café Américain in Paris.[16]

Nevertheless, in an age when public relations and press agentry were still rudimentary and the interview not yet invented, the private lives of Hindle and Wesner were not town topics. A male impersonator who appeared solo did not shock public sensibilities; the sentiments expressed by the songs were so highly conventionalized that no realistic correlative was conceived. Even when Hindle played a parlor scene called "Love and Jealousy" with Blanche de Vere, it was taken simply as "a very finished piece of acting" (New York *Clipper* September 24, 1870: 199). The personal "masculinity" of these women was, in fact, neutralized by their disguises, just as Boulton's femininity had been made acceptable by his stage performances in dresses.

On stage the *female* impersonator could flaunt a courtesan's wardrobe and coquettish behavior without falling foul of the censure aimed at a woman behaving in such a way. The *male* impersonator could replicate a young rake's swagger and dash, without being condemned for practicing such behavior in real life (Plate 15). Figures that were highly sexualized and consequently highly threatening were made acceptably attractive. However, the popularity of the raffish male impersonator and the tantalizing female impersonator who played otherwise condemned social roles suggests that they rendered these roles not so much innocuous as accessible. (That they were not innocuous is clear from an Atlanta city ordinance of 1870 prohibiting performers from wearing the garb of the opposite sex on stage. A reporter commented, "The City Fathers of Atlanta must be a queer old party" (New York *Clipper* July 23, 1870: 126).) The accessibility results partly from the stage frame but more, paradoxically, from the reversal of sexes.

The benefits transmitted between performer and audience were thus reciprocal. Homosexual men and women as well as heterosexual transvestites could experiment with gender shuffling in a context that won them approbation and indulgence;[17] the audience could savor sexually provocative behavior because it had ostensibly been neutralized by the transvestism. The acts' polymorphous potential proved attractive at a time when gender identities were severely defined by costume and manners. Both styles of performance functioned as wish-fulfillment. Male impersonation responded to woman's longing for the freedom and license available to young men. Female impersonation responded to man's longing for woman's colorful trappings and the strategy of vulnerability. Vicariously they could experience the potential offered by changing sex. Both *emplois* were soon to be neutered by the encroaching gentility of the late Victorian stage. For a more genteel audience, Vesta Tilley would return male impersonation to the principal-boy tradition, and Julian Eltinge would refine female impersonation to an asexual elegance – and both would be known for the faultlessness of their private lives.[18] But at their inception, glamour drag and male impersonation on the variety stage were potent sublimations of sexual anxiety and valuable techniques for enlarging the spectrum of gender identities.

NOTES

1 See also Mayer (1974). The transference of allure from the boy player to the actress is touched on in Senelick 1990: 33–43.

2 See also Fletcher (1987); Goodman (1895: 3–28). The substitution of pathos for verisimilitude in male impersonation is evident in the critical comment on her Smike in 1838: "Her small and pretty figure did not suit well for the representation of the overgrown boy of nineteen, but her dress was perfect, her look was unexpressibly wretched, and her voice and nuances heart rending" (Goodman 1895: 35).

3 According to S 1901: 313. However, in Second Empire Paris, one of the stars of the *café chantant* was a man who lived as a woman; see Legludic (1874).

4 Hirschfeld also cites the homosexual German writer Emil Mario Vacano who was a circus rider under the names Miss Corinna and Signora Sangumeta.

5 I use "homosexual" strictly for convenience, since neither the term nor the notion of an exclusively homosexual personality was current at this time. See, *inter alia*, McIntosh (1968) and Weeks (1980/1: esp. 116–17).

6 All quotations from Louis Hurt's letters to Ernest Boulton, April, 1870, and from the subsequent legal proceedings derive from *The Trial of Boulton and Park* (1871); lively accounts of the case can be found in Roughead (1931: 147–84), and Bartlett (1988: 134–43). Additional details of the medical examinations appear in Pearsall (1969: 464). Reports of the preliminary hearings in magistrate's court, where the evidence was more damning, were carried in the New York *Clipper* (May 28, 1870, and following dates).

7 Also see New York *Clipper* (January 30, 1875: 350); and Odell (1937: 465–66). I was able to make the connection between Ernest Boulton and Ernest Byne when I acquired a number of carte-de-visite photographs of him: the English portraits had Boulton written on the backs, the American ones had Boulton, Byne, or both. A physiognomic comparison clinched the identification.

8 Toll (1974: 140) quotes this, and says the appeal lay in the fact that this gender cross-over "threatened no one" (144), but this begs the question. *Why* did it threaten no one?

9 The archeologist Mme Dienlafoy was accorded by the French government the privilege of wearing male attire fashioned by her husband's tailor, at a time when transvestite women in Berlin and St Petersburg were regularly arrested.

10 *The Phunny Phellow*, a pro-Union humor paper published in New York, often ran cartoons about women in uniform; e.g., see the issue for December, 1862: 4.

11 Data on Annie Hindle are hard to come by. My account of her life and career is based on "Stranger than fiction" (1891); Graham (1902: 214–15); and the columns of the New York *Clipper* and the San Francisco *Figaro* in the 1870s and 1880s.

12 A Mrs J. Taylor appeared at a benefit at Moy's (the Royal Standard) on July 9, 1850, portraying "The middy on the shore," "The waggoner," and "The

acting schoolboy"; and in the 1860s Kate Harley sang "Away down Holborn Hill" in male character dress (Stuart and Park 1895: 40; and Mander and Mitchenson 1965: plate 29).

13 Vivian seems, by all accounts, to have been a nasty character, although he enjoyed popularity as a *lion comique* in the San Francisco area where he settled. In 1872, he collected a group of friends to vandalize the shop of a San Francisco tailor who had advertised Vivian's non-payment of bills ("Sensation by a comic singer" 1872); and in 1878 he was charged with defrauding a hotel keeper out of five weeks' board (New York *Clipper* April 27, 1878: 39). He died penniless in Leadville in March, 1880, and was buried in an unmarked grave; it took seven years for the Elks, who were eager to dissociate themselves from him, to erect a monument over it.

14 For lesbianism in the Victorian English theater, see Ellis (1936: II, 214–15). His informant naively believed that most relationships were non-sexual: "the fact is that the English girl, especially of the lower and middle classes, whether she has lost her virtue or not, is extremely fettered by conventional notions. Ignorance and habit are two restraining influences from the carrying out of this particular kind of perversion to its logical conclusions."

15 A blonde burlesque star took to wearing men's clothes in imitation, and even Hindle was referred to as "a character vocalist of the Ella Wesner type" (San Francisco *Figaro* October 8, 1871). A good description of Wesner's act at the beginning of her career can be found in the New York *Clipper* (December 18, 1872: 302).

16 Other isolated cases that crop up hint that the American theater often harbored lesbians with a penchant for cross-dressing. In 1876, for example, a French-born actress working in San Francisco who affected masculine attire was shot and killed by a Frenchman who found her in bed with his fiancée at the San Miguel Hotel ("A woman's mania for wearing male attire ends in death" 1876: 221).

17 This is supported by the account of a modern transvestite who manages to introduce his cross-dressing to "normal" friends by appearing in amateur shows in drag ("Edwina" 1963: 52–4).

18 For Vesta Tilley's permutations of male impersonation, see Senelick (1982). For Eltinge's innovations, see Senelick (1992) and Marybeth Hamilton's chapter in this volume.

6

THE TRAVESTY DANCER IN NINETEENTH-CENTURY BALLET

Lynn Garafola

More than any other era in the history of ballet, the nineteenth century belongs to the ballerina. She haunts its lithographs and paintings, an ethereal creature touched with the charm of another age. Yet even when she turned into the fast, leggy ballerina of modern times, her ideology survived. If today the art of ballet celebrates the *danseur* nearly as often as the *danseuse*, it has yet to rid its aesthetic of yesterday's cult of the eternal feminine. Like her nineteenth-century forebear, today's ballerina, an icon of teen youth, athleticism, and anorexic vulnerability, incarnates a feminine ideal defined overwhelmingly by men.

The nineteenth century did indeed create the mystique of the ballerina. But it also gave birth to one of the more curious phenomena of ballet history. Beginning with romanticism, a twenty-year golden age stretching from the July Revolution to about 1850, the *danseuse en travesti* usurped the position of the male *danseur* in the corps de ballet and as a partner to the ballerina (Plates 16 and 17). Stepping into roles previously filled by men, women now impersonated the sailor boys, hussars, and toreadors who made up "masculine" contingents of the corps de ballet, even as they displaced real men as romantic leads. Until well into the twentieth century, the female dancer who donned the mufti of a cavalier was a commonplace of European ballet.

In real life, donning men's clothing meant assuming the power and prerogatives that went with male identity. Cross-dressing on the stage, however, had quite different implications. Coming into vogue at a time of major social, economic, and aesthetic changes, it reflected the shift of ballet from a courtly, aristocratic art to an entertainment geared to the marketplace and the tastes of a new bourgeois public.

Thus the *danseur* did not vanish in Copenhagen, where August Bournonville guided the destiny of the Royal Theater for nearly five decades, or at the Maryinsky Theater in St Petersburg, where Marius Petipa ruled the Imperial Ballet for a similar tenure. On these courtly stages the male remained, even if eclipsed by the ballerina.

Where he fought a losing battle was in those metropolitan centers that stood at the forefront of the new aesthetic – Paris and London. At the prestigious cradles of ballet romanticism in these cities, the Paris Opéra and King's Theatre, he was edged gradually but firmly from the limelight by a transformation in the social relations of ballet as thoroughgoing as the revolution taking place in its art.

Unlike the theaters of the periphery, where government control of arts organization remained intact, those of the European core operated, or began to operate, as private enterprises.[1] Entrepreneurs stood at the helm, with subscribers paying all or a substantial share of the costs – even at the Paris Opéra which continued to receive partial subsidy from the government after losing its royal license in 1830. This change in the economic structure of ballet placed the audience – particularly the key group of moneyed subscribers – in a new and powerful position. It led to a new kind of star system, one based on drawing power rather than rank, while eliminating, for purposes of economy, the pensions and other benefits traditionally accruing to artists in government employ. The disappearance of the male dancer coincided with the triumph of romanticism and marketplace economics.

The ban on male talent was not, strictly speaking, absolute. Even in the second half of the century in England and on the continent, men continued to appear in character roles such as Dr Coppélius, the doddering lovestruck Pygmalion of *Coppélia*, parts that demanded of dancers skill as actors and mimes and could be performed by those long past their prime. Men on the ballet stage were fine, it seemed, so long as they left its youthful, beardless heroes to the ladies and so long as they were elderly and, presumably, unattractive.

Initially, then, the "travesty" problem defines itself as one of roles, specifically that of the romantic hero, who incarnated, along with his ballerina counterpart, the idealized poetic of nineteenth-century ballet. In the new era opened by the July Revolution, this aesthetic and the styles of masculine dancing associated with its expression became gradually "feminized." Scorned by audiences as unmanly, they became the property of the *danseuse en travesti*, that curious androgyne who invoked both the high poetic and the bordello underside of romantic and postromantic ballet.

Although travesty roles were not unknown before 1789, they were rare, especially in the so-called *genre noble*, the most elevated of the eighteenth century's three balletic styles.[2] Indeed, its most distinguished exponents were men, dancers like Auguste Vestris, who brought a supreme elegance and beauty of person to the stage and majestic perfection to the adagios regarded as the touchstone of their art. No one embodied more than the *danseur noble* the courtly origins of ballet, its aristocratic manner, and the masculinity of a refined, leisured society.

Already by 1820, the *danseur noble* appealed to a very limited public –

97

connoisseurs and men of refined tastes. To the increasing numbers from the middle classes who began to frequent the Paris Opéra in the later years of the Restoration, his measured dignity and old-fashioned dress betrayed, like the *genre noble* itself, the aristocratic manner and frippery of the Ancien Régime.

In the changing social climate of the 1820s, then, a new kind of gendering was under way. The men about town who formed the backbone of the growing bourgeois public saw little to admire in the stately refinements of *danseurs nobles*. Their taste, instead, ran to the energized virtuosity of *danseurs de demi-caractère* like Antoine Paul whose acrobatic leaps and multiple spins offered an analogue of their own active, helter-skelter lives. The high poetic of ballet, the loftiness of feeling embodied by the *danseur noble*, came to be seen as not merely obsolete, but also unmanly. With the triumph of romanticism and the new, ethereal style of Marie Taglioni in the early 1830s, poetry, expressiveness, and grace became the exclusive domain of the ballerina. At the same time, advances in technique, especially the refining of *pointe* work, gave her a second victory over the male: she now added to her arsenal of tricks the virtuosity of the *danseur de demi-caractère*. By 1840, a critic could write, "If male dancing no longer charms and attracts today, it is because there is no Sylphide, no magic-winged fairy capable of performing such a miracle and doing something that is endurable in a male dancer" (*Le Constitutionnel*, quoted in Guest 1980: 1).

In appropriating the aesthetic idealism and virtuoso technique associated with the older genres of of male dancing, the ballerina unmanned the *danseur*, reducing him to comic character and occasional "lifter." But her gain had another effect, more lasting even than the banishment of the male from the dance stage. Beginning with romanticism and continuing throughout the nineteenth century, femininity itself became the ideology of ballet, indeed, the very definition of the art. Ideology, however, turned out to be a false friend. Even as nineteenth-century ballet exalted the feminine, setting it on a pedestal to be worshipped, its social reality debased the *danseuse* as a worker, a woman, and an artist.

From the romantic era with its triumphant bourgeoisie and market ethos came the dual stigma of working-class origins and sexual impropriety that branded the woman dancer well into the twentieth century. The great ballerinas continued, by and large, to emerge from the theatrical clans that had survived from the eighteenth century, a kind of caste that trained, promoted, and protected its daughters. (Taglioni, for instance, arrived in Paris in 1827 with a brother to partner her and a father who coached her, choreographed for her, and acted as her personal manager.) The rest, however, belonged to the urban slums. "Most of the dancers," wrote Albéric Second in 1844, "first saw the light of day in a concierge's lodge" (*Les Petits Mystères de l'Opéra*, quoted in Guest 1980: 25). Bournonville (1979: 52) summed up the lot of the majority succinctly – humble origins, little education, and wretched salaries.

Poverty, naturally, invites sexual exploitation, especially in a profession of flexible morals. (Liaisons sweeten almost every ballerina biography.)[3] In the 1830s, however, the backstage of the Paris Opéra became a privileged venue of sexual assignation, officially countenanced and abetted. Eliminating older forms of "caste" separation, the theater's enterprising management dangled before the elect of its paying public a commodity of indisputable rarity and cachet – its female corps of dancers.

Imagine for a moment the inside of the old Paris Opéra. Descending tier by tier from the gods, we move up the social scale until, finally, we stand at the golden horseshoe of wealth, privilege, and power where, in boxes three deep on either side of the proscenium, sit the pleasure-minded sportsmen of the Jockey Club.

As the Opéra's most influential *abonnés*, the occupants of these *loges infernales* – all male, of course – enjoyed certain privileges: the run of the *coulisses*, for example, and entry to the Foyer de la Danse, a large room lined with barres and mirrors just behind the stage. Before 1830, lackeys in royal livery had warded prying eyes from this warm-up studio. When the new regime turned the Opéra over to private management, the Foyer de la Danse acquired a different function.[4] No longer off limits to men of wealth and fashion, before and after performances it became an exclusive *maison close*, with madams in the shape of mothers arranging terms. Nowhere was the clash, evoked time and again in lithographs and paintings, between the idealized femininity of balletic ideology and the reality of female exploitation so striking as in the Opéra's backstage corridors.

The commerce in dancers' bodies was not peculiar to Paris. In London, remarked Bournonville, it lacked even the pretension of gallantry that accompanied such exchanges across the Channel. To be sure, some dancers did eventually marry their "protectors." Many more bore children out of wedlock, sending them in secrecy to distant relations or country families to be reared. Nor did marriages between dancers fare well in this atmosphere of libertinage: one thinks of the choreographer Arthur Saint-Léon, Fanny Cerrito's on- and off-stage partner, who, jealous of the gifts showered on his beautiful and brilliant wife (which he could neither duplicate nor reciprocate), left the field of battle to his competitors.[5] The association of ballet and prostitution was so pervasive that Ivor Guest in his history of ballet under the Second Empire makes a special point of noting the Opéra's good girls – model wives, midnight poets, authors of books of religious reflections. But such cases were only exceptions. For pleasure-loving Paris, dancers were the cream of the *demi-monde*.

Aesthetics today stresses the dancer's symbolic function: it views physical presence as the form of dance itself. In the nineteenth century, however, the *danseuse* was first and foremost a woman. Like her audience, she saw the the task of ballet as one of charming the sensibility, not elevating the mind. Tilting her face to the *loges infernales*, flashing the brilliants of her latest protector, making up with coquetry the shortcomings of technique, she presented herself as a physical synecdoche, a dancer without the dance. For the nineteenth-century public, ballet offered a staged replay of the class and bordello politics that ruled the theater corridors.

Conventional wisdom has it that there were two sorts of romantic ballerinas: "Christians" who evoked romanticism's spiritual yearnings and supernal kingdoms, and "pagans" who impersonated its obsession with exotic, carnal, and material themes (Gautier 1932: 16). But this paradigm, invented by Théophile Gautier to describe the contrasting styles of Marie Taglioni and Fanny Elssler, is at best misleading. For no matter how patly the virgin/whore scheme seems to fit the ideology of romanticism, it ignores both the dancer's totemic reality – her position within the social order of ballet – and that troubling third who articulated the common ground of the period's balletic avatars of Eve. As an emblem of wanton sexuality, feminized masculinity, and amazon inviolability, the *danseuse en travesti* symbolized in her complex persona the many shades of lust projected by the audience on the nineteenth-century dancer.

Unlike the older genre distinctions based on body type, movement, and style, romanticism's female triptych aligned balletic image with a hierarchy of class and sexual practice. If Taglioni's "aerial, virginal grace" evoked romanticism's quest for the ideal, it also summoned to the stage the marriageable *démoiselle*, chaste, demure, and genteel. So, too, Elssler's "swooning, voluptuous arms," like her satins, laces, and gems, linked the concept of materialism with a particular material reality – the enticing, high-priced pleasures of a *grande horizontale*.

The travesty dancer practiced none of these symbolic feminine concealments. As shipboys and sailors, hussars and toreadors, the proletarians of the Opéra's corps de ballet donned breeches and skin-tight trousers that displayed to advantage the shapely legs, slim corseted waists, and rounded hips, thighs, and buttocks of the era's ideal figure. Like the prostitutes in fancy dress in Manet's *Ball at the Opera*, the *danseuse en travesti* brazenly advertised her sexuality. She was the hussy of the boulevards on theatrical parade.

The masquerade of transvestism fooled no one, nor was it meant to. The *danseuse en travesti* was always a woman, and a highly desirable one (a splendid figure was one of the role's prerequisites). She may have aped the steps and motions of the male performer, but she never impersonated his nature. What audiences wanted was a masculine image deprived of maleness, an idealized adolescent, a beardless she-man. Gautier, in particular, was repelled by the rugged physicality of the *danseur*, that "species of monstrosity," as he called him (1932: 44). "Nothing," he wrote, "is more distasteful than a man who shows his red neck, his big muscular arms, his legs with the calves of a parish beadle, and all his strong massive frame shaken by leaps and *pirouettes*" (1932: 21).

His critical colleague, Jules Janin, shared Gautier's prejudices: even the greatest of *danseurs* paled against the delicate figure, shapely leg, and facial beauty of the travesty dancer. Janin, however, added another element to Gautier's list of characteristics unbecoming in a male dancer – power. No real man, that is, no upstanding member of the new bourgeois order, could impersonate the poetic idealism of the ballet hero without ungendering himself, without, in short, becoming a woman in male drag. Janin's remarks, published in the *Journal des Débats*, are worth quoting at length:

> Speak to us of a pretty dancing girl who displays the grace of her figure, who reveals so fleetingly all the treasures of her beauty. Thank God, I understand that perfectly. I know what this lovely creature wishes us, and I would willingly follow her wherever she wishes in the sweet land of love. But a man, as ugly as you and I, a wretched fellow who leaps about without knowing why, a creature specially made to carry a musket and a sword and to wear a uniform. That this fellow should dance as a woman does – impossible: That this bewhiskered individual who is a pillar of the community, an elector, a municipal councillor, a man whose business it is to make and . . . unmake laws, should come before us in a tunic of sky-blue satin, his head covered with a hat with a waving plume amorously caressing his cheek, a frightful *danseuse* of the male sex . . . this was surely impossible and intolerable, and we have done well to remove such . . . artists from our pleasures. Today, thanks to this revolution we have effected, woman is the queen of ballet . . . no longer forced to cut off half her silk petticoat to dress her partner in it. Today the dancing man is no longer tolerated except as a useful accessory.[6]

As the concept of masculinity aligned itself with productivity, the effeminate sterility of the *danseur* became unacceptable to ballet's large male public.

But in defining power as male, Janin implicitly defined powerlessness as female. In photographs of the *danseuse en travesti* posed with her female counterpart, the modern eye notes a curtailment of scale, a reduction not only in the height and girth of the masculine figure, but in the physical contrast of the imaged sexes. What is missing, above all, is the suggestion of dominance, that intimation of power that even the most self-effacing *danseur* communicates to his audience. In appropriating the male role, the travesty dancer stripped that role of power.

In eliminating the *danseur*, ballet turned out the remaining in-house obstacle to sexual license. With the decline of the clan, only his lust, that last bastion of power, stood between the *danseuse* and the scheme so artfully contrived by the entrepreneurs of ballet for the millionaire libertines of the audience. For what was the Opéra if not their private seraglio? Thanks to the travesty dancer, no male now could destroy the peace of their private harem or their enjoyment of performance as foreplay to possession.

In appearance, the feminine androgyne laid claim to another erotic nexus. Tall, imposing, and majestic, she added to the charm of wantonness the challenge of the amazon, that untamed Diana who so fascinated the nineteenth-century imagination. In Gautier's description of Eugénie Fiocre as Cupid in *Néméa*, note the sapphic allusions:

> Certainly Love was never personified in a more graceful, or more charming body. Mlle. Fiocre has managed to compound the perfection both of the young girl and of the youth, and to make of them a sexless beauty, which is beauty itself. She might have been hewn from a block of Paros marble by a Greek sculptor, and animated by a miracle such as that of Galatea. To the purity of marble, she adds the suppleness of life. Her movements are developed and balanced in a sovereign harmony . . . What admirable legs! Diana the huntress would envy them! What an easy, proud and tranquil grace! What modest, measured gestures! . . . So correct, rhythmical and noble is her miming that, like that of the mimes of old, it might be accompanied by two unseen flute players. If Psyche saw this Cupid she might forget the original.
>
> (quoted in Guest 1974a: 200)

Fiocre, an exceptionally beautiful woman who created the role of Frantz in *Coppélia*, was one of the most famous travesty heroes of the 1860s and 1870s. Like a number of Opéra dancers, she shared the boards with a sister, whose shapely limbs commanded nearly as much admiration as her sibling's. By far the most fascinating sister pair of the century were the Elsslers – Fanny, the romantic temptress with the body of a "hermaphrodite of antiquity" (Gautier 1932: 22) and Thérèse, her partner and faithful cavalier. For over ten years they danced together, lived together, and traveled together. On stage they communicated a veiled eroticism, while offstage their relationship suggested a feminized relic of the older clan system.

A giraffe of a dancer at 5'6", the "majestic" Thérèse served her diminutive sister in the multiple roles reserved in an older era for the ballerina's next of kin. She handled all of Fanny's business affairs, decided where and what she should dance, and staged, without credit, many of the ballets and numbers in which they appeared. As a woman, however, Thérèse lacked the clan's patriarchal authority, while as a dancer she would always be without the wealth and power of the "protectors" who increasingly materialized behind the scenes – promoting favorites, dispensing funds as well as maintaining dancers and their impoverished families. Indeed, one such protector, the self-styled Marquis de La Valette, who became Fanny's lover in 1837, eventually destroyed the sororial ménage: his scorn for the ex-dancer who shared her bed forced Thérèse to leave.

One expects that the likes of the Marquis de La Valette relished the sight of his Elssler girls charming *confrères* of the *loges infernales*. But one also suspects that the travesty *pas de deux* was not so completely unsexed as the household he ruled. Certainly, it had been neutered by the substitution of a woman for the man, but that hardly means it was devoid of erotic content. Might not audiences have perceived in the choreographic play of female bodies something other than two women competing to whet the jaded appetites of libertines? Consider Gautier's account of a duet performed by the two Elsslers:

> The pas executed by Mlle. T. Elssler and her sister is charmingly arranged; there is one figure in particular where the two sisters run from the back-cloth hand in hand, throwing forward their legs at the same time, which surpasses everything that can be imagined in the way of homogeneity, accuracy, and precision. One might almost be said to be the reflection of the other, and that each comes forward with a mirror held beside her, which follows her and repeats all her movements.
>
> Nothing is more soothing and more harmonious to the gaze than this dance at once so refined and so precise.
>
> Fanny, to whom Theresa has given as ever the more important part, displayed a child-like grace, an artless agility, and an adorable roguishness; her Creole costume made her look ravishing, or rather she made the costume look ravishing.
>
> (1932: 24)

Thérèse had choreographed *La Volière* (*The Aviary* in English), which like her other ballets and dances made no use of men: she cast herself in the masculine role. Yet despite the differences in their attire, what struck Gautier was the oneness of the pair: he saw them as refracted images of a single self, perfect and complete. In evoking an Arcadia of perpetual adolescence untroubled and untouched by man, the travesty duet hinted at an ideal attainable only in the realms of art and the imagination – not the real world of stockbrokers and municipal councillors.

But dancing by its very nature is a physical as much as a symbolic activity. In the formalized mating game of the travesty *pas de deux*, two women touching and moving in harmony conveyed an eroticism perhaps even more compelling than their individual physical charms. The fantasy of females at play for the male eye is a staple of erotic literature, a kind of travesty performance enacted in the privacy of the imagination. Ballet's travesty *pas de deux* gave public form to this private fantasy, whetting audience desire, while keeping safely within the bounds of decorum. For ultimately, sapphic love interfered with the smooth functioning of the seraglio as much as the obstreperous male. In the case of the Elsslers, where Thérèse seems to have animated her choreography with something akin to personal feeling, the incest taboo coded as sisterly devotion what might otherwise have been construed as love. And one cannot help thinking that the buxom travesty heroes of the Second Empire and subsequent decades flaunted an outrageous femininity to ward off the sapphism immanent in their roles. In so doing, however, ballet robbed the *danseuse* of erotic mystery.

Today, thanks to the example of the Ballets Trocadero, we are apt to think that travesty in dance inherently offers a critique of sexual role playing, but the travesty dancers of nineteenth-century ballet offered no meditation on the usages of gender, no critical perspective on the sexual politics that ruled their lives, no revelation of the ways masculine and feminine were imaged on the ballet stage. What they exemplified was the triumph of bordello politics ideologized as the feminine mystique – a politics and an ideology imposed by men who remained in full control of ballet throughout the century as teachers, critics, choreographers, spectators, and artistic directors. The advent in 1909 of Diaghilev's Ballets Russes with its dynamic new aesthetic shattered the travesty paradigm. Seeing real men on the stage in choreography that exploited the strength, athleticism, and scale of the male body simply electrified audiences, causing them to look anew at the travesty dancer. But the audience itself had changed dramatically. The new following for ballet came from the highly sophisticated milieu of *le tout Paris*. The great connoisseurs, collectors, musical patrons, and salonnières of the French capital – many of whom were women – replaced the sportsmen and *roués* of the *loges infernales*. At the same time a new androgynous thematic and iconography, particularly evident in works created for Nijinsky where images of sexual heterodoxy transgressed rigid categories of masculinity and femininity, regendered the ideology of ballet, ending the reign of the feminine mystique. The era of the *danseuse en travesti* had come to an end.

NOTES

1 For the dramatic changes in the organization of the Paris Opéra after the Revolution of 1830 see Guest (1980: 22–5). In England, nineteenth-century ballet appeared exclusively in a commercial setting. John Ebers, a former ticket agent, assumed the management of the King's Theatre in 1820, an association that ended in bankruptcy in 1827. He was succeeded in 1828 by Pierre Laporte, who, with the exception of the 1832 season, controlled the opera house until his death in 1841, whereupon Benjamin Lumley, in charge of finances since 1836, assumed the theater's management. In the hands of this solicitor/impresario, Her Majesty's (as the King's Theatre had been renamed) entered upon an era of glory. In the 1830s and 1840s, under the management of Alfred Bunn, the Theatre Royal, Drury Lane became another important venue for ballet. During the latter part of the nineteenth century up to the eve of the First World War ballet lived on in the music-halls, above all the Empire and Alhambra, see Guest (1954: 33, 46, 83–7, 128–31); Guest (1962); Guest (1959).

   In France, it should be noted, the commercial boulevard stage was the breeding ground for theatrical romanticism. Long before the Paris Opéra's *Robert le Diable*, usually considered the official point of departure for romantic ballet, spectacular techniques and supernatural effects were commonplace in the melodramas and vaudevilles of the popular theaters. Ballet was an important component of these spectacles. Indeed, it was at theaters like the Théâtre de la Porte-Saint-Martin, which maintained a resident troupe and regularly presented new ballets and revivals, that the aerial style of dancing associated with romanticism began to crystallize early in the 1820s. Among the talents associated with the flowering of romantic ballet at the Paris Opéra who gained early experience on the boulevard stage was Jean Coralli, who produced several ballets in the Théâtre de la Gaîté. Guest (1980: 4–5, 13–14, 16, Appendix D, 272–4); Winter (1974: 178–9, 193–7).

2 Some instances of gender swapping prior to the nineteenth century are Marie Sallé's appearance as Amour in Handel's *Alcina* (which Sallé choreographed herself) and the three graces impersonated by men in *Plathée*, Jean-Philippe Rameau's spoof of his own operatic style. The lover in disguise *à la* Shakespeare's *Twelfth Night* was a popular conceit that called for cross-dressing. I am grateful to Catherine Turocy for this information. For the response of the London audience to Sallé's performance, see Migel (1980: 25).

3 Fanny Cerrito's liaison with the Marqués de Bedmar, Carlotta Grisi's with Prince Radziwill, Fanny Elssler's with the Marquis de La Valette, Pauline Duvernay's with (among others) La Valette, and Lyne Stephens, and Elisa Scheffer's with the Earl of Pembroke are a few of the romances that dot the ballet chronicle of the 1830s, 1840s, and 1850s.

4 For the changes introduced by Dr Louis Véron at the Paris Opéra after the Revolution of 1830, see Guest (1980: 28). Under Ebers, the Green Room built at the King's Theatre performed a similar function as the Foyer de la Danse, while at Drury Lane, Bunn allowed the more influential patrons the run of the *coulisses*. Procuresses "of the worst type" circulated backstage at Drury Lane, among them the blackmailing beauty specialist known as Madame Rachel

(Guest 1980: 36–7, 113).

5 Migel (1980: 218). Married in 1845 (to the chagrin of Cerrito's parents who had hoped for a son-in-law with a fortune or at least a title), the couple broke up in 1851. Shortly thereafter, her liaison with the Marqués de Bedmar became public knowledge. When rumors began to circulate in 1844 about Cerrito's impending marriage to Saint-Léon, the ballerina's London admirers, headed by Lord MacDonald, created a public disturbance when Saint-Léon appeared onstage. During one performance, the dancer stopped before their box and with a "sarcastic grin" and an "indescribable gesture" hissed menacingly at Lord MacDonald. The word *cochon* was heard to leave Saint-Léon's mouth, a gross impertinence coming from a dancer. Saint-Léon's written apology appeared in *The Times* a few days later (Guest 1974b: 85).

6 March 2, 1840, quoted in Guest (1980: 21).

7

"I'M THE QUEEN OF THE BITCHES"

Female impersonation and Mae West's *Pleasure Man*

Marybeth Hamilton

"Stop where you are! The show is over!" With those words, on October 3, 1928, detectives from the New York City vice squad leapt on to the stage of the Biltmore Theater and clapped their hands over the actors' mouths. The offensive production was *Pleasure Man*, a play by Mae West, set behind the scenes at a vaudeville show. Its crime: "endangering the morals of youth and others" through the "degenerate" antics of its supporting cast, the very men the police had silenced – a troupe of female impersonators.

That female impersonators should have attracted the vice squad may seem a laughable overreaction. Most likely, however, it does not seem altogether incomprehensible. Even in late twentieth-century America, female impersonation remains illegitimate performance. Apart from a few (very recent) exceptions, its practitioners are consigned to the margins of show business, to a netherworld of bars and nightclubs far removed from the entertainment mainstream.

At the heart of that stigmatization lies the perception of female impersonation as a homosexual practice. As a theatrical specialty it is consequently regarded as "extreme, bizarre and morally questionable," an illicit parading of sexual deviance (Newton 1972: 6). As anthropologist Esther Newton has argued: "The work is defined as 'queer' in itself. The assumption upon which both performers and audiences operate is that no one but a 'queer' would want to perform as a woman" (Newton 1972: 7).

Yet, though we take female impersonation's inherent "queerness" for granted, in fact that assumption is relatively recent. When *Pleasure Man* was raided in 1928, such sentiment did not hold nearly the sway it does now. Quite the contrary: for the fifty years prior to *Pleasure Man*'s premiere, female impersonation had been viewed as wholesome amusement, particularly suitable for women and children. Its practitioners had ranked among the most popular performers in vaudeville, and a few had entered motion pictures. It was only in the 1930s that our own assumptions gained prominence – that this form of theater was stigmatized as "queer in itself" and removed from the panorama of family amusement, banned across country by municipal ordinances forbidding male cross-dressing on stage.

In the first few decades of the twentieth century, in short, female impersonation acquired a new set of meanings that branded it illicit, illegitimate performance. Yet while historians have long recognized that this stigmatization happened, they have not fully explained where those new meanings came from and why they gained prominence when they did.

Mae West's production of *Pleasure Man* illuminates this new disreputability. In the 1920s West was Broadway's most notorious playwright and actress, the creator of a series of lurid productions. With *Pleasure Man* she staged her most controversial piece, a deliberately sensational play that toyed with the meaning of female impersonation, explicitly linking this respectable tradition to the styles and manners of New York's gay subculture.

This chapter begins by examining female impersonation in American vaudeville, focusing on its original connotations of "wholesomeness." It then turns to *Pleasure Man*, which depicted a troupe of impersonators in vaudeville – and destroyed those "wholesome" connotations altogether. The play illuminates the complex social and cultural changes that were destabilizing a respectable form of performance, for it redefined female impersonation in unforgettable fashion. After *Pleasure Man* – at least for those who had seen it – female impersonation would never be the same again.

> I have some lady impersonators in the play? In fact I have five of them. But what of it? If they are going to close up the play and prevent these people from making a living because they take the part of female impersonators then they should stop other female impersonators from appearing on the Keith Circuit.
>
> (Mae West, quoted in the *New York World*, October 3, 1928: 4)

Mae West's defense of her play, though unarguably self-serving, highlights a crucial analytical point: that up to the time of the *Pleasure Man* raid, female impersonation had been lauded as family amusement. For decades, it had been a mainstay of the most spotless of showbiz arenas: the Keith Circuit, which presented "big-time" vaudeville to America's genteel middle class.

The work of theater historian Robert Toll provides indispensable insight into this phenomenon. The next few pages summarize Toll's discussion (in his book *On with the Show*) of late Victorian female impersonation, in which he traces the roots of this vaudeville tradition and analyzes its solidly middle-class appeal. It sustained that appeal, his analysis makes clear, because (appearances to the contrary) it was not ultimately transgressive. As staged in turn-of-the-century vaudeville, female impersonation affirmed and celebrated the most traditional middle-class sexual norms.

To a degree difficult to imagine today, female impersonation at the turn of the century was one of the most popular of theatrical specialties. Several impersonators boasted nationwide followings. The best known – Francis Leon in the 1870s, Julian Eltinge in the 1910s – were among the most renowned entertainers of their day. Even as late as the 1920s this form of performance had lost none of its appeal. "There are more female impersonators in vaudeville this season than ever before," noted the trade journal *Variety* in 1923. "Three impersonators in one bill at a split house recently is viewed as a record" (Toll 1976: 256).

At the heart of female impersonation's broad-based popularity lay its unimpeachable respectability. Its very prominence in vaudeville makes that fact clear. From its beginnings in the 1880s, vaudeville marketed itself as "clean wholesome amusement," geared at the genteel urban middle class. Assembling its programs from a range of popular perform-ance traditions (minstrelsy, melodrama, variety, burlesque), vaudeville spotlighted only those that could be successfully sold as "family amuse-ment" – as one manager, writing in *Variety*, defined it: "entertainment for the masses, children and adults, to be given without bringing a blush or a shiver" (October 27, 1916: 3).

Female impersonation fitted that demand perfectly. Indeed, so esteemed for wholesomeness was this form of performance that simply labeling it "respectable" does not do it justice. At the turn of the century female impersonation was deemed *particularly* suited to middle-class taste, *particularly* fit for genteel women and children. Emerging as a theatrical specialty in minstrel shows in the late 1860s, it was created with precisely that public in mind.

While to an 1860s American audience cross-dressed male performers were nothing new, professional female impersonators decidedly were. The distinction is important. In the minstrel show before 1860, male comics had occasionally performed as women – usually in the service of bawdy satire, as in the stock character of "The Funny Old Gal," a caricature of an aging woman played by a burly comedian in frumpy clothes.

But that was a very different phenomenon from what emerged in the late 1860s and 1870s, as the minstrel show attempted to take advantage of a growing middle-class (and female) entertainment market. Appealing to that middle-class market meant respecting its concern with gentility and decorum. Out went the minstrel show's raunchy humor; in its place came a new theatrical specialty: specialist female impersonators, who built their careers solely on their ability to impersonate women, a skill they sold as a remarkable feat.

For late nineteenth-century theater managers seeking to pull in "respectable" crowds, female impersonation proved an unbeatable draw. In part, that appeal can be traced to the content of impersonators' performances, which validated some cherished cultural norms. Unlike their minstrel show predecessor, "The Funny Old Gal," female impersonators did not lampoon femininity. Their performances were serious, even reverential; they celebrated femaleness rather than mocking it.

And, crucially, they celebrated a construction of femininity that gave them an in-built middle-class appeal. From Francis Leon, who impersonated lovely ladies of fashion, to Julian Eltinge, who presented a demure ringletted child and a "dainty young miss in a pink party dress," the best-loved impersonators embodied and celebrated the Victorian feminine ideal. Their performances exalted those qualities deemed essential to respectable womanhood – delicacy, gentility, modesty, and grace.

Yet the fact that female impersonation upheld feminine norms does not explain why it was so astoundingly popular. It does not explain the phenomenon of Julian Eltinge, whose thirty-year reign as one of vaudeville's top performers brought him a nationally distributed fan magazine and ardent admirers from coast to coast. It does not explain the tremendous enjoyment culled by the respectable from these performances – the thrill that kept them on the edge of their seats for each of Eltinge's female sketches.

What thrilled and astonished fans about the best-loved impersonators was the apparent truth of the illusion. "I'll never forget the first time I saw him," recalled a vaudeville prop man of an Eltinge performance: "I couldn't believe it was a man. He was the most beautiful woman I ever saw on Keith's stage and that includes Lillian Russell and Ethel Barrymore and all the rest" (Toll 1976: 239).

Though the prop man marveled at Eltinge's beauty, his real *wonder* was directed elsewhere: at this male performer's ability to project convincing femininity, replicated down to the most minute detail. To contemporary observers, it was a remarkable feat, one that inspired endless awestruck comment. "There is not, from the time of his entrance until he quits the stage, the slightest suggestiveness of a disguised member of the sterner sex," rhapsodized a Leon admirer in the 1870s – praise that Eltinge's fans echoed forty years later (Toll 1976: 243). His impersonations, his admirers argued, were uncanny:

> He does not . . . force his voice to an unnatural soprano pitch, but maintains a natural tone, speaking very deliberately, so that it is a low contralto. There is, therefore, no incongruity between the woman's appearance and the spoken word. He walks with the short

steps of a woman, but with the recognized gait required by the slightly hobbled dress.

Altogether lacking in "incongruity," Eltinge so unerringly recreated feminine nuances that he even captured the peculiar step demanded by a lady's high-fashion attire.

To turn-of-the-century middle-class audiences, this seemed a thrilling and altogether incredible feat. It confounded one of their most basic assumptions: that men and women were fundamentally different species, in habits of thought, feeling, and action separated by a deep and unbridgeable divide. That men were aggressive, competitive, active; that women were gentle, spiritual, passive; and that no common ground existed between these polarized positions: to nineteenth-century middle-class Americans these were indisputable biological facts.

In this context, impersonators' popularity may seem perplexing – the very ease with which they crossed gender boundaries might seem to challenge these rigid assumptions. But in fact their performances did precisely the opposite. Billing themselves as "female illusionists," impersonators were lauded as skilled magicians, able to conjure themselves across gender boundaries that all observers believed to be fixed and immutable.

Therein lay the secret of impersonation's middle-class appeal: it turned on that most awe-inspiring of skills of performance – the ability to perform an act of magic. Done successfully, *Variety* noted, it constituted a "thing of wonderment." Audiences marveled at Julian Eltinge as they did at the likes of Harry Houdini: at the conjurer's skill by which he transgressed nature's barriers, went from man to woman, crossed what they saw as an unbridgeable divide.

"It is a libelous and treacherous portrayal of show people, and one that demands retraction to the thousands it so falsely paints and so grossly insults" (*Billboard*, October 13, 1928: 42). The sheer fury of *Billboard*'s attack on *Pleasure Man* indicates the raw nerve that West's show had struck. Like the bulk of the Broadway community, *Billboard* saw *Pleasure Man* as a slander on show people – and on female impersonators in particular. The rage was overstated, but the journal did have a point. *Pleasure Man* presented a sharply untraditional reading of female impersonation – one that concertedly undermined all its connotations of wholesomeness.

Pleasure Man subverted the fundamental premise of the vaudeville tradition: that in masquerading as women, impersonators accomplished a magical transformation, crossed a rigid, unbreachable gender divide. *Pleasure Man*'s female impersonators, on the contrary, were effeminate to start with. For them portraying women was no act of magic, but an expression of a "womanly" sexual self.

Pleasure Man established this subversive vision by taking its audience behind the scenes, spotlighting a group of female impersonators before and after their vaudeville performance. In Acts I and II, we observe the impersonators backstage, still dressed in everyday male attire and preparing for the evening's show. That device gave these scenes a tantalizing power: by taking viewers behind the curtain, West's play purported to offer a privileged glimpse of female impersonators "as they *really* are."

What they "really are," the play argued, was flamboyantly effeminate. Even when dressed in male attire, *Pleasure Man*'s female impersonators minced as they walked, postured suggestively as they stood, and took up bits of needlework while relaxing backstage. Police officers characterized their mannerisms as befitting a group of "proud young girls": in one scene a male character threw open a door to find a female impersonator changing clothes; the impersonator pulled a kimono around himself and screamed "like a frightened woman."[1]

The impersonators' effeminacy involved more than just mannerisms: as the play presented them, they were biological males who lived out a feminine social identity. Some impersonators – like "Bunny" and "Peaches" – went by female names; all referred to themselves as "women" and "girls" and addressed their fellows with feminine pronouns. And not only did their slang evoke "womanish" images – so did the tone in which it was delivered: giddy and shrill, punctuated by bitchy insults and hysterical shrieks.

Finally, the female impersonators' effeminacy extended to their taste in sexual partners. Like women, they slept with men. This fact was made unmistakable in countless instances of acid-tongued banter: in Peaches's complaint about a clumsy ex-lover ("Men are such uncouth things"); and in bawdy exchanges scattered throughout the play, exchanges laden with sexual double entendres and leering allusions to male anatomy.

> STAGEHAND: Have you had your cream-puff this morning?
> PARADISE: Oh, I always eat early – you know it's the early bird that catches the worm, dearie.
>   . . .
> BUNNY: Peaches dear, did you see that glorious Adonis directing traffic at Broad and Main Street?
> PEACHES: Do you mean the one on the horse, dearie? You know that's the statue of some General.
> BUNNY: Oh, perhaps it's General Coxey.[2]

While vaudeville hailed impersonators as virile men transforming themselves through magical skills of performance, Mae West suggested a far more sensational reading: that female impersonation was a vehicle of homosexual self-expression, a means for gay men to flaunt their true sexual selves. That was certainly the only reading possible for the Act II performances of *her* female impersonators. Taking the stage at a post-performance party, a dozen impersonators cavorted in women's clothes, singing musical numbers rife with gay slang ("I'm the Queen of the Bitches") and delivering a succession of comic "bits," rapid-fire one-liners that directed their humor at police raids and male lovers.

1st BOY: I hear you're working in a millinery shop.
2nd BOY: Yes, I trim rough sailors.
3rd BOY: My, what a low-cut gown you've got.
4th BOY: Why, Beulah, a woman with a back like mine can be as low as she wants to be.
1st BOY: I hear you're studying to be an opera singer.
2nd BOY: Oh, yes, and I know so many songs.
1st BOY: You must have a large repertoire.
2nd BOY: Must I have that too?
3rd BOY: Oh, look, I can almost do the splits.
4th BOY: Be careful, dearie, you'll wear out your welcome.

What *Pleasure Man* suggested, in the end, was a radical redefinition of female impersonation, linking onstage cross-dressing to offstage effemi-nacy and equating the latter with homosexuality. To our eyes, certainly, it comes across as a dubious, politically reactionary enterprise. By equat-ing effeminacy with homosexuality, the play appears to perpetuate one of the most hackneyed of homophobic stereotypes.

Yet, as historian George Chauncey has noted in his pathbreaking study of New York City's gay history, in the 1920s that equation was no mere stereotype – it had a firm basis in gay social reality. By the 1920s New York City had developed a thriving homosexual subculture. And effeminate style predominated in that subculture, far more than it does today.

In 1928 New York housed a growing gay community, one which dated its emergence to the turn of the century when a network of bars, bathhouses, and other meeting-places took root in Harlem, Greenwich Village, and the Lower East Side (Chauncey 1986). New York was not the only American city to see the rise of a gay underworld during those years. As newspaper accounts, medical case histories, and personal correspondence testify, such subcultures took root in major centers across the nation, as gay men and women made their sexual desires the basis of a personal identity and a distinctive social style (D'Emilio 1983).

At the heart of that style, for gay men, lay what Chauncey has described as the "culture of effeminacy": the use of "womanish" banter and mannerisms – even female names and feminine pronouns. Chauncey's investigation of New York's early gay community suggests that, far more commonly than in later years, gay men found in effemi-nate style the clearest means of participating in a gay social world. He writes:

More gay men in the 1920s than today *did* adopt effeminate mannerisms: they provided one of the few sure means of announcing one's sexuality. But acting like a "fairy" was more than just a code; it was the dominant role model available to men forming a gay identity, and one against which every gay man had to measure himself.

(Chauncey 1986: 29–30)

To signal homosexuality in the 1920s, in short, men adopted effeminate style – or, to put it another way, they impersonated women. For some men that impersonation became a way of life, a persona both public and private; for others, it was adopted to fit the occasion, set aside for working hours but put on at night, as part of participation in New York's vital homosexual nightlife. There, effeminate style set the tone, particularly at what became New York's largest gay social event – its series of drag balls, held six or seven times each year at Harlem's Rockland Palace, the old Madison Square Garden, and the Astor Hotel and often attended by thouands (Chauncey 1986).

Pleasure Man unearthed that underworld effeminate style and placed it under the Broadway spotlight. It was the play's replication of gay social reality that ultimately damned it in the eyes of its critics. Theater writers and practitioners, in particular, were outraged. In their view West was little more than a crass pornographer, exploiting a time-honored theatrical tradition as a pretext for showcasing "degenerate antics," usurping the artistic terrain of Broadway for something that belonged in the underworld streets. "There was not a trace of playwriting in it," fumed drama critic George Jean Nathan in the December, 1928, *American Mercury*. "The thing was a mere lifting over to a theatre stage of the kind of Harlem 'drag' that the police peremptorily raid."

In some ways the theater community was right. Mae West was unarguably an opportunist. Convicted two years previously for onstage obscenity, West specialized in raunchy plays that retailed dirt to the Broadway public. Her interest in female impersonators was clearly exploitative: they provided a convenient pretext, a shrewd means of flaunting censorable stage content. In 1928, New York state law forbade open stage depiction of homosexuality. Yet West managed to depict gay culture's most sensational elements (and deny any sensational intent) by exploiting the link between mainstream vaudeville tradition and the female impersonation at the heart of gay style.

Yet, though West's lurid intentions are undeniable, she was hardly as inventive as her detractors made out. Critics accused her of singlehandedly perverting female impersonation: of fabricating a connection between the sexual underworld and the the world of the theatrical female impersonator; thus opening the stage to sexual deviants whose perform-

ances were foreign to dramatic tradition. Yet there was theatrical precedent, however lowly, for the kind of performances *Pleasure Man*
showcased. Indeed, what West's play uncovered on Broadway was not
just the style and slang of New York's gay community, but an underground tradition of female impersonation, one that had existed as long
as vaudeville's but had hitherto resided in very different quarters.

For information about that tradition, one need only have turned to
Jimmy Durante, whose long experience as a nightclub pianist had given
him an intimate knowledge of underworld nightlife. Durante got his
first job in a gay bar on New York's Bowery; after the club was raided in
1905, he went to work at Diamond Tony's, a run-down saloon on Coney
Island. As he remembered in 1930, both Diamond Tony's and the
neighboring club Jack's staged a brand of female impersonation not too
dissimilar to that offered in *Pleasure Man*.

> At our place and Jack's, the entertainers were all boys who danced
> together and lisped. They called themselves Edna May and Leslie
> Carter and Big Tess and things like that. You know. Just like the
> first joint I worked in. When they had sung their numbers, they sat
> at the tables the way hostesses do today, "spinning their web," as
> they called it. Some of them were six feet tall and built like
> Dempsey, so it was never very healthy to make nasty cracks.
>
>   Outside of the queer entertainers, our place was no different
> from most of the others. The usual number of girls hung out there,
> and the customers were mostly on the level; that is to say, they were
> not interested in our entertainers any more than they would have
> been in the freaks that filled the Surf Avenue sidewalks.
>
> (Durante and Kofoed 1931: 54–5)

A native of New York's Bowery, Durante had an insider's knowledge
of underworld amusements like burlesque theaters and concert saloons
– venues, located in the city's slums, that offered raunchy diversion to
working-class men. Within that world, his comments suggest, female
impersonators were a common attraction. That perception was confirmed by others – vice investigators, in particular, whose ventures into
underworld nightlife introduced them to the tradition of the "fairy
impersonator."

Like all performance traditions, this one was marked by a set of
conventions. The underworld impersonator masqueraded as female.
That, however, was virtually the only convention he held in common
with his vaudeville counterpart. Unlike such performers as Julian
Eltinge, he made no pretense of showcasing a skill of performance, of
attempting to impress observers with impeccable recreations of feminine
detail. The whole thrill of his stage appearances lay, on the contrary, in
the fact that he was not, technically, performing at all. He was displaying

115

his real, offstage self – as (in turn-of-the-century terms) a "fairy," a "third sexer," a being who straddled the gender divide.

Drawn from the ranks of the gay underground, the underworld impersonator used the stage to flaunt an illicit offstage sexual self. In so doing, he followed a pattern shared by other performers in underworld theater. In these theatrical spaces, stage life and street life tended to merge: female dancers, too, gave raunchy performances that suggested an offstage identity as a prostitute. And like Durante's female impersonators, who sat with patrons "spinning their web," the women followed their dances with "audience work," mingling with customers to sell drinks and sex.

Vice investigators loathed all underworld theater, with its promiscuous mingling of patrons and performers, its blurring of the boundary between the stage and the street. Yet, perhaps not surprisingly, they viewed its female impersonators as the most pernicious spectacle of all. One turn-of-the-century investigator reported:

> If you want to understand the full measure of the harm that can be done by masqueraders of this sort, you should go, as I have gone, to some of the concert halls on the Bowery, and see in what fashion they make their appeal to the boys and men who constitute almost their entire audience, and with what evil intelligence the audience responds to their insinuations of word and action. These denizens of the slums know too well the awful horror which the masquerades may be made to suggest.
>
> (*New York Herald-Tribune*, April 14, 1895)

What was most horrendous to this vice investigator was the sheer familiarity of these spectacles to lower-class patrons and the reading the performances so clearly invited. The boys and men in that Bowery audience *knew* to respond with "evil intelligence" – they *knew* that these impersonations connoted not acts of magic but the "awful horror" of homosexual sex.

So long as that knowledge was limited to "denizens of the slums," vaudeville female impersonation could continue to flourish, with the middle class continuing to read it as thrilling yet wholesome theatrical magic. Yet it seems clear that – well prior to the *Pleasure Man* premiere – that traditional reading had come under strain. While the most renowned vaudeville impersonators remained as popular as ever, they were framing their performances to cope with new challenges – rumors circulating among their middle-class audiences about female impersonation's possible "deviant" meanings.

Take, for example, Julian Eltinge. In the 1910s Eltinge remained one of the most popular performers in vaudeville. But his publicity took on a defensive new slant, carefully framed to alleviate doubts about the nature of his private identity. "JULIAN ELTINGE ISN'T EFFEMINATE WHEN HE GETS HIS CORSETS OFF" trumpeted one press notice.

> This is Julian D. Eltinge, a handsome, healthy young man, filled with the joy of life, bubbling over with spirits, a strong young athlete who covered right garden for the Harvard baseball team, and who has every appearance on the stage of a charming young woman, who sings divinely and dances as lightly and gracefully as a ballroom belle.
>
> There is nothing feminine about Julian, for when off the stage he will get into a game of poker, can beat Bob Hilliard playing pinochle, can row in a varsity eight, or can eat chop suey with the sticks and talk nonsense with the ladies. Julian is certainly all right.
>
> (Julian Eltinge clippings file, Billy Rose Theater Collection at Lincoln Center)

He was all right, the article insisted, in that he was a genuinely masculine male: an athlete, a gambler, an adventurous rake. In taking the stage dressed as a woman, he performed a supreme act of magic. It was sheer skill of performance – not an offstage effeminacy – that enabled him to cross that gender divide.

"There is nothing feminine about Julian," his publicity stressed. Clearly, it is necessary to insist on that point only if one fears that one's readers believe precisely the opposite. In stark contrast to earlier vaudeville impersonators, Eltinge felt compelled to surround his performances with assurances of his offstage masculinity. It was only those assurances that could counter a growing awareness among his middleclass fans: that female impersonation could hold a sensational meaning – it could imply not a professional skill of performance but a sexually deviant offstage self.

That that awareness existed seems indisputable; where it came from is more difficult to pin down. Certainly, it must have stemmed at least in part from the growing visibility of New York's gay community. Vice investigations, police raids, and press exposés – to say nothing of what could be seen on the streets – by the 1910s were familiarizing middleclass New Yorkers with the city's expanding homosexual subculture. That familiarization may well have brought with it a sense of how gay men "impersonated women" – both as a means of expressing a gay identity and as participants in underworld theater and nightlife.

The turn-of-the-century medical profession played a key role as well. In a voluminous body of literature describing and classifying sexual abnormality, it brought cross-dressing under scientific scrutiny, deeming it a key symptom of "sexual inversion." As conceptualized by European sexologists Richard von Krafft-Ebing and Havelock Ellis, "sexual

117

inversion" defined gay men and women as victims of a medical disorder, a dysfunction compelling them to adopt not just the sexual preferences but the appearance and behavior of the opposite sex. Through theories of inversion, cross-dressing reentered the culture defined as a symptom of a pathology. Indeed, according to some medical theorists, cross-dressing constituted a pathology unto itself; by 1910, studied and analyzed, it acquired its own name: "transvestism" (Chauncey 1989b: 87–117; Katz 1983: 145–7).

Gay streetlife and medical literature were exposing middle-class audiences to new ideas and influences; but, just as crucially, the most basic middle-class beliefs and values were already in the process of change. The early years of the twentieth century saw the decline of Victorian "separate spheres" ideology, the belief that men and women were mentally, emotionally, and psychologically different. By the 1910s, scientific studies were undermining that belief; and young middle-class women were actively flouting it, adopting male habits (smoking, drinking) and male vocations (college attendance, professional careers) to express a new middle-class conviction of the basic similarity of the sexes' talents and temperaments.

All performance traditions, in order to flourish, must bear some relation to social reality. Yet the traditional reading of vaudeville impersonation suited a world that was rapidly fading. It suited a world where men and women were deemed to be starkly and fundamentally different, separated by biologically-rooted distinctions. Only there could a convincing female impersonation seem as baffling and as thrilling as an act of pure magic.

For the two decades prior to *Pleasure Man*'s premiere, female impersonation had been losing its capacity to move audiences to "wonderment"; it may well have been provoking their prurient curiosity. Mae West, for her part, addressed that curiosity – far more baldly and sensationally than anyone else had dared.

In March, 1930, after repeated delays, Mae West stood trial for *Pleasure Man*. From the beginning the cards were stacked in her favor. The prosecution faced the near-impossible task of convicting a production staged eighteen months previously – a production for which they had no script (West claimed no script had ever existed) and whose crucial actors were conspicuously absent (all the female impersonators, West reported, had joined the navy) (*New York World*, April 4, 1931: 1).

The trial swiftly descended into a tangle of cross-accusations. The state accused West of "parading degeneracy," but lacked any evidence to back up its charges. Mae West, for her part, denied everything: all the sexual double-entendres, all the connotations of homosexuality. The police, she claimed, had faulty memories – or were on a campaign to "get

Mae West." Faced with such sharply conflicting testimony, the jury collapsed in a seven-to-five deadlock.

So Mae West, more or less by default, was cleared. But female impersonation most decidedly was not. As the 1930s proceeded, it became increasingly stigmatized, pushed from the stages of respectable theaters.

There was no more eloquent testimony to this process than the fate of Julian Eltinge. Still a vaudeville headliner as late as the 1920s, at the end of the decade he migrated to Hollywood – but found his entry to movies effectively banned by a new city ordinance outlawing male cross-dressing on stage. A 1931 comeback proved of little avail. The only forum open to Eltinge was the stage of a cheap Hollywood nightclub. Barred from appearing in women's clothes, he attempted to compensate by displaying his costumes on a clothes rack and gesturing alongside them. As one might expect, he performed to a virtually empty theater. His "comeback" collapsed within a week (Slide 1981: 51).

As Eltinge's fate indicates, within an astonishingly short period of time female impersonation's past connotations vanished. By the late 1930s, it held only one meaning: it was purely and simply an act of "degeneracy." Government legislators now understood it as a vehicle of homosexual nightlife. By banning female impersonation, they sought to keep that nightlife sharply curtailed. In the eyes of the press and the medical profession, impersonators were deviant, perverse, and potentially dangerous. "BAN ON FEMME IMPERSONATORS, SAYS DETROIT MD, ONE WAY TO STOP SEX MURDERS" was by no means an exceptional *Variety* headline (April 7, 1937).

"How many thousand female impersonators do you think there are in the country?" Mae West had demanded after the *Pleasure Man* raid. "Are they going to put them all out of business?" (*New York World*, October 3, 1928: 4). West's words proved prophetic. By the end of the decade female impersonation was thoroughly demonized. Impersonators were no longer seen as performers – they were performing homosexuals. In a culture that demonized homosexuality, that was enough to push them from the mainstream. As West had predicted, most of America's thousands of female impersonators were indeed put out of business.

NOTES

1 Police officers' observations are quoted from the *New York Sun*, March 26, 1930: 27, and the New York District Attorney's memoranda on the *Pleasure Man* case, held in the District Attorney Case Files (case # 174, 820–1/2, People vs. Mae West et als), Municipal Archives, New York City.

2 All quotes from Mae West, *Pleasure Man* (1928), unpublished manuscript held in the Mae West Collection, Library of Congress, Washington DC.

9 Louisa Fairbrother (1816–1890) as Abdallah in the extravaganza *The Forty Thieves* performed at the Lyceum Theatre April 15, 1844. One of the many breeches roles of the day. (Victoria and Albert Museum/Theatre Museum Collection.)

Mary Anne Keeley

10 Mary Anne Keeley as Jack Sheppard. Engraving by R. J. Lane, 1839. (Laurence Senelick Collection.)

11 Omar Kingsley as Ella Zoyara. (Photo: Silsbee, Case, Boston. Laurence Senelick Collection.)

12 Eugene as a minstrel wench. (Photo: Laroche, London. Laurence Senelick Collection.)

13 Top: Park (kneeling) and Boulton (seated). (Photo: Oliver Sarony, Scarborough.) Below: Earnest Byne (Boulton). (Photo: Napoleon Sarony, New York. Laurence Senelick Collection.)

14 Annie Hindle in costume and makeup. Presumably taken from a photograph. (New York *Sun*. Laurence Senelick Collection.)

15 Hetty King, emptying her pipe, in one of the most popular costumes for male impersonation – the sailor.

16 Travesty dancer Caroline Lassiat, *Paquita* (1846). (Lynne Garafola
Collection.)

17 Travesty dancer Céline Celeste, *The French Spy* (1831). (Lynne Garafola Collection.)

18 Miss Stormé DeLarverié, male impersonator. Reproduced with her kind permission.

19 Gautam, an 11-year-old gotipua performer, dancing at the 1986 ISTA Congress in Denmark. (Photo: Torben Huss.)

20 Venus Xtravaganza in *Paris is Burning*, a film by Jennie Livingston. (Photo: Jennie Livingston.)

8

SLIDING SCALES

Notes on Stormé DeLarverié and the Jewel Box Revue, the cross-dressed woman on the contemporary stage, and the invert

Elizabeth Drorbaugh

[T]he female possessed of masculine ideas of independence; the viragint who would sit in the public highways and lift up her pseudo-virile voice, proclaiming her sole right to decide questions of war or religion, or the value of celibacy and the curse of women's impurity, and that disgusting anti-social being, the female sexual pervert, are simply different degrees of the same class – degenerates.

(William Lee Howard, *New York Medical Journal*, 1900)

Perversity, the dumping ground at the turn of the century for women who confounded norms of sex, gender, and sexuality, was a restive place from which proprietary norms continued to be disturbed, since labeling degenerates did not seem to make them go away. Degeneracy, relegated to the category of "wrong," became a necessary boundary: one could not otherwise fully comprehend "right." The women of Howard's nightmare were sexual and masculine in behavior, dress, and attitude. They crossed boundaried genders and assailed his assumptions of propriety. He most likely would have preferred to dispel them from humanity altogether than be subjected to their difference, but he marked himself indelibly in relation to them when he declared their lesser position. In effect, they clamored harder to be looked at, to be evaluated, and to be discussed. The varieties of women in cross-dress – from male impersonators to butch lesbians to passing women – have continued to provoke curiosity and even dread as they have tweaked (and sometimes wrenched) proprietary relations of sex, gender, and sexuality.

Research on women's cross-dressing has been characterized by pockets of activity which have hummed more loudly and more harmoniously recently, but from separate, not yet integrated, spheres. Many of us writing have found ourselves at the "beginning" again, pulling in pieces of information and trajectories of thought from disparate places in order to lay some groundwork for further consideration. The work has been exciting, but frustrating because knee-jerk responses and generalizations continue to be real risks. None the less, valuable research has been done on women's cross-dressing in such areas as women who have performed on stage in cross-dress (e.g. research by Lisa Merrill 1985. Laurence Senelick 1982), passing women (Allan Berube 1979, Julie Wheelwright 1989), lesbian theories (Judith Butler 1991, Carole-Anne Tyler 1991), lesbian popular culture (JoAnn Loulan 1990, Joan Nestle 1987), feminist performance theories (Sue-Ellen Case 1990, Kate Davy 1989, Jill Dolan 1988), and sociology and anthropology (Holly Devor 1989). One may be struck by the variety of areas within the field of study, but research on men's cross-dressing far exceeds that on women's in quantity, and while quantifying difference in this way sets a minefield, my point is that women's cross-dressing is comparatively underexplored.

In this chapter I will be looking at male impersonation on stage, beginning with the loosely structured rubric of the invert, a nineteenth-century term used to describe a man or woman who cross-dressed and whose behavior was generally considered to be cross-gendered, and who, in the early twentieth century, was pathologized as homosexual. My topic will be the Jewel Box Revue, a company of one male impersonator and up to twenty-five female impersonators, who toured the United States from the late 1930s to the early 1970s.

One may wonder how to classify the performers of the Jewel Box Revue as assuredly as William Lee Howard might have. How have they been read and how might we read them today? "Real" perverts or "just" performers? Curios? Specimens? Womanish, mannish, hermaphroditic? Homosexual, heterosexual, bisexual, confused? Is there anything resembling a reliable body of criteria for discernment, or do labels themselves merely replicate conventions of reception? While inversion connotes a fixed state in inverse proportion to stable norms of the sex–gender system, I hope to point to how it more advantageously may be understood as an unstable turning-about of these standards.[1]

The invert in my study of the Jewel Box Revue is Stormé DeLarverié, the solitary male impersonator of the show, who says that she began wearing men's clothes both on and off the stage shortly after joining the company (Plate 18). Parrying questions from her audiences about her "real" self, she has elided a fixed identity by destabilizing her inversion. Following an introduction to the Jewel Box Revue and brief history of the invert, I will take up a discussion of inversion and identity so as to begin to develop a flexible framework for viewing the cross-dressed woman on the contemporary stage.

AN INTRODUCTION TO THE JEWEL BOX REVUE

The Jewel Box was the name of the bar-club in which a nascent company of "Femme-Mimics" performed for eight years beginning in 1939. This followed the earliest beginnings of the company in 1936 or 1938 at the Venetian Causeway bar in Miami (private conversation with Stormé DeLarverié). By 1942, the company of what later became known as "twenty-five men and a girl" began a limited tour as the Jewel Box Revue, eventually playing clubs and theaters nationwide for over thirty years, from improvised stage spaces in tiny, crowded bars to the Apollo Theater in Harlem and the Loew's State Theater on Broadway. Unusual for its time, the Jewel Box Revue was a multiracial troupe which included at one point white, black, Latino, and (one) Native American performers. Touring the deep south during times of legislated bigotry was doubly risky for the interracial company of gender impersonators.

The Jewel Box Revue was a two-hour-long performance of songs, dances, and theatrical sketches that was compared, sometimes favorably and sometimes disparagingly, with vaudeville. The songs and dances and their exotic locales such as Paris or an evocation of the "Arabian Nights" were changed from year to year, but the Revue's format remained essentially the same, as did the traditional opening number which established the frame of female impersonation. Beginning in 1958, according to Stormé, the company sang "You can't do a show without girls" which was composed for the show. In this upbeat number the spirited company (of only the men, not the girl), paraded around the stage and sang. As the men put on wigs and padded costumes, feathers and furs, thereby openly transforming themselves in/as performance, at least a faintly ironic tone must have permeated the stage as the pleasures of show girls were extolled.[2] Frank Quinn, reviewing the show for the *New York Mirror*, described the number as a spectacle of "half-man, half-woman attire for a 'Boys Will Be Girls' sequence . . .", noting that the featured artists for the show were costumed as Cleopatra, Helen of Troy, Madame Butterfly, Madame Du Barry, Mata Hari, and a comic Lady Godiva (Quinn n.d.). Not all of the men performed exclusively as women. Some occasionally discarded the illusion to play men, returning to female impersonation later.

Stormé DeLarverié, the "girl" of "twenty-five men and a girl," performed in the company of the Jewel Box Revue for fourteen years, from January, 1955, until September, 1969.[3] The daughter of a black mother and a white father, she cut a dashing figure both on and off stage. She was described by the filmmaker Michelle Parkerson as bringing "a distinctive style and fashion sense to the mystique of male impersonation – à la Harry Belafonte" (Parkerson 1987a: 3). In addition to performing in the show, she was its stage manager, musical arranger, and "mother to the chorus" (Parkerson 1987a: 3).

Stormé did not appear in the opening number. However, unbeknownst to the audience at the top of the show, it was she who introduced the Jewel Box Revue. Intoning a welcome to the audience, her rich, low voice was commonly mistaken for that of a man. The outermost frame, then, was not the opening number's ode to female impersonation, but the disembodied voice of a woman being read as a man. At the end of the show, Stormé closed the frame by announcing the performers to take their bows, and by taking one herself, after which, as she says, she "hit the last note and the curtain fell" (private conversation with Stormé DeLarverié).

During the show, the men performed in drag, as did Stormé, but it was not until late in the show that, playing a man on stage, she was discovered to be a woman in a number subtitled "The Surprise." The revelation of Stormé as the promised girl was preceded by nearly two hours of the audience trying to break the code. Who exactly was the "true" woman among the twenty-six performers? A reviewer of the 1958 production at Lowe's on Broadway noted that "A surprise in the finale, 'Alaharajah's Dream', has Storme De Laviere [*sic*] revealed as the only 'Miss' in the company. Storme sings the production songs in a rich baritone" (Quinn 1958). Stormé's voice had not given her away. Referring to her so-called baritone voice, Quinn still marked her as a man. He continued, saying "We look for flaws in the illusion [of female impersonation] but find few. Only the voices – sounding like impersonations of Tallulah Bankhead – are keyed too low" (Quinn 1958). It is ironic that Quinn discredits the "too low" voices of female impersonation by calling to mind women's voices, such as Tallulah Bankhead's deep husky voice and Stormé's "baritone." The odd example of a woman's low voice as the inappropriate vocal choice for a female impersonator points to the erroneous but exacting nature of the mythology of what constitutes "true" femininity and "true" masculinity. Furthermore, when Quinn unthinkingly implies the inadequacy of women's voices he champions the mythology of absolute masculinity and femininity; accordingly, impersonation can only ever be the failed copy.

The critics generally acknowledge the Revue's attempts at verisimilitude in gender impersonation.[4] However, the Revue contained both comic and serious songs and sketches which would have tugged at verisimilitude, and which recall the conditions of William Lee Howard's proper woman/degenerate woman. The Revue's comedic performances, through their humor, conceivably established the parameters of amusingly "wrong" gender impersonations against which the serious performances were judged.

In his book *Coming Out Under Fire*, Allan Berube recounts "three basic wartime styles of GI drag" which are similar to what appears to have been featured in the Jewel Box Revue. The three styles Berube lists are "the comic routines, chorus lines or 'pony ballets' of husky men in dresses playing for laughs; the skilled 'female' dancers or singers; and the illusionists or caricaturists, who did artistic and convincing impersonations of female stars" (Berube 1990: 70). The comic "husky men in dresses," in contrast with the serious "artistic and convincing impersonations," may have helped to generate some frictive difference on an otherwise sliding scale of sex and gender performance. As will be discussed later, ascriptions of ironic or gay overtones of the show were also used to try to justify the intentions and thereby pin down the performance.

Male and female impersonation enjoyed what has been called its golden age of popularity as family entertainment during the first twenty years of the twentieth century. (Berube 1990: 72; Senelick 1982: 33).[5] But when vaudeville declined in popularity in the mid-1920s, so did gender impersonation. By 1933, when the Hollywood Motion Picture Production Code banned the performance of "sexual perversion or any inference of it," the feared conflation of (homo)sexuality with gender impersonation caused male impersonation seemingly to evaporate and female impersonation to go underground in the cities where it became (happily for some) adult entertainment in nightclubs. "queer joints," and formal drag balls (Berube 1990: 73). In 1955, Francis Renault's obituary pronounced him "Last of [the] Major Femme Mimics," observing that female impersonation had "fallen into disrepute and [is] confined mainly to a few cafes located in various cities. It's no longer a type of entertainment that could be viewed by the family trade, but is confined mainly to curiosity seekers" (Berube 1990: 74, citing *Variety* 1955: 64).

Meanwhile the Jewel Box Revue played on. A program note for the Revue tried to counter the bad press on female impersonation by saying that the company's producers, "[r]ecognizing that female impersonation is true art, and not the burlesque it had come to be . . . decided to bring back the glories of a neglected field in entertainment" (souvenir program, n.d.; Theater Collection at Lincoln Center). By implying that burlesque was *passé* and popular entertainment *declassé*, the producers tried to confer an elitist tradition on theatrical transvestism. The program's description of the producers as extravagant connoisseurs intimated their relationship to high standards of artistry by juxtaposing elite socio-economic appreciation of "true art" with the panache of large-scale spectacle.

The Jewel Box Revue toured the country throughout the 1940s, 1950s, 1960s, and early 1970s, decades of great flux in sex and gender roles as well as in race relations. Despite that, the Jewel Box Revue remained remarkably consistent, continuing to play year after year in the same basic format of song and dance numbers revolving around female impersonation.

A BRIEF HISTORY OF THE (FEMALE) INVERT, WITH A CONSIDERATION OF HER IMAGE ON THE CONTEMPORARY STAGE

In the late nineteenth century, sexologists Richard von Krafft-Ebing and Havelock Ellis and others used the term "invert" or "sexual invert" to distinguish women and men whose behavior and appearance were contrary to prescribed sex and gender roles. Medical writers thereby assumed the hegemonic discourse of the heterosexual paradigm. As historian George Chauncey has argued, however, the medical profession did not coin nor did it create the identity of the "invert" (or of the homosexual, either) at the turn of the century, as some researchers have indicated (Chauncey 1989b: 90).[6] In another essay arguing the permeable contexts of defining homosexuality, Chauncey cites a Navy trial witness who said that he had first heard the term *invert* in the *theater world*, not from the medical or other specialized literature (Chauncey 1989a: 313). The term's application in the theater usefully points out that the idiom preceded the medical profession's employment of the term.

Medical investigators categorized and tried to explain an existing subculture of which they seemed to be only dimly aware (Chauncey 1989a: 314). While William Lee Howard, Freud, and others were perplexed by the inversion of sex and gender in almost any venue, that of performance escaped their censure for a time. Critical and popular acclaim of such female performers as the music-hall male impersonator Vesta Tilley and actress Charlotte Cushman, who played Shakespearean men's roles, helped to reinforce cross-dress as an acceptable form of entertainment in this period. The popular novelty of male impersonators on the stage in the 1860s occurred roughly twenty years before the term *invert* was first used in medical journals.[7]

Women in the late nineteenth century were beginning to question the circumscription of their social place by sex and gender roles. Increasing numbers of women were entering the workforce, suffrage was being fought for and was won, and there was a resexualization of women after their having been assumed to be "passionless" (a middle-class belief in particular). As evident in this all-too-brief account, the arenas of sex, gender, and sexuality for women were in flux.[8] The theater may have offered spectators some latitude for imagining more elastic social roles, accounting for some of the popularity of the male impersonator and cross-dressed actresses.

Notably, the popularity of the female invert on the stage and the quickening of the women's movement precede the medical profession's deepening analysis of inversion. As the medical writer/researchers were picking out the "bad seeds" of the sex-gender system, such as the invert and the virago of the women's movement, their resolve was being strengthened to address pathology and not simply deviance. Thus, as Chauncey has argued, the medical profession employed "the instrumentality of the perverse" in pathologizing objectionable thought and behavior so as to shore up lax boundaries of the sex-gender system (Chauncey 1989b: 103ff.).[9] Not too long after charges of perversity achieved currency in medical and popular literature, and pathology marked deviance as threatening, the invert on stage and the women's movement started to decline in popularity. The medical profession was not the cause of their decline, but through "the instrumentality of the perverse" it seems to have been a contributor, its tracts employed by those whose stake in the sex-gender system was socially, culturally, and economically based, and likewise at risk.

Returning to the historical use of the term *invert* in order to reconsider male impersonation may appear at first to be regressive, but defining what constitutes inversion, like cross-dressing, is fortunately tricky. Inversion is usually understood as a radical reversal *within* masculine/feminine polarity. It is contextualized by the binary: one must recognize the binary and risk accepting it in order to comprehend what it means to cross. Boundaries, therefore, are kept in place.

The prospect of destabilizing what are customarily viewed as inversion's rigid boundaries may be undertaken through Judith Butler's approach to arguments of origin and of how heterosexuality is naturalized (Butler 1991). Pitting homosexuality as the supposed (bad) copy against heterosexuality as the original is nonsensical, Butler points out, arguing that they are interdependent since each defines the other by contrast. She says that "[W]ere it not for the notion of the homosexual *as* copy, there would be no construct of heterosexuality *as* origin. Heterosexuality here presupposes homosexuality" (Butler 1991: 22, emphasis in the original). She points out that if it can be accepted that the notion of homosexuality as the copy is required before heterosexuality can be conceived of as the original, then it can be said that homosexuality is the original, and heterosexuality is the copy. She continues,

> But simple inversions are not really possible. For it is only *as* a copy that homosexuality can be argued to *precede* heterosexuality as the origin. In other words, the entire framework of [homosexuality as the bad] copy and [heterosexuality as the] origin proves radically unstable as each position inverts into the other and confounds the

possibility of any stable way to locate the temporal or logical priority of either term.

(Butler 1991: 22)

Correspondingly, then, not only the inverted, but the norm that is implied, are interrelated and unstable. What may have appeared to be a solid identity or norm is actually a continual liquefaction. Yet establishing the "essential" nature of inversion will continue to seem paramount as long as the elemental polarity of masculine and feminine is (mis)recognized as origin.

Butler's use of the term *invert* as a noun and as a verb stems from what she calls "the logic of inversion" whereby something or someone is transformed into its opposite through the excess of a binary (Butler 1991: 25). Since a binary is a closed system, that which seems "excessive" to it may still be contained by the system. Butler gives as an example the butch lesbian who constitutes herself as:

> capable, forceful, and all-providing . . . [The butch] who seems *at first* to replicate a certain husband-like role, can find herself caught in a logic of inversion whereby that "providingness" turns to a self-sacrifice which implicates her in the most ancient trap of feminine self-abnegation . . . In effect, the butch inverts into the femme or remains caught up in the specter of that inversion, or takes pleasure in it.

(Butler 1991: 25, emphasis in the original)

The femme who "orchestrates" sexual exchange may invert to a butch as well, as Butler notes, and, like the butch, may take pleasure from it (Butler 1991: 25).

Butler's application usefully points out the mercurial qualities of sex, gender, and sexuality that correspond to inversion, and which contrast with historic usage following that by medical writers in the late nineteenth and early twentieth centuries. Their typically anti-feminist and homophobic discourse about "the intermediate sex," "the mannish lesbian," and the (homosexual) invert were, as historian Carroll Smith-Rosenberg observes, "spatial and hierarchical images concerned with issues of order, structure, and difference [notably of the sex–gender system]. 'Inversion' turns predictable and ordered hierarchies upside down" (Smith-Rosenberg 1989: 275).[10] The supposed stability of sex and gender such that they can be reliably reversed is predicated on an unquestioning acceptance of the essential and opposing natures of masculinity and femininity. However, the invert cannot remain within normative frames; she can be returned only to an intermediate and fluid space of what she is not: not-woman, not-man. Inversion thus may be recognized as unstable and not as the tidy reversal of

127

sex-gender norms that are suggested by the common definition of inverse.

THE JEWEL BOX REVUE, GENDER IMPERSONATION, AND THE INVERT

In Michelle Parkerson's film, entitled *Stormé: The Lady in the Jewel Box'*, Stormé off-handedly explains her involvement with the Jewel Box Revue as something that "just happened."[11] "One day the show needed help," she says, so she "went to help out for six months," as "kind of a gag" because "they needed somebody," and she "stayed for fourteen years." It is not uncommon for a lesbian in cross-dress to be the MC for a drag show in a gay bar. If the Jewel Box was a gay drag bar, Stormé's role as lesbian MC is a possible subtext for "helping out" with the show. Lesbian or not, the risk of being read by the Jewel Box Revue's "family" audience as a lesbian or sexually "wrong" because she cross-dressed may have prompted Stormé to avoid labels of identity, not only as a performer but on the streets. Much about Stormé is hidden (and kept private by those who have known and worked with her), and her efforts to shroud facts in gauzy references may have been an attempt to keep the inquiring gaze off her and on the show. Stormé claims that very soon after she first started singing with the Jewel Box Revue, she commenced to dress only in men's clothing both on and off the stage. Her performance in the Revue and her performances of self in film and newspaper interviews and, to use Erving Goffman's phrase, "everyday life," hinge on her role as invert.

Stormé insists that she moved and sang in the Jewel Box Revue in the same ways as when she was known as Stormy Dale, a big band singer touring the country in the 1940s, and that, by extension, she has always "been herself" when she has performed, no matter what the context.[12] "All I did was cut my hair and change," she says in the Parkerson film. "I walk the same, I talk the same. And it took me a long time and I paid the price for it." Punctuating her remarks on the Jewel Box Revue and her performance of inversion, she says that "the funny thing was I never moved any different than when I was in woman's clothes." Conflating her performance of inversion on the street and on the stage, she relates that "Some say sir and some say ma'am, and that's the way it is. But I never change expression. It makes no difference to me. And that's the way it is." (Parkerson: 1987b).

In publicity photographs of her as a big band singer and as a male impersonator, her gendered persona differs subtly in her gaze, more markedly in her appearance. A photograph of her as the singer Stormy Dale shows a tall, slim woman, whose nearly shoulder-length curly hair softly frames her face. She smiles sweetly, even coyly, at the camera, a flower behind her ear. By contrast, in a series of publicity photographs for the Jewel Box Revue program, she seems to coolly regard the camera, or she looks away, her facial features in studied repose. Unfortunately, the photographs cannot convey how Stormé moved and sang, which is where she locates the consistency of her performance as interchangeably masculine or feminine.[13]

The producers of the Jewel Box Revue made every effort to recontextualize gender impersonation as an expression of normative sex and gender values. The show was billed as "family entertainment" which featured the "amazing deception" of "femme-mimics." The souvenir programs for the Jewel Box Revue were showpieces of audience education. Maneuvering the Revue into historical and mythological traditions, the programs announced:

> "It's an old mannish custom," explains Danny Brown [a co-producer of the show] to people who think guys getting done up in gals' clothes is something new and unique. And because it's a far cry from Juliet to Hopalong Cassidy, it's hard for most of us to realize that the immortal Shakespeare created his greatest feminine role, Juliet, knowing it would be portrayed – not by a woman – but by a young man. For in the days of the Elizabethan theater, all feminine roles were played by young men, and this custom prevailed until after the Reformation.
>
> As a matter of fact, when the boys of the Jewel Box Revue are asked how it feels to be wearing long hair for their stage appearance, they recall how loss of masculinity has always been synonymous with loss of hair. Remember Samson? And Hercules? And Billy the Kid and Buffalo Bill, the Wild West heroes, weren't they almost vainly proud of their long flowing bobs? Female impersonation, men making the ladies look to their laurels in the matter of fashion finery, and such, has long been with us, and Danny and Doc [Benner, a co-producer] in their Jewel Box Revue have maintained the art in its true and original sense.
>
> (souvenir program, n.d.; Theater Collection at Lincoln Center)

Why Juliet was selected as Shakespeare's "greatest feminine role" is unclear. But the program notes' objective is in crystal relief: to draw parallels between the revered, mythic performance past and the Jewel Box Revue. Values of artistry, tradition, aesthetic purity, and hypermasculinity are ushered in to help assure the stature of the show.[14] Similarly, the Revue's "amazing deception" was used to reinstate traditional sex and gender values by implying them to be the truth behind the deception: impersonation's verisimilitude was in homage to so-called "true" femininity and masculinity.[15]

Arguments for the acceptability of permutations of sex, gender, or sexuality try to align them with established norms, but the sex–gender system's chilly response to deviance has not been allayed, even over time. In 1989 in New York City, female impersonator Charles Busch starred in a play entitled *The Lady in Question*. On the night I saw the show, Busch sashayed downstage center after the curtain call, warmly greeting us, and abruptly presented us to ourselves as his "cross-over audience." With flicks of his wrist he seemed to indicate that the left and right sides of the house were criss-crossed, the lightly ironic tone of his delivery conveying the slightest disdain for the inadequate phrase. He told us that a reviewer who enjoyed the show used the phrase "cross-over audience" to describe the surprising variety of assembled spectators. Busch's subtle reapplication of the phrase to his current audience had that inverse effect that labels often do: the audience was left undefined or insufficiently defined, meaning that our identity(ies) exceeded representation.[16] The term "cross-over audience" held no real significance for us. Uncertain of the implied center or more aptly the inferred "right" side of the house to be on, the audience laughed after momentary stupefaction: from where did we cross over and to what, exactly? Perhaps homosexuality was implied. But nobody had quite *said* that.

At this point a distinction between "seeing" and "reading," terms used by Peggy Phelan for analyzing performance, may usefully be made (Phelan 1989: 50). In her differentiation of the terms, seeing perceives but it does not derive meaning in performance (which is broadly defined). Reading, on the other hand, proceeds from seeing to construct a narrative of meaning. To illustrate their difference, seeing cross-gendered appearance and behavior would not itself constitute making a judgment through a normative lens. However, reading homosexuality onto cross-gendered appearance and behavior would construct a meaning, especially causality, for what is seen.[17] A second example may be found in "passing women," women who appear wholly as men and hence "pass" for men. A passing woman is not perceived as an invert because she is seen as a man. This example derives from Phelan's sense of seeing a passive kind of perception which, when seeing nothing that is markedly different or out of the ordinary, sees "nothing." Inversion, on the other hand, must be actively read in Phelan's sense. For example, a passing woman who has been discovered may be understood as an invert since she is at once seen as a man, and read as a woman. The tension between seeing a man and reading a woman passing as a man is usually so acute that spectators commonly marvel at having been fooled (Berube 1979: 20). Publicity for the Jewel Box Revue tried to make the most of this, educating the audience to see the men as women while reading them as men, as artists, and as part of a venerated tradition of cross-dressing on stage. In the case of *The Lady in Question*, Busch's critic reads the audience as one which crosses over, indicating that seeing the assembly was jarring in some way, perhaps because disparate (and normally segregated?) groups of people were present. While reading homosexuality may or may not have been at issue, some sort of traversed boundaries are imagined in the word cross-over which literally hinges on separateness. In effect, cross-over (like cross-dress) implies transgression, thereby inviting readings which likely will reify and not question boundaries.

Readings of homosexuality occur often enough that cross-dressers who identify themselves as heterosexual are usually regarded with suspicion. As Butler points out, "[S]exuality always exceeds any given performance, presentation, or narrative which is why it is not possible to derive or read off a sexuality from any given gender presentation. And sexuality may be said to exceed any definitive narrativization" (Butler 1991: 25). A fundamental question is whether a normative strategy is being employed to explain cross-dressing through the narrative of homosexuality, as has been popular since the early twentieth-century medical writers.

In Reno, Nevada in 1962, *Variety* chronicled the censorship of the Jewel Box Revue which occurred as a result of "readings" of homosexuality. On February 28 and again on March 21 prior to the Revue's scheduled appearance in the area, Reno City Council members were reported to have passed an ordinance by a five-to-one vote prohibiting local shows in which one sex impersonated another. The action was aimed directly at the Jewel Box Revue, according to *Variety*, in response to the "local citizenry and clergy" who had protested the revue's attracting " 'an undesirable element' " (*Variety*, March 21, 1962; Theater Collection at Lincoln Center).[18] None the less, the Revue went on as scheduled. Having voted to ban the Jewel Box Revue before seeing it, some city officials belatedly went to see the show. Assistant City Attorney Glen Dilly announced that the revue "did not appear to be vulgar or obscene but in my opinion, it did violate the city ordinance" – passed by the Council in order to close the Jewel Box Revue in the first place (*Variety*, March 21, 1962). A *Variety* headline for the story read "Bare Bosoms Have Reno's Tacit OK But Would Bar Femme 'Personators," bringing to view how women's sexuality on stage for a presumably heterosexual audience was permissible in the averted eye of the law, while inversion which may have confused the heterosexual "seeing eye" was not.

Two years later in New York, homophobia was demonstrated when on March 14, 1964, as *Variety* reported, "as before [in New York City], the revue was picketed at the Apollo by grand Harlemites, with signs reading 'the dregs and drags of society,' 'my son the queen,' etc." Nevertheless, the picketers "didn't prevent an SRO house at early evening . . . Sunday show." As standing-room-only crowds packed the house, the threat of inversion which can be legislated against or demonstrated against was shown to be more phantasmic than real.

The sex and gender disruption provoked by inversion is not always read as threatening, or even as objectionable. The former manager of the Apollo Theater, Bobby Shiffman, said that the Jewel Box Revue was

> a most unusual show. It was something that was away from the normal fare of the Apollo. It was glamorous. It was good family entertainment. It was wholesome. There was nothing sleazy about it. It was a show that people came back to see time and time again.
>
> (Parkerson 1987b)

The Jewel Box Revue toured nationwide for decades to a host of performance spaces, including the black theater circuit, which included the Howard Theater in Washington DC, the Baltimore-Royal Theatre, the Uptown Theater in Philadelphia, and the Regal Theater in Chicago, as well as the Apollo Theater in New York. In view of Shiffman's and the press's largely favorable reviews of the Jewel Box at the Apollo, such as that from the *New York Amsterdam News*, it may appear that comparatively less restrictive norms concerning the Jewel Box Revue's gender representation occurred in the black community at the time. If this is true, it may be because blacks (and gays and lesbians) have been skewed from the white (and heterosexual) social paradigms within which social roles are enacted and enforced. None the less, it is noteworthy that, as Michelle Parkerson has said, the demise of the Jewel Box Revue "in the early seventies was prompted by violent homophobic boycotts staged by black nationalist groups which claimed the Jewel Box undermined the black male and the black family, and promoted homosexuality in the black community" (Parkerson 1987a: 4). The Revue and particularly inversion were not thought "safe" by a variety of groups, both critical and popular, who were concerned by what they considered to be representations of homosexuality.

The possible disruption of sex and gender norms by inversion is often relieved when the reading focuses on how well the copy matches the so-called original, in other words, how skilled the performers are as gender illusionists. A reviewer from the *New York Amsterdam News* on March 3, 1973, considered the Jewel Box Revue in this light, saying

> The men [of the Jewel Box Revue] made believe they were women [and] did it with grace and charm. Their voices had feminity [*sic*] written all over it and the grace with which they move about the stage gave the impression of a ballet dancer. The show was a masterpiece.
>
> (Theater Collection at Lincoln Center)

Allusions to ballet and "high art," moreover, were employed to underscore the integrity of the production while implying the artistry of gender impersonation. The critical eye bears its authorial privilege to represent a readership's collective conscience and tastes. In the trade papers such as *Variety*, a typical response to the show was a knowing wink at homosexuality; in the black newspaper of Harlem, the *New York Amsterdam News*, the response was appreciation of the performers' having stepped into the guise of the other; in a majority newspaper such as the *New York Mirror*, the performers are graded – and then marked down – on the not-quite perfect illusion of feminine signifiers (by using female voices to evidence the incorrect vocal choice of the male performer, for example).

But what of Stormé and the reviews of her performance in the Jewel Box Revue? In the reviews she is seldom if ever mentioned, although she contends in Parkerson's film that people on the street often recognized her and that she was the one whom they remembered. As the MC and the sole woman in the show, it would stand to reason that Stormé's performance should have been noticeable by dint of being different, but perhaps there lies the logic's failure. In the face of the sex–gender system's castration anxiety, difference is coopted as the exception which proves the rule; difference is, at best, shifted outside the frame of what is considered to be important. At issue is not only her performance of inversion but her race as well. Since the multiracial company of the Jewel Box Revue was performing gender and not racial identity overtly, perhaps race was the blind spot in critical reception.

While a more rigorous inquiry into the politics of race in the reception of the Jewel Box Revue is technically beyond the scope of this chapter, to ignore it completely at some level would be to comply with the erasure of Stormé. Perhaps by (re)phrasing the question as "In what ways could racial difference affect her role and its reception?" we may approach the subject. According to the billing of the Revue, one "girl" serves as the men's played-back inversion. She rectifies the potentially unsettling gender play and alludes to heterosexual presence just by being there. Would a woman of any color achieve specifically this, or would racial readings of her color complicate an ostensibly "simple" gender impersonation? It is likely that a racially othered woman in male drag was particularly arresting in her compounded status of inverted race, sex, gender, and sexuality. As Michelle Parkerson has observed of male impersonation, the idea of women putting on the "attire of power and privilege, *and* doing it with such grace, is very threatening . . . This power shift is especially disconcerting when embodied by a black woman, let alone one who is now 66" (at the time of filming) (quoted in Pisik 1987: n.p., emphasis in the original).[19]

Furthermore, Stormé's difference as the sole woman performer could have signified to critics her supposedly lesser presence, which is to say

133

that, while she was visible on stage, she was overshadowed by her use value to mirror the men doubly. She was the negative image of their impersonations, and, as a woman, her lack differentiated her and affirmed them as men.[20] Her erasure is systemic since the economy of the Same – which recognizes the masculine and disregards the feminine, assumes white and suppresses other races – was, and continues to be, prevalent.[21]

When Stormé is reviewed, the overall tenor of the reviewer's response to the Jewel Box Revue is characteristically represented in her notice: favorable reviews of the show tend to mention her voice while unfavorable reviews tend to mention her appearance, echoing traditional gender-coded ways of appraising men and women. Stormé's voice in the favorable reviews is consistently reported as a "baritone" instead of as a contralto, indicating that seeing her as male is unexamined, and even that her illusion has become a laminate. On the other hand, in the unfavorable reviews, the critics disparage her appearance as being *too* masculine, as if the illusion is too real, as if the playfulness turned serious. The differentiations, while subtle, are important because the swill from the insidiously fluid question "When is enough, and what is too much?" has potentially nasty complications due to endowing the polarity of masculinity and femininity with absolute worth.

As we have seen, the sex–gender system's governance of appearance, behavior, and sexual object choice reinscribes the system's dominance through the repetition of normative images which themselves become the "true." Hence, Stormé performs as the copy of men, who are the original in one case, while the men perform as the copy of women, who are the original in another case. The implied aesthetic in watching male and female inverts is to see how well they measure up, how well they reproduce (but do not take over) the system. A question arises as to how we might qualify an "original." When do we know a real woman? When do we know a real man? When we see one? (Those who know a handsome passing woman, a beautiful male transvestite, or a fetching hermaphrodite may understand the double bind.) It would seem that analyzing sex and gender is a bit like being caught inside an Escher print of slipping forms and copies, which is to say, illustrating Butler's point, that originals and copies are unstable performative acts which may be said to materialize continually.[22]

A trajectory from this territory of false starts might be to pose different ways of seeing and reading so as to disengage the comparison of the copy to the original ("performed" sex versus "true" sex). But emphasizing seeing by disengaging all meaning would be most difficult, and emphasizing reading would risk a pedantic tone. Would the simultaneity of seeing-with-reading that defines the invert be useful in any way for helping to unmask the supposedly all-powerful sex–gender system?

Upon seeing the palimpsestic gender, we might read the real sex. As we thus would recognize inversion, we might query essential masculinity and femininity. Yet relying on the truth value of a "real" sex indicates that inversion is a deviation from truth, and sex-gender norms are recuperated. The palimpsest is not necessarily helpful.

Stormé is seen as a man, known (or thought . . . what of hermaphrodites?) to be a woman, and read as an invert. However, and this is an obvious but important point, her reading does not end there. The invert is not simply read as an invert; as I have discussed, the invert is read as well, homosexuality being one of the more common readings which come to resemble arguments for due cause of deviance and consequently pathology. Readings of Stormé's inversion that are discussed or implied in Parkerson's film and in interviews with Stormé in print suggest that her audiences are consistently jarred by her inversion which is believed to be the stable referent. Stormé continually is asked for her identity, for her "true" sex and "true" self in reaction to her being seen as disparate signs while being read as either a woman or a man (and she has been read as both). Her audience requests her autobiographical authority to end their anxious speculation.

This faith in not only a "true" sex but a "true" self is evident throughout the programs of the Jewel Box Revue which feature side-by-side photographs of the male performers in and out of their female personas. The program touts "Amazing Deception!," curtailing negative readings of cross-dress by foregrounding the proof of both the "truth" of mimesis and a faith in the real, or true. In an enduring romance with platonic truth, a common if reactionary response to inversion is a persistent belief that something real lies behind the deception, a belief that is addressed by the program copy. In this performative moment the graft of the character onto the performer is gauged to weaken and peel, in turn revealing the actor's real self. The audience becomes engaged with the truth behind the facade, and not the inversion itself. But, as will be discussed in the next section, Stormé often eschews her autobiographical authority and a true self, preferring that her audiences come to their own conclusions. As a result the audiences remain engaged with the uncomfortable inversion for which they have no defensive identification label or coding of Stormé and from which they have no relief.

NOTES ON THEORIZING INVERSION AND IDENTITY

When seeing a man cross-dress we may read the construction of "woman." When we see a woman cross-dress as a man, the "real" in our culture, what do we see? We may read power. But if we read (a construction of) a man, that which is supposedly not constructed, faith in the real may begin to break down. Does this undermine the realness of masculine and feminine coded behaviors and appearances? Or does inversion refer to and thereby reinscribe true masculinity and femininity?

Over the course of several interviews shown in Michelle Parkerson's film, Stormé repeats that she wants people to "see what they want to see" in her. Her reluctance to claim an identity of sex, gender, or sexuality for herself is a perplexing and provocative example of what some post-modernists and post-structuralists argue, which is that she claims no authority about her identity which keeps slipping; moreover, she cannot nor will she label what her audiences should perceive about her, suggesting a performance parallel to Barthes's "Death of the author."[23] She has killed off the "author" in her, while forcing us to authorize her. We long to stabilize who she is in order to read her, but she refuses to define herself for us, to give us her autobiography.

In Parkerson's film at one point, Stormé says, "I model myself after me." Outside the array of normative images of the white, heterosexual sex–gender system, Stormé's arresting single moment of staking an identity happens without relation, except, as she claims, to herself. It may be said that for her, mimesis and representation as repositories of the faithful copy of a true original have dropped out; in her view, she is both the copy and the original.

Stormé's reluctance to "name" herself was deeply confounding at first when I read or heard her repeated divestments of self-identification. How does one approach thinking or writing about her? And isn't this the same consternation that her audiences have expressed?

In the chatty style of the book *Female Impersonation* by Willard Avery, an occurrence of reading Stormé is recounted:

> It is amusing to Stormé to see the numbers of people who think of her as "one of the boys," simply because she is appearing – as a boy – in a revue with boys who masquerade as girls. Recently, when she was asked whether she preferred to be called "he" or "she," her reply was "Whatever makes YOU feel the most comfortable."
>
> (Avery 1971: 63)

Despite what may be called her generosity in this instance, Stormé has occasionally seemed ambivalent about others' uncomfortable reactions to the ambiguities she presents. Audiences of her variously public and private stages have not always been approving. Were the shifting identities stilled and then reliably defined, the discomfited audience member could rely on some measure of stability. What Stormé called the "uncomfortable" perception results not from a view of inversion as end result, but of the frictive relationship between what "should" be and what appears to be. That is to say, the destabilizing itself is more riveting than either its agent or its result.

This seems to have been the case in Avery's recounting, above.

136

Audiences were transfixed by what was impossible to comprehend, even though they saw, in Phelan's terms, a man, and read a woman (at least after having been told that during the Revue); actually, they still couldn't comprehend what appeared to them to be an inconclusive and therefore disruptive ambiguity. So they went to the "source," who told them they could rely on whatever perception would put them at ease. But, in effect, and importantly, Stormé did not solve the puzzle. To take advantage of this point and to jump ahead a bit, the perception of destabilization *in process* – which results largely from a rather supreme ambiguity, in this case confusion even in the face of knowing – is the ephemeral space for subversion of sex and gender norms by means of inversion, particularly provocative for theatrical production.

In the Parkerson film Stormé alludes to what seem to have been difficult periods in her life when the ambiguity of her identity caused her to suffer significant losses of an undisclosed kind. Referring in the film to racial and gender ambiguity, Stormé says that

> I grew up hard in New Orleans with *my mixed blood* . . . So I was my own responsibility and I kept the touch of class. And it was very easy. All I had to do was just be me. And let people use their imaginations. It never changed me. *I was still a woman.*
>
> [author's emphasis]

What she calls the "mixed blood" of race is transferred in just a few sentences to sex–gender inversion, suggesting that her racial and gender identities were sometimes conflated in difference. Stormé claims her favorite expression is "It ain't easy being green" with which she seems to refer to an uneasy place of identity (Parkerson 1987b). Her ambivalence at being outside customary forms of identification seems to be a liminal zone of faith (and despair) in a representable self. Not fitting into white, masculine or feminine, and therefore recognizably "truthful" forms derails her. Instead of radicalizing the performance of herself as she might have done, she defuses the site of tension over whether to fit and be fixed or to not fit and be fixed by obviating the role of her authority. Like a filmy specter, she'll come into focus if the spectator trains his or her eye, but she dismisses anything more specific, repeating only, "That's the way it is. And that's the way it is" (Parkerson 1987b).

Upon reflection of "the slippery ontology of mimesis," in Elin Diamond's phrase, it would seem that mimesis itself is unstable in a way that is similar to inversion's instability and consequent subversive potential. If in Diamond's words mimesis is "realism at its most naive," and if realism "*produces* 'reality' by positioning its spectator to recognize and verify its truths" (Diamond 1990: 60), then mimesis could arguably possess the real, subverting faith in it by slipping into its place.[24] Reality, not to mention realism and mimesis, depends upon its repetition for its (re)creation, and truth. Reality, and with it realism and mimesis, are inconstant. Hence, if mimesis is naive realism and realism produces "reality," then it is conceivable that gender impersonation could become the "real marker," thereby displacing (not replacing) the truth of a real gender. This would be accomplished in the domain of the visible in which "seeing is believing." In its continual performance (its pro-duction), mimesis would supersede the notion of the real if momentar-ily, holding the audience transfixed as they believe while not believing. Mimesis in gender impersonation positions spectators to recognize and verify the "truth" of the sex–gender system's reproduction while it also elides the system, since the truth of gender is produced by as well as on the inappropriate body. The fascination with the illusion begins to supersede the real even as it depends on it, the threat of which helps to explain recurring problems with male impersonation such as the impro-priety if not the objectionable homosexuality of the invert, the stigmati-zation of the butch lesbian, and the invisible history of the lives of women who at their death were discovered to have passed as men.[25]

Lesbian writer and activist Joan Nestle, in an interview shown in Parkerson's film, says that

> Entertainers like Stormé challenged us to cross lines. They did it for us in their presentations but they made our imaginations ex-plore the potential of leaving gender or playing with gender . . . For women to do it was much more perplexing for the society . . . Duplicating in some way a power that was very privileged [may be why] male impersonators may be even more threatening . . . [They] certainly have posed . . . an erotic allure and challenge that makes them compelling.

Nestle concludes saying that "I think their invisibility is not an acci-dent." Perhaps the female invert and the male impersonator in particu-lar are so arresting that their invisibility is more of a defensive maneuver than an offensive display of power in the sex–gender system. At the close of Nestle's remarks, the next rather Spartan shot in the film is of a Jewel Box marquee advertising "twenty-five men and a girl." Why was it enough to cast only one "girl" to offset the twenty-five female imperson-ators? Neither the film, nor the interviews, nor the reviews, and certainly not Stormé provide an answer. My supposition is that the "girl" is predominantly functional. Even her artistry is in the service of female impersonation in this particular case. Similar to Irigaray's mirroring woman, the girl's value reflects that of the show and that of the men. This is not to say that Stormé's performance was superfluous. It truly was a key. However, the locus of Stormé's power, if it may be called that, on stage in the Jewel Box was as the inversion of the inversion, or the "surprise" that called attention to the gender impersonation as mimesis, not the real thing, and, further, (re)introduced heterosexuality since the presence of men with women is customarily read to signify that. Stormé's performance served as a neutralization of what the reviewer Frank Quinn called "boys will be girls" by making clear, as Stormé said, the fact that what the men added, she took away (Parkerson 1987b), that the impersonation and play with sex and gender norms was "just" perform-ance, and that the binary of masculinity and femininity could remain intact. In the Jewel Box Revue, inversion was not explicitly a device for subversion. The static "reality" of sex, gender, sexuality, and the domi-nant order have helped to ensure that the show has a broad appeal. "Amazing Deception" of the Jewel Box Revue could only be amazing, and acceptable, if the unbelievable happened in convention's shadow.

The more subversive project on stage would be to illuminate the mercurial quality of sex, gender, and sexuality, to continually displace normative binaries lest they be reasserted, and to disengage reactionary readings. Stormé's performance as the female invert on stage and in everyday life began to accomplish this through her resistance to being "read."

GYMNASTICS OF LOGIC

Theorizing inversion now may seem regressive when performance theorists are pushing for change beyond conventional language and approaches to sex, sexuality, and gender. But the binary of masculinity and femininity is still quite secure and until it has been reliably destabi-lized, old language forms will continue to reflect the entrenched system and infect our efforts on behalf of change. (A measure of real progress would be that over change's slow, resistant course, inversion eventually becomes nonsensical.) As Butler, Tyler, and others have demonstrated, however, norms are not permanent, but are repeated and (re)natural-ized, and in their (re)creation lies potential for change.

Stormé's dismissal of identity places a wedge between the binary and the reception of her as the invert. In a sense, her disavowal of a stable sense of self rooted in sex and gender codes renders her the invert's invert: she appears as who she is not and she is disclaimed either way. Hers is an ontological trip, like slipping on a banana peel. In Phelan's sense, seeing and reading Stormé DeLarverié in the Jewel Box Revue may register a rapidly changing series of perceptions, such as: Stormé *is* not-a-man. Stormé is *not* a man. Stormé is not a woman. Stormé is not *not* a woman.

The gymnastics of inversion's logic depend upon the degree to which masculinity and femininity are recognized as absolutes. The more abso-lute the gender, the more violent the twists of logic employed to compass inversion. If masculinity and femininity were not absolutes, the chaotic ontology above would lack a driving momentum prompted by the perceptions of shifting identity. That is, the jarring effect registered by disbelieving eyes, which pick up and discard possible explanations of what is seen, would soon dissipate. From this perspective, then, the essential and opposing natures of masculinity and femininity are an advantage. Inversion's fascination may be said to lie in enticing and frustrating uncertainties, which are in relation to the promise held by certainty, in the face of the sex–gender system.

Within these theoretical permutations may lie some of the social and theatrical potential for transvestism and the prospects for destabilizing convention. The jarring effect of colliding visual images, viz. "seeing," and values, viz. "reading," is the unstable locus of change. Rupture cannot effect progressive change unless it is transpiring. After it has transpired, its value has expired, and at this point normative values may reinstitute themselves. While the binary may rock back into place, the repetition of performative acts of sliding identities can continue to perturb phantasmic normalcy. Inversion's restive place thereby gains some theoretical ground.

Acknowledgments: Stormé DeLarverié, George Chauncey, Jr, Lesbian Herstory Archives (New York), Michelle Parkerson, Judy Rosenthal.

NOTES

1 The term sex–gender system, coined by Gayle Rubin (1975), argues that the biological differences between women and men are structured and then conflated as social differences, and that, broadly speaking, in terms of sexual labor relations, men exchange women, but not the other way around.

2 The Busby Berkeley film *Dames* features a similar song. In light of the Hollywood mania for the showgirl film during the 1930s, the irony may have extended in some measure to a form of parody, but at some remove, as the song for the Jewel Box Revue was composed much later.

3 It is likely that she was not the first male impersonator cast in the Revue. At least one other woman served as MC in the history of the company, although dates and records are sketchy. Unfortunately, none of the programs are dated, and a chronology of casts and of shows is very difficult to determine. It is possible that the Revue for part of its history was made up only of men.

4 For a probing analysis of theories of cross-dress and its reception, see Tyler (1991).

5 In contrast to recordings of critical and popular acclaim, C. J. Bulliet, in his book on female impersonation, which was published and later reissued around the time of gender impersonation's heyday and the Jewel Box Revue's beginnings, said that comparatively little interest was shown in women who cross-dressed in everyday life or in actresses who played men's roles on the stage (Bulliet 1933: 8–9). Bulliet blandly asserted that "Maude Adams as Peter Pan, Sarah Bernhardt as Hamlet have none of the interest of Julian Eltinge or Edward Kynaston. They are accepted as sexless and mild –

to be considered as artists, not as persons" (Bulliet 1933: 9). Contrast Bulliet's version of the "passionless" woman with what Lisa Merrill has described as expressions of lesbian love, not romantic friendship, by ardent women admirers who wrote letters to Charlotte Cushman (private conversation with Lisa Merrill).

6 For an opposing view, see Katz (1983).

7 "Invert" was synonymous with "queer" which likewise described cross-gendered appearance and behavior, but not necessarily homosexuality. "Pansy" and "fairy" were terms which marked gender inversion and were used sometimes to imply homosexual object choice. They were terms used expressly for men, unlike "invert" and "queer" which were used as much to describe women. "Queer" and "fairy" have been recuperated for contemporary usage, as in, for example, the groups Queer Nation and Radical Faeries. The Radical Faeries use cross-dress as part of their gender manipulation and exploration of sexuality in rituals and celebrations (see Dorff 1990). The pansy became a code word for homosexuality, but also denoted cross-gendered appearance and behavior (see Jeffries 1990).

8 For further reading on the medical profession's analyses of sex and gender roles and the medical literature's effect on the women's movement, see Chauncey (1989b): 98, 103ff.

9 Bulliet skirted homosexuality (and fetishism and narcissism) in women when he quoted Dr Bernard S. Talmey as saying that "[w]oman takes it for granted that her clothes, just as her body, have an erotic effect upon the male. Hence female clothes awaken in woman a complex emotion akin to the sight of the female body. Woman becomes sexually excited by her own clothes. For this reason clothes are to woman of the greatest importance. The desire for beautiful clothes is an irradiation of the sex instinct" (Bulliet 1933: 11; no citation given).

10 In this article Smith-Rosenberg writes about the female invert who appropriated her "pathology" as a tool of subversion. See also Newton (1989).

11 Primarily a series of interviews with Stormé DeLarverié, the film also includes interviews with lesbian writer and activist Joan Nestle, former Jewel Box Revue performer Robin Rogers, and former Apollo Theater manager Bobby Shiffman. Photography and memorabilia from the Jewel Box Revue are shown as well.

12 The difference in her first name's spelling surely indicates stage and street personas at some variance, that of Stormé and that of Stormy. Her given name is Stormé DeLarverié.

13 In watching Stormé in Parkerson's film, and in speaking with her myself, I did not notice conventionally masculine movement.

14 Elsewhere in the program the co-producers are introduced under the headline "Meet the BOY-OLOGICAL EXPERTS!" One imagines that there is plenty in this program that may be read by those in the audience who would understand encoded messages of homosexuality. *Variety* reviews the show on March 9, 1960 with a sly wink, saying, "The Newspapers advertise the show as 'Amazing Deception.' Maybe so, but the magic is not the kind that Thurston [presumably a magician] provided. It's more up Krafft-Ebing's line, but it is so gay, all of it . . . If they weren't advertised as female impersonators, nobody would have been fooled." The reference to Krafft-Ebing presumably is to his research on inversion and the pathology of homosexuality.

15 This is not to say that readings of homosexuality are necessarily unreasonable. Gay camp-drag deliberately plays against normative sex and gender roles and appearances from a gay man's point of view. Gender bending, or the arresting "genderfuck" of the Cockettes, an infamous drag company in

San Francisco in the late 1960s and early 1970s, on which Martin Worman has written (Worman 1990), stems from a gay perspective which is understood to be outside the sex–gender system. Lesbian performance regularly features cross-dressing, as, for example, at the WOW Cafe, a performance space and very loosely knit company which is located in New York City. My point is that a spectator from within the heterosexual paradigm may react to inversion's sex–gender difference by reading homosexuality, thereby constructing a causal narrative of what is seen. (This discussion anticipates another about the terms "reading" and "seeing" which will follow.)

16 In Phelan's view representation never adequately reproduces the "real." For development of her theory on the "real," see Phelan (1992).

17 In a paper/performance, I explored Phelan's use of "seeing" and "reading" in the context of feminist experimental performance. I focused on a production of Oscar Wilde's *Salomé* performed by a company of all women and one man which was presented in the spring of 1989 at Performance Space 122 in New York City (paper delivered at Performance Studies International Conference at New York University, October, 1990; Pleasure and Politics: The 4th Annual Lesbian, Bisexual, and Gay Studies Conference at Harvard University, November, 1990; Flaunting It: The First Annual Lesbian and Gay Graduate Students Conference at University of Wisconsin/Milwaukee, 1990).

18 A *Variety* reporter conducted an informal survey of people who saw the show and reported that "the majority" said "they witnessed nothing objectionable. Several women patrons of the show reported they had seen it more than one time" (*Variety*, February 18, 1962).

19 Parkerson's observation, which warrants further study, leads me to acknowledge that, owing to the necessarily limited scope of this chapter. I must abbreviate the inquiry into race so as to more fully develop the theme of sex/gender inversion.

20 For a discussion of the woman as the mirror, see Irigaray (1985). For an expansion of Irigaray's ideas applied to feminist performance, see Diamond (1990). For a reevaluation of Irigaray's ideas, see Tyler (1991).

21 For a discussion of the economy of the Same and the far-reaching implications for women, see Luce Irigaray (1984).

22 This suggests a riddle of "When is an invert not an invert?" which finds an answer (one answer) in "When she's a man," instead of "When she's a 'man,'" which is an answer to "What is an invert?" Making sense of the riddle depends upon whether one believes that there are more than two sexes and two genders. Individuals who have both male *and* female chromosome pairs come to mind, for example. A second example might be a hermaphrodite who identifies as a woman. In the first instance, that of biological exceptions, and in the second, that of (failing) identity, lie the foundations for the riddle, urging once again an avowal of the shifting cartographies of sex, gender, and sexuality.

23 This was suggested by Lesley Ferris in a private conversation. Please see the Introduction to this collection.

24 For this section I am in debt to Elin Diamond's ideas which are discussed in her essay on "Mimesis, mimicry, and the 'true-real.'" In the article she investigates issues of "truthful" representation and feminist performance in order to postulate possibilities for social change.

25 For example, in 1988, jazz musician Billy Tipton was discovered to be a woman upon her death. Passing as a man, she had lived with a wife and two adopted sons, and led a jazz trio.

9

IT'S NEVER TOO LATE TO SWITCH

Crossing toward power

Alisa Solomon

"I'm a man," sings Stanley, flexing formidable biceps beneath a torn undershirt in *Belle Reprieve*, the 1991 Split Britches-Bloolips collaboration based loosely on *A Streetcar Named Desire* (Plate 6). Two men in work overalls join in the chorus: "I'm a man, spelled M-A-N, ow ow ow ow ow." That the two men accompanying Stanley seem awkward, fake, even dainty as they try to preen in macho poses while Stanley struts with the assured strength of a construction worker, is just one of the countless gender-bending ironies in a performance that explores the relationship between narrative and social conformity, between the yoked constraints of naturalism and naturalized notions of gender: the two chorus members are "real" men (Bette Bourne and Precious Pearl of the London drag troupe Bloolips); Stanley is played by a "woman" (Peggy Shaw of New York's lesbian-feminist company, Split Britches). The production, Brechtian in style if not in structure, makes the categories of male and female strange; through performance it puts them – embodies them – in the quotation marks so common to contemporary theory.

Of course, much of that theory recognizes "woman" as a social construction (often citing de Beauvoir's pithy formulation, "One is not born a woman, but rather becomes one" (de Beauvoir 1952)). But *Belle Reprieve* punches "maleness" into the same critical relief – and does so in a way that takes into account the relationship between social roles and social power, a point often glossed over, or ignored entirely, in much current theoretical discourse about gender and transvestism.

Most discussion of cross-dressing, whether on stage or in the streets (another distinction rarely examined), focuses on instances of men playing women. While, granted, such instances have a long tradition in the history of theatre, and are more abundant in contemporary popular culture as well, to make male-to-female drag the point from which all discussion of cross-dressing follows simply reinstates the presumption of the male as universal; he remains the standard, the given, even when wearing feather boas and four-inch stilettos.

Indeed, the man in drag has even been said to epitomize femininity far better than a woman ever could. As Jan Kott has remarked, "When an actress is asked to act a woman, walk like a woman, sit like a woman, sip tea like a woman, she will at first be surprised and ask: 'But *what* woman?' . . . Femininity can only be acted by a man" (Kott 1984: 124). Leaving aside the points that Kott's assertion says a lot about what kinds of roles women have traditionally been relegated to, and that his observation applies only to certain theatrical styles, it begs one important question: if femininity is best performed by men, why isn't masculinity best performed by women?

Perhaps it is, though superficially, at least, the idea seems absurd: first, unlike many female characters, male characters rarely exist on traditional stages for their gender alone – they are statesmen, soldiers, salesmen, not merely men. More important, as the presumed universal, maleness is more invisible in its artificiality. Sociological studies have demonstrated that maleness is assumed, unless proved otherwise. Shown photographs of people with characteristics of both sexes, participants in such studies tend to see a man if there is any male signifier – such as a moustache – regardless of what else – such as breasts – might also be present (Devor 1989: 47–9). Meanwhile, simply flipping through the pages of any popular women's magazine, through all its step-by-step instructions for molding the body and face into an idealized version of femininity, provides instant and ample evidence for a constructionist view of women. Perhaps the artificial nature of femininity is most literally – and grotesquely – demonstrated by the tens of thousands of American women who get breast implants every year, despite their exorbitant expense and their grave dangers.

Precisely because "man" is the presumed universal, and "woman" the gussied-up other, drag changes meaning depending on who's wearing it, depending on which way the vestments are crossed. And since femininity is *always* drag, no matter who paints on the nail polish and mascara, it's easy to caricature. Frou-frou, sequinned drag queens are often taken to be a joke, a misogynist mockery made of tawdry tinsel and bedecked bitchiness that, like blackface, is a kind of dressing down by dressing up. Misogynist drag (which by no means includes all instances of male-to-female cross-dressing), like racist blackface, reassures, making fun of the socially subservient class by parodying it, always reminding the viewer that the power-granting penis remains – what a relief! – just beneath the skirts. This is slumming; in the end it restores and reifies the standing order.

If men dressed as women often *parody* gender, women dressed as men, on the other hand, tend to *perform* gender – that is, they can reveal the extent to which gender, as Judith Butler suggests, is a "regulatory fiction" – and thus it often takes very little for women to be designated as

145

cross-dressers (Butler 1990: 141). A Sunday *New York Times* fashion supplement in May 1992 described male-inflected high-style designer wear – not only intended and tailored for women, but extremely tight-fitting as well – as drag (Hochswender 1992). This designation was applied to Karl Lagerfeld's black dresses with white shirts and black ties, as well as to Dolce & Gabbana's neckties worn with leather bustiers. If a woman wears drag when she dons a *dress* or *bustier*, or a deliberately silly foot-wide necktie that hangs to her thighs (designed by John Richmond and featured in a photograph, in the *Times* article), what is she doing when she puts on clothes specifically intended for men? When her transvestism is not transplanted into titillating high-priced couture? This non-disruptive commodification of drag, these fashions that accentuate breast and hips, simultaneously capitalizing on and reining in a disruptive practice, are like seventeenth-century breeches parts, in which women played male roles as a means of showing off their legs. (Indeed, Nell Gwynn and her rival Moll Davis danced jigs in afterpieces, to give their audiences a further gander at their gams, unencumbered by text, lot and other actors.) To label these fashions as drag is to draw the line, to say it's sexy for women to take on a little power, a little *hint* of power; nothing more.

But in the theater, which by its very nature can investigate and undo conventions of representation, women in drag can do far more than display their legs; they can call into question the social conventions of gender roles and gender representation, and, as a result, the very category of gender. Without making any trans-historical or trans-cultural claims for the meaning of female-to-male drag, I'd like to look at a few examples from the last couple of decades of women playing men on the American stage, to examine what can happen when the borderlines of gender are transgressed toward power instead of away from it, toward a critique of gender roles instead of toward a parody of them.

I WOULDN'T WANT TO BELONG TO A CLUB THAT ACCEPTS PEOPLE LIKE ME AS MEMBERS: EVE MERRIAM'S THE CLUB

One thing that happens when the borderlines of gender are transgressed toward power is that those in power defensively miss the point. Eve Merriam's *The Club*, in which four gentlemen, a page, a waiter, and a pianist in an Edwardian men's club, drink, play billiards, sing songs, and tell jokes (while keeping an eye on the ticker tape), opened Off-Broadway in 1976 to reviews by one male critic after another who dismissed the show because its cast of seven women failed to convince the audience that they were really men. In the *New York Times* Mel Gussow chided, "Did she [Merriam] think we wouldn't notice the latent femininity under the blustering masculinity?" (Gussow 1976). And Douglas Watt in the *Daily News* complained that one actress in particular "didn't fool me for a minute" (Watt 1976). Of course she wasn't really trying to.

Other critics were more obtuse – and more vicious. "The idea itself is the sort of thing one would expect to find in a girl's boarding school on parents' weekend," wrote Howard Kissel in *Women's Wear Daily*. "Not being any of the girls' parents, I found it hard to indulge" (Kissel 1976). Perhaps most befuddled of all was Rex Reed whose *Daily News* review railed, "This impudent, worthless bore would be laughed out of town if performed by men. To see women impersonating the stuffiness and arrogance of male supremacy seems alarmingly like watching whites perform a minstrel show in blackface. It's a gross insult to everyone." *His* parting insult: "Sadly, this 'club' looks more like an evening spent in a lesbian bar" (Reed 1976).

Of course, if Reed couldn't recognize that women impersonating men are not analogous to whites in blackface for the obvious reason that their relative social positions are reversed, one could hardly expect him to understand that the show would not only be laughed out of town if performed by men, it wouldn't *exist* if performed by men. Reviewing the show for the *Village Voice*, Erika Munk explained, "There was little attempt at deception; nor could there be, given the singing voices. Instead of the [camp] transvestite combination of contempt and identification, there was a lighter mockery, a more modest imitation, no loss of self" (Munk 1976). With a few exceptions, critical response to *The Club* divided across gender lines (much like the critical response to the 1991 film *Thelma and Louise*, where men also failed to appreciate – even resisted – the implicitly feminist critique). Indeed, Merriam credited Munk, Edith Oliver (*The New Yorker*), and Marilyn Stasio (*Cue*) with saving the play from an early closing (in Betsko and Koening 1987: 294).

While some plays produced by various feminist collectives in the 1970s represented men in wicked caricature, *The Club* was certainly the first in a mainstream theater (Circle in the Square) to make fun of men so openly – and in so lighthearted a way. Built of authentic period songs ("Oh what a blissy when we kissy," "Come and whisper yessie, Tessie") and jokes ("What do they call a man who's lucky in love? A bachelor." "Do any of you chaps believe in clubs for women? If every other form of persuasion fails." "Oh, if only there were a way of falling into a woman's arms without falling into her hands!"), the 90-minute show ridiculed men by showing how absurd they are when they ridicule women. The brilliance of the play is precisely that it doesn't go to extremes. The material, irritating as it may be, is not as virulent and hateful as misogynist humor can get. (Think of Lenny Bruce, Andrew Dice Clay.) Indeed, as Munk pointed out in her review, *The Club*'s humor is the same as the humor still driving contemporary sitcoms.

To be sure, revealing the genteel nastiness of common male banter could make even semi-conscious men uncomfortable, but the parallel and deeper uneasiness no doubt came from the self-conscious, presentational performance style. How much easier it would be to take the satire if spectators couldn't tell that the performers were women. But then, what would be the point? The all-woman cast creates a guilty, or at least embarrassing, tension as the targets of such jokes aren't supposed to know about them – much less throw them back in the tellers' faces. More than that, male privilege itself is called into question if women cannot only do what men can do (the show's costumes, sets, lights, and musical arrangements were all done by women), but actually "be" men. What confers male privilege if not some intangible aura of masculinity – and how potent, how sure, is that quality when women can put it on as easily as they put on top hats and tails? These questions would hardly be raised if the impersonations were thoroughly convincing: they depend on a recognition of transvestism; they depend on self-conscious performance.

As if to stretch further this widening, unsettling gap between sex and gender, Merriam adds a scene in which the "gentlemen" rehearse for their club's spring revue – in which one of the "men" plays a "woman," and rather ineptly at that. "She" trips over "her" skirt, minces about, and cowers with pleasure as the "men" fight over "her." The scene hilariously sends up the artificiality of femininity, and does so successfully only because it's refracted through a sly representation of masculinity.

Just as the jokes don't get vulgar or extreme, the male impersonations remain subtle and seductive. There's no swaggering or flexing, no belching or bellowing. If in part that's because of the characters' class status, it's also another indication that masculinity need not be – often must not be – exaggerated to be performed. While the actors worked on sitting with their knees apart and broadening their gestures, in emotional terms, performing maleness means reducing facial expressiveness, reining in exuberance, holding back – the opposite of what drag queens do.

It's hard to say whether *The Club* would be as effective now, more than fifteen years later – now, that is, in this age of Madonna, when the play's ironic stance toward gender has become so taken for granted. None the less, much as it may have harked back to such nineteenth-century American male impersonators as Annie Hindle, *The Club* offered a pioneering, subversive critique of gender inequities, and a heady suggestion of gender instability.

PASSING NARRATIVE: SIMONE BENMUSSA'S *THE SECRET LIFE OF ALBERT NOBBS*

In 1982 Simone Benmussa brought *The Secret Life of Albert Nobbs* from Paris's Compagnie Renaud-Barrault, where she had been working since the late 1950s, to London and then to the Manhattan Theater Club (MTC), a major Off-Broadway subscription house. Based on a short story by the Irish writer George Moore – which was itself based on a nineteenth-century newspaper story – the play unfolds the tale of Nobbs, the head servant of a hotel in Dublin who lived as a man, but was discovered upon his death to be a woman.

Fragmented and spare, the production's set, with its disconnected doors and window frames, reflected the play's somber mood of isolation. The action proceeds through a disjunctive, interrupted series of narrations, beginning with the disembodied voice of the writer George Moore, telling a friend, Alec, of the astonishing Albert Nobbs (played in New York by Glenn Close), while Nobbs and co-workers go about their business. Soon the scene shifts to the diegetic present, and Albert takes on the action Moore has been describing. When Nobbs is forced to share a bed with a visiting worker, Hubert Page (Lucinda Childs), her true identity is revealed. The narrative leaps back as Nobbs explains how she was forced to take on masculine garb to find work after she fled from a job where her love for her employer went unrequited. This narrative is in turn interrupted by a brief exchange in which Nobbs enters the diegetic present tense of her own tale, and converses with the voice of a woman who suggests she dress as a man.

Soon Page confesses that he, too, is really a woman, whose drinking, battering husband drove her to seek her own way – taking on her husband's clothes and profession. Page surprises Nobbs, suggesting that he marry a woman, as Page has done, and the rest of the play follows Nobb's fruitless courtship of a hotel maid.

Though such a summary sounds linear and conventional, the story is repeatedly broken, not only as it leapfrogs in time, but by repeated interventions from the voice of Moore. This "collision between the 'here' of theatrical representation and the elsewhere of narration," Elin Diamond has suggested, "produces a play of signifiers that makes it impossible for the audience to consume a unified image of feminine identity" (Diamond 1985: 281). At the same time, Moore's male voice symbolically circumscribes the stage space in the constraints of male domination: as Diamond points out, Nobbs is confined within Moore's narrative, bereft of identity, bereft of representation – in Page's words, a "perhapser."

Thus gender indeterminacy parallels the denial of self-narrative; cross-dressing strips Nobbs of sexuality and self. The play presents

Nobbs as having to make an artificial choice between a career and living within her own body, as strangled by the very fact of gender; thus, in a manner quite different from *The Club*, it takes a cold look at gender and scoffs at its arbitrariness. On the other hand, because Nobbs's condition as a "perhapser" is liberating only in an economic sense – and indeed lethal in an emotional and, eventually, literal sense – it's difficult to read the play as providing any giddy revelation about gender indeterminacy.

Perhaps this is why a program insert at MTC insisted that the play "is not about a transvestite." Rather, the note explained, the play reveals the compulsion for "a woman to cease to be a woman in order to work." In this sense, *The Secret Life of Albert Nobbs* represents what Marjorie Garber calls, in *Vested Interests*, the "progress narrative" (Garber 1992: 70) – the use of cross-dressing as "an instrumental strategy rather than an erotic pleasure and play space." Such narratives, she argues, are unconvincing because "they rewrite the story of the transvestic subject as a cultural symptom . . . [and because] the consequent reinscription of 'male' and 'female' . . . reaffirms the patriarchal binary and ignores what is staring us in the face: the existence of the transvestite, the figure that disrupts" (Garber 1992: 70).

What Garber fails to acknowledge is that the figure of the transvestite can disrupt in any number of different ways – and one of them is through the "progress narrative." In other words, a woman's disruption of her own oppression can be as powerful and destabilizing as tweaking the binary. In *Albert Nobbs*, of course, it doesn't feel powerful because, like all narratives in the play, the "progress narrative" is interrupted too, left incomplete. The play impugns the gender system and its patriarchal economy, but offers no way out. Perhaps that's because the narrative representation of transvestism – that is, the fact that the story is about a woman playing a man (as opposed to a story about a man, who is played by a woman) – is itself restricted by the narrative framework. As Diamond writes:

> Benmussa's achievement in *Albert Nobbs* is to induce narrativity in the audience while insisting on the coercive effects of a male narrative that (inevitably) refuses or diminishes and distorts the experience of female subjects. Albert's story – or rather Moore and Alec's storytelling – indicts the practice of enacting or telling any woman's story, including those cultural myths and histories that women and men "naturally" consume, inhabit, and perpetuate
> (Diamond 1985: 283)

– among them, gender roles.

THE DRAG THAT IS NOT ONE: HOLLY HUGHES'S *THE LADY DICK*

If there is no way out of the gender system within a transvestic narrative, one solution is to flout and parody narrative structure altogether, as so much experimental theater had been doing for a decade or two when the WOW (Women's One World) Cafe opened its doors in New York's East Village in 1982. The all-woman space, run by a collective comprised of anyone who showed up at its weekly meetings, frequently appropriated and wreaked havoc with familiar forms. Early productions on the postage-stamp stage included lesbian versions of well-known fairy tales, fantastical feminist revisionings of 1950s television programs, homoerotic rewrites of Harlequin romances, sapphic redactions of Shakespeare.

While, in certain respects, WOW women are camp followers of Charles Ludlam's Ridiculous style, mixing high and pop culture with mischievous abandon and insinuating sexual double entendres at every turn, WOW departs from the Ludlam-Ethyl Eichelberger-Charles Busch traditions by assuming – and therefore constructing – a lesbian specta- tor. Taking lesbianism and feminism as givens, not as issues to be exposed, debated, agonized over, or resolved, shows at WOW operate outside the normative system of gender representation – and as a result, perhaps even outside of the normative system of representation itself, which, at least in psychoanalytic theoretical terms, depends on sexual difference.[1]

Heterosexuality is not only not compulsory on WOW's stage, it doesn't exist. And as a result, the lesbian performer is not defined against some "norm" and singled out by her "otherness." (Nor is "woman" defined against "man" since men don't exist either. If they're needed for the plot, they're represented by women in a mock-reluctant drag, or even, with cunning metonymy, by a suitcoat on a hanger.) Here, the lesbian is the universal (which is one reason that criticisms of WOW's frequently amateur performance skills are completely beside the point).

In this context, drag can be vastly complicated and strangely ethereal. Not only because it points to a species outside its own ecology, but because it continually denies men *any* representation: a lesbian in male clothing, after all, is not dressed as a man, but as a butch.

One of the more sophisticated WOW pieces to dance around this conundrum was Holly Hughes's 1985 play *The Lady Dick*, a steamy Raymond Chandleresque yarn set in a lesbian bar with a cheesy floor show. Here the title character – "half Clint Eastwood and half Angela Davis"[2] – narrates her escapades in genre tough-talk: "When all the other girls started looking for shelter from the storm, I started looking for the storm"; "What an angel she is. Takes away the sins of the world and stuffs them in her bra."

151

Building mood more than plot, the play is a series of long speeches by the bar's various denizens, punctuated by suggestive banter between them. The Lady Dick, flirting with bar patrons, is given no case to solve; Hughes is more interested in the mystery of her oxymoronic title. *The Lady Dick* appropriates, most literally, a narrative form typically the domain of men. Hughes's audacity comes not only from placing a woman into the macho role of the crusty detective, but from then denying that character his usual function. What's a detective story, after all, without a plot, without a murder? There are moments in the play when the dick aims an index finger at a bar patron or two and shoots, but almost as soon as the victim crumples to the floor, she's on her feet again. Corpses hold no interest when the living, present, performing body seethes with so many of its own delicious mysteries.

The Dick – named Garnet McClit – enters in the first scene in a shiny green strapless prom dress. Soon she strips out of the dress. "For three years I was treading water in the secretarial pool," she explains. "I was about to go down for the third time. Next time I knew I'd be doing the dead man's float in suburbia. I got desperate." Her solution? Going shopping for a new outfit. As she puts on a baggy double-breasted suit she sings:

> A butch is a woman
> Who looks like a man
> Depending how close you look
> A femme is a female
> Sometimes she may be male
> Sometimes she don't want to cook
> A femme can be fatal
> A butch can be prenatal
> Some walk like their moms
> Some walk like their dads
> It's never too late to switch

To suggest the capacity to "switch" – indeed the production's very demonstration of such a switch – is to step beyond the possibilities promised in *The Club* and deferred in *Albert Nobbs*. Judith Butler has written, "in both butch and femme identities, the very notion of an original or natural identity is put into question; indeed, it is precisely that question as it is embodied in these identities that becomes one source of their erotic significance" (Butler 1990: 123).

In *The Lady Dick*, where butch and femme are not identities but performances, that question gets even touchier. As McClit lets her long hair cascade from beneath a fedora, as Holly Hughes herself rushes onto the stage toward the end of the performance in a green prom dress like the one McClit discarded, to spew out a stream-of-consciousness monologue about falling in love and driving too fast, masculinity and femininity are not only questioned. They are reduced, as Sue-Ellen Case has remarked, to sex toys (Case 1989: 297).

PERFORMING GENDER: SPLIT BRITCHES AND BLOOLIPS'S *BELLE REPRIEVE*

Through some ten years of their own work at WOW, Peggy Shaw and Lois Weaver of Split Britches have staged, celebrated, parodied, and reversed butch-femme identities in autobiographical cabaret (*Anniversary Waltz*), fractured fairy tales (*Beauty and the Beast*, with Deb Margolin), and non-linear, multi-layered drama (Holly Hughes's *Dress Suits to Hire*). Their explorations entered new dimensions when they joined forces with Bloolips on *Belle Reprieve*.

Interlacing Split Britches's self-conscious butch-femme performance style with Bloolips's radical drag queen aesthetic produced an exciting proliferation of genders, pointing to realms beyond the binary. With Shaw cast as *Streetcar*'s Stanley, Weaver as Stella, Precious Pearl as Mitch, and Bette Bourne as Blanche, virtually any given pairing on stage could be read as simultaneously homo- and heterosexual.

The production refers to *Streetcar*, but is not really an adaptation of it. Retaining barely a handful of lines from Williams's text, the show is a four-part invention on themes the script evoked in improvisational workshops among these avatars of homo, pomo performance: the influence of heterosexual imagery on gay and lesbian eroticism; the mythological power of cinematic icons; the appeal of butch-femme and macho-sissy role-playing in lesbian and gay subcultures; the whole messy meaning of gender itself. There's also a tap dance or two.

Perhaps most important, as suggested by the production's title – a none-too-subtle pun on Belle Reve, the name of the family estate Blanche has lost to creditors – *Belle Reprieve* sets out to offer the characters a reprieve from the stifling constraints of naturalism by placing them inside a liberating, non-narrative form. After all, as the characters discuss as they approach the rape scene in *Streetcar*, in naturalism, violence against women is inevitable. But rather than remain subjected, like Albert Nobbs, to this narrative order, the characters in *Belle Reprieve* break down the structure.

In a hilarious outburst toward the end of the play, Bette/Blanche complains, "I want to do a real play. With real scenery, white telephones, French windows, a beginning, middle, and an end. What's wrong with a plot we can all follow? There isn't even a drinks trolley."[3] Shaw/Stanley replies, "Okay, you want realism. I'll give you realism."

BETTE/BLANCHE: You mean like in a real play?

SHAW/STANLEY: If that's what you want.

BETTE/BLANCHE: With Marlon Brando and Vivien Leigh?

SHAW/STANLEY: You think you can play it?

BETTE/BLANCHE: I have the shoulders.

SHAW/STANLEY: I have the pajamas. Okay, let's go for it. "It's just you and me now, Blanche."

For the first time in the 90-minute performance, the actors actually begin to perform a scene from *Streetcar*. But almost immediately Bette/Blanche, frightened, retreats to the non-narrative margins. And Shaw/Stanley understands because, as this beer-drenched butch explains to the fluttering queen, "We're in this together. . . . We are the extremes, the stereotypes. We are as far as we can go . . . ." And then they share a little music-hall number.

While Stanley and Blanche offer the most blatant impersonations of masculinity and femininity in *Belle Reprieve*, they also reveal the less exaggerated masculinity and femininity of Mitch and Stella to be provisional as well. (Precious Pearl has said that he felt less authentic playing straight Mitch than he does under the whiteface, glitter, and fancy frocks of a typical Bloolips extravaganza.[4]) Gender here – until the impossibility of the rape scene touches its limits – is in constant flux. Indeed, throughout the performance run, Shaw raked in adoring fan mail from gay men.

Belle Reprieve points in exciting new directions not only because, by self-consciously using drag that crosses both toward and away from power, it puts masculinity as well as femininity into critical relief. More than that, it envisions the rejection of the power structure itself, obliterating domination through the playful disruption of its most confining expressions.

NOTES

1 For a further discussion of the lesbian performer and representation see: Dolan (1988), and Davy (1986).
2 Quotes from *The Lady Dick* are taken from my performance notes and from the text published in *The Drama Review*, T 131 (fall 1991): 199–215.
3 Quotes from *Belle Reprieve* are taken from my performance notes and from an unpublished manuscript.
4 Interview with Alisa Solomon, January, 1991.

10

CRISSCROSSING CULTURES

Peggy Phelan

The first part of this essay is reprinted from my 1988 article, "Feminist theory, poststructuralism, and performance" (*The Drama Review: A Journal of Performance Studies* 32, 1: 107–27). That argument was divided into four parts: it was my intention that it would grow in complexity and controversy as it went along. In fact, however, it is the first section – reprinted here – that has caused the most distress.

I

When Richard Schechner invited me to attend the September 1986 International School for Theatre Anthropology (ISTA) Congress entitled The Female Role as Represented on the Stage in Various Cultures, I anticipated an international moan and groan about the difficult paradoxes inherent in "representation" in general, and a kind of multilingual opera about the different politics of representing "the female role" cross-culturally. More wrong I could not have been.

The congress, hosted and organized by Eugenio Barba, was not at all concerned with the politics of representation. Issues of cultural hegemony, as well as issues of gender and sexual dominance/submission, were ignored: Barba explicitly stated in the program notes that the congress was not interested in the psychological/political consequences of the performer's roles.[1] Although the reasons why Barba chose not to pursue these issues are extremely important as an indication of where some European "third theater" is (and is not) locating itself, it is unfair to criticize the conference for not doing what it never intended to do. The focus of the conference was on what Barba calls "the actor's energy." Barba believes that a study of the use of the actor's energy on a "'biological' level . . . permits us to make an intercultural examination of the various theatrical traditions, not as historically determined systems but as [physiological] technique." Energy exists at a visible and an invisible level; Barba is interested in the "invisible" energy which emerges on (and in) the "pre-expressive level." Interestingly enough, Barba's pre-expressive level (see Barba 1986a: 135–56) is strikingly similar to what psychoanalytically inclined feminists call the "pre-Oedipal stage." In both ideas, there is a kind of Nietzschean romanticism, an ache for one's "best self," which can be seen only by continually turning back, by a continual turn away from the hubbub of competing meanings. (Nietzsche: "The most essential question of any text is its *hinterfrage* [back question].")

In the effort to reclaim and isolate both the "pre-expressive" and the "pre-Oepidal," a similar hope to understand the construction of meaning (literal and symbolic) is at work. Pre-expressive energy, for Barba, "refers to something intimate, something which pulses in immobility and silence, a retained power which flows in time without spreading through space." For Laura Mulvey: "The pre-Oedipal, rather than an alternative or opposite state to the post-Oedipal, is in *transition* to articulated language: its gestures, signs, and symbols have meaning but do not transcend into the full sense of language" (1986: 10). Just as Barba wants to isolate that intimate and immobile silence which underlines the energy one sees and hears, Mulvey wants to isolate the language of "gesture, sign, and symbol" which is not yet attached to a fully expressive language. In both projects, that which precedes "full sense" – or full expression – is important because it is in the pre-formed gesture/sound that one can perhaps find a way to rejuvenate and manipulate the rigid coding of performed expression and spoken language.

In order to make this clear, let me propose a distinction between "reading" (constructing a narrative in a full language) and "seeing" (a chaotic observation that does not fit into a narrative – either the movement narrative or the narrative of a sentence). At the pre-expressive level and the pre-Oedipal level, "seeing" is dominant because full narratives have not yet been formed and therefore "reading" is impossible. Both the pre-expressive state and the pre-Oedipal period posit a recoverable phase in which differentiation, opposition, and dualism are not yet operative. Hence, for Barba, the pre-expressive level is of interest as a site for the study of "pure" energy, and as a tool to develop an actor's training; hence the pre-Oedipal is of interest to those who want with Mulvey to upset and undermine the psychological/philosophical narrative of difference and opposition – particularly as it relates to gender, "power knowledge," and erotic desire.

Barba's investigations of the actor's energy were based upon various cross-cultural performances of the female role. The eastern dance forms represented at the Congress – Balinese dance drama, Indian Kathakali and Odissi, Japanese Kabuki, and Chinese opera – proved to be the most disturbingly interesting. These eastern theatrical roles are essentially mythic and, as Roland Barthes has remarked, myth "organizes a world which is without contradiction because it is without depth, a world wide open and wallowing in the evident, it establishes a blissful clarity: things appear to mean something by themselves" (1972: 143). Such classical female roles played by men or women do not, by definition and design, penetrate the "identity" of any female; they are surface representations whose appeal exists precisely *as* surface. "Reading" them depends not on plausibility or coherence but rather upon an immediate recognition of the comic artifice *and* reverent idealization which organizes the image the dancer projects. But the substance and style of these dances are perhaps not the most interesting thing about them; for Barba it was the crucial discipline of the training; for a group of western participants (primarily from the US and Canada), it was the contradictory portraits these dances created, not of femaleness *per se*, but of the social/political imaginations which they serve and express.

I'd like to discuss these issues in terms of one dancer: an 11-year-old boy named Gautam, the gotipua performer (Plate 19). Admittedly, this discussion wrenches the dance from its context. I am not trying here to analyze the intricacies of gotipua, but rather trying to isolate the terms of address operative between the spectator and the performer.

Gautam's hot pink costume and elaborate make-up (lips painted berry red, face painted with flowers), are conventional tropes of seduction. As a child, Gautam, with his ability to look non-male, was perhaps the most literally convincing of all the performers. While several women performers played the male role, Gautam's youth and his silence pointed out another implicit aspect of the "power knowledge" system operative in the role division of classical dance. A child can play the part of an adult female, but not of an adult male. The child is "closer" to the woman than to the man.

On a more complicated level, however, the excess and surplus encoded within Gautam's surface femininity reminds the spectator of the absence of the female (the lack) rather than of her presence. The choreography of gotipua is punctuated by a series of tableaux in which the dancer rests squarely in front of the spectator and smiles seductively. He gazes boldly at the spectator and holds his smile. The directness of his seductive appeal is disarming, and it is that directness which paradoxically illuminates the way in which the dance is addressed to the male spectator. No one forgets that the dancer is male; the invocation of the non-male is controlled by the security of the male's body. As a substitution for the female in the sphere of visual desire, Gautam's dance questions the function of erotic substitutions – what Freud called fetishes – in the incitement to desire which all performance exploits. The fetishized female *image* so perfectly encoded in Gautam's costume, make-up, and movement works not to bring "the female" into the spectacle of exchange between spectator and performer but to leave her emphatically outside. In place of the actual female, a fetishized image is

157

displayed which substitutes for her and makes her actual presence unnecessary.

Freud's analysis of fetishism elucidated the ways in which all fetishes function as phallic substitutes, a reassuring projection of male narcissistic fantasy. The fantasy generated by Gautam's performance is the fantasy of exchange *between* men *about* women. In other words, "the female role" turns out to be another reinforcement of the primacy of desire between men for men/boys (the male homoerotic), and the inequitable power relationship between the spectator and the performer (the young boy flatters the male spectator's physical and visual prowess). In short, the fetishized female image reinforces rather than subverts the structure of the patriarchal unconscious.

Much of this reading of Gautam's dance is indebted to a western feminist discourse, a discourse not addressed or summoned by the dance itself. I'm treating the dance not as a series of movements but as a western visual representation. My reading is obviously indebted to feminist re-readings of Freud, a revisionary project which has had the most important consequences for the criticism of film. Feminist film criticism has been the discourse most attentive to the relationship between the position of the spectator and the construction of "gendered texts." Employing psychoanalysis as a method, feminist film critics have outlined the complex relationships between visual pleasure, the conventions of camerawork in Hollywood film, and the structure of the patriarchal unconscious, in order to uncover the inscription of desire in narrative and avant-garde film. Central to the first generation of this project has been an analysis of the male gaze. If a feminist critical analysis of gender issues in performance is going to be written, however, it must begin not with an analysis of the male gaze, but rather with a re-examination of the economy of exchange between the performer and the spectator in performance.

[*End of Part I of "Feminist theory, poststructuralism, and performance."*]

II

Avanthi Meduri has argued that my discussion of Gautam from a western feminist point of view violates the integrity of the dance itself.[2] By ignoring the mythological structure which informs gotipua and its reception for an Indian audience I appropriate it and thereby perpetuate the structure of colonialist knowledge which renders the Indian as always "other" in relation to the North American. The charge of appropriation, given the political history of the United States, is a serious and vexed one.

And yet, to some extent, all representation – critical, artistic, political – practices appropriation (minimally at the level of the sign). The moral and ethical problems of representational appropriation arise when such theft maintains, rather than questions, the degrading and familiar crimes of institutional power knowledge – colonialism, sexism, racism, homophobia (and that's just the most familiar list). While seeking to subvert the unmarked structures of sexism and misogyny within this instance of cross-dressing, and trying to give some flavor of the context of *the conference* in which I saw the dance (explicitly not India, and "mythic" in Barthes's sense rather than in Meduri's), perhaps my discussion of Gautam unwittingly exemplified colonialist appropriation.

But perhaps Meduri's critique of my essay also serves to illustrate the relative comfort people now feel with understanding sexism and misogyny – "we've been through all that, let's get on with the big questions of political rape, economic abuse, and racism." These *are* big questions, but I do not believe we are all through with sexism and misogyny. Nor have we come close to understanding how misogyny is laced, with so much arsenic, into colonialism, racism, homophobia, and class bias.

The appropriation of woman at the heart of male cross-dressing cannot be simply declared "celebratory" or "misogynist" without accounting for the role of race, class, sexuality, economics, and history which determine that appropriation. A rigidly dichotomous ethics of appropriation results in a naive representational politics. An extremely complex and slippery use of appropriation can be seen in Jennie Livingston's controversial film, *Paris is Burning* (1990).

Livingston's documentary focuses on cross-dressing as a means of investigating the politics of culture, knowledge, and power. She employs some of the common ethnographic devices for displaying community: intertitles explaining specific lexical markers seemingly "unique" to this community (but translatable none the less), interviews with articulate informants, a significant change within the community under observation, and voice-overs marking the consequences of that change. In part a visual threnody for a pre-AIDS culture, the film is nostalgic for a future her informants had dreamed of in a more vital past. The loss of that future haunts the speakers' dreams for economic success and idealized femininity. The impossibility of realizing these dreams frames the space of this particular theater. The balls documented in *Paris* are masquerades of absence and lack which enact the masochistic power and genuine pleasure of symbolic identification so crucial to both capitalism and erotic desire.[3] Part of that symbolic identification is with the power connoted by whiteness (which is different from "identifying as white") and another part of that identification stems from a desire to reverse the seeing/being seen dyad. The walkers admire "whiteness" because it is unmarked and therefore escapes political surveillance. For these men who are simultaneously over-seen and under-represented, appropriating whiteness can be a paradoxical gesture. On the one hand, it is complicitous with the notion of whiteness as an unmarked part of "ideal beauty" and, on the other, the marked appropriation comments on that "normative" notion of beauty. But the force of feeling one does not conform to that model, that one is always other than the model, leads to a desire to revise and/or enhance the physical body which does not conform to that model. Currently, "black women [in the US] spend as much as three times more than white women on cosmetics and skin care products" (Kerr 1991). And those who benefit from this spending are, by and large, (white) men.

III

Paris is Burning chronicles the competitive balls staged in Harlem clubs (most of the film was shot at the Imperial Elks Lodge) between 1987 and 1989. The models who walk and compete for huge trophies during the ball are Latino and African-American gay men, transvestites, and transsexuals, most of whom are poor. Livingston illustrates the structures of the communities, the balls, and the vocabulary in which the balls are staged. Participants are performing legends, mothers, up and coming legends, or children. They compete in contests for Military Realness, Butch Queen Realness, Best Bangee Boy and Bangee Girl. They belong to houses, which under the seemingly thin bond of fashion and style, knit members together into the fabric of family. Their family names are taken either from the stars of the fashion industry – St Laurent, Chanel, Armani – or from the most captivating member of the house – Pepper Labeija, Willie Ninja, and Angie Xtravaganza – who serves as the mother of the family. In adapting the corporate name/logo of the most expensive fashion designers as their own, the children both appropriate and mock the intentional "exclusiveness" of these labels. In adapting the name of the mother as against the name of the father the houses valorize the femininity which they emulate in the balls themselves. The architecture of that femininity, however, is thoroughly masculine. And it thoroughly reflects the psychic-political structure of capitalism.

The driving force of an appropriative capitalism insists on affirming the "have-not" condition of commodity desire. Economic "lack" everywhere infiltrates sexual and political–psychic lack in *Paris is Burning*. The boasting pride of the children who have bought breasts for their mother Angie Xtravaganza is the pride of reversal: they convert the "no" of the Law of the Father into the double "yes" of the Mother. The children want to be mothered and to be given the nurturant pleasure associated with breasts. (Psychoanalytically, the male child's desire to ingest the maternal breast is a formation influence on his castration complex. Just as he wanted to devour her breast, she, he fearfully believes, wants to consume his penis.)[4] Being unable or unwilling

160

to face the heterosexual imperative leaves political, economic, racial, and class imperatives also imperilled.

The gender play operative within *Paris is Burning* involves much more than cross-*dressing*. And the stakes are higher than most theoretical speculation around gender generally allows. Driving the mechanism of these performed identities is a notion of "the real." Realness is determined by the ability to blend in, to go unnoticed. The extravagant costumes and personae displayed at the balls are serious rehearsals for a much tougher walk – down the "mean streets" of New York City. The balls are opportunities to use theater to imitate the theatricality of everyday life – a life which includes show girls, bangee boys, and business executives. It is the endless theater of everyday life that determines the real: and this theatricality is soaked through with racial, sexual, and class bias. As one of the informants explains, to be able to look like a business executive is to be able to be a business executive. And yes, given the impoverished politics of appearance which allow "opportunity" and "ability" to be connoted precisely by the way one looks, this is too true to bear.

Realness is not a static concept – any more than race, sexuality, or identity itself are static. Dorian Corey, one of the the wisest informants in the film, is a light-skinned African-American who dresses *à la* Marilyn Monroe in part because when he began performing the "showgirl look" was the apex of drag. That "showgirl look" was emphatically white. The younger and darker-skinned teenagers who dress as "bangee girls" have a radically different idea of what the ideal drag performance is about. And yet, both performances appropriate the constructed image of "the woman" and in that appropriation celebrate and reinterpret it.

Woman remains available to further reinterpretation in part because she is that which can never be internalized as identity for men and in part because each repetition of that image marks its perpetual (re)construction. Woman is the figure of disguise, of masquerade. In imitating her, the cross-dresser makes visible his own desire to be disguised. Within the economy of patriarchal desire which frames – although does not completely define – gay male cross-dressing, the figure of the woman is appropriated as a sign to validate male authority. His authority is determined by how fully he can "wear" her; in wearing her, however, he (like Gautam) renders her actual presence unnecessary. In this sense, gay male cross-dressing makes manifest the psychic structure of "traditional heterosexual culture" – which is to say, male homosocial culture. Woman is a necessary point of tension because she reflects and assures male authority. The inability to internalize woman makes her representation a substitute for a substitute, a fetish.[5] "She" disguises his desire for the phallus – and the competition to wear her well merely makes room for the displacements operative in all erotic exchange.

A re-presented woman is always a copy of a copy; the "real" (of) woman cannot be represented precisely because her function is to re-present man. She is the mirror and thus is never in it. Her narrowly defined but ubiquitous image represents the frenzy of man to see she who makes him him. (Woman is man's always-mother.) In the film, Willie Ninja teaches young women how to walk like women – to be "models." These walkers are in turn imitated by Ninja's compeers at the balls. A man teaches a woman how to walk and she models that walk for another man to imitate. He imitates another man's idea of what a woman walks like and, given the slippery politics of appearance, what a woman "is." Homophobia demands that the woman continue to be placed between the bodies of the two men – but she is just a foil for the central relationship between the men.[6] At the balls, he then displays that walk for the approval of other men.

As "mothers," women's bodies retain the possibility of being entered and evacuated by other bodies. Within the tight literalness of the western psyche, women cannot themselves enter the body of men; they can internalize men but they cannot be internalized by men. Men's inability to internalize the woman fully accounts for the projective anxiety of castration which traditional heterosexual culture represses and gay male drag fetishizes. Gay male cross-dressers *resist* the body of woman even while they make its constructedness visible. The bodies of women do not "penetrate" these men because they do not erotically desire women. This is in part why the misogyny which underlies gay male cross-dressing is so painful to women. As Marilyn Frye puts it: "gay men's effeminacy and donning of feminine apparel displays no love of or identification with women or the womanly. . . . It is a casual and cynical mockery of women."[7] But it is something more than that as well.

Within the film world of *Paris*, walking in a ball is at once a celebration of one's grandest ambitions to charm, seduce, and attract, and an admission that what one most admires is perennially hostile and imper-vious to such admiration. Masochism is an integral part of the spectacle; pain is never too far from the parade of costume and Protean self-invention demanded by the discriminating spectators/performers who watch the show – spectators who no matter how critical are ever so much "safer" than the spectators on the street, the subway, the line for the movies.

The filmic spectators who watch *Paris is Burning* have a different relation to the performance than the spectators/performers recorded within the film. The filmmaker addresses her spectator as external to the community – in keeping with the law of the genre of ethnographic film. Ethnographic law insists that the film will function as the liminal figure who sutures "them" to "us." The film must then maintain the distinction between "them" and "us" so as to justify its address and its powerful

liminality. As Jackie Goldsby points out in her terrific review of *Paris,*
Livingston

> can tell this story because her identity is not implicated in it . . .
> This is not to say that Livingston shouldn't have made the film, or
> that a "black" film necessarily would have been different. It is to
> suggest, though, that the cultural and social privilege of the film-
> maker is inscribed into the film however unobtrusive she strives to
> be.
>
> (Goldsby 1991: 11)

That cultural and social privilege is the privilege of a non-interrogated
whiteness. The danger of this particular form of liminality is that it
allows the white spectator to be flattered, rather than chastened, by the
ideological critique of white capitalist culture embodied in the balls. The
distinction between symbolic identification and identity is in danger of
being lost by the form of spectatorial address Livingston employs. Some
of the walkers want to *pass* as white, but they do not want to *be* white.
This is a crucial difference.

As bell hooks remarks in her blistering review of the film, "Livingston
does not oppose the way hegemonic whiteness 'represents' blackness, but
rather assumes an imperial overseeing position that is no way progressive or counterhegemonic" (hooks 1991: 62). While hooks implicitly
subscribes to the overly simple idea that reflexivity about whiteness
would have "saved" the film from its appropriative hegemonic grasp, she
forcefully denounces the uncritical praise of the film's methods. hooks's
critique is severe but it should be noted that she is writing against the
adoring voices of reviewers ranging from Vincent Canby to Essex
Hemphill.[8] Hemphill, for example, remarks enthusiastically: "We are
not exposed to any of Livingston's judgments, if she has any, of the
subjects. The authentic voice of this community emerges unfettered"
(Hemphill 1991: 10). The wish to hear an authentic and single voice is
very strong, but representation is never transparent.

The specific and important achievement of *Paris* is that it opens up the
possibility of seizing an appropriative epistemology not *about* cross-
dressing but indebted to its wisdom. Livingston's film does not enact the
radical epistemology of her subjects – it sticks too close to the rules of
ethnographic documentary to experiment with crisscrossing filmic identities. But despite these failures *Paris is Burning* is still an important film –
if only because it comes so close to being an astonishing documentary
about something that may be unfilmable.

The balls Livingston documents and the film with which she documents them are precisely alike in their revulsion for and adoration of the
real. Ontologically, cinema detests the real because it must remain a
celluloid shadow of it, a trace of something always receding and absent.

163

At the same time, cinema loves the real because in tracing and framing the real, it gains power and definition. Similarly, those who walk in the balls win for *imitating* – rather than being – the real. The walks both perpetuate the aspiration to be real and mark again the artifice that makes it, always, impossible to be real (and not only for the walkers). Cheryl Lynn's "Got to be real" haunts the sound-track while the camera restlessly wanders out of the clubs into the streets of mid-town and finds white, heterosexual couples chatting in well-coiffured hair and trim suits. The walkers want to believe that such people are real in order to have something to imitate *and* define themselves against. But realness has become such a fluid term that these heterosexual white couples seem exceptionally artificial just by virtue of being framed within a film that is so relentlessly concerned with the fine gradations of the (relative) real. All film is preoccupied with these calibrations because ontologically film is excluded from the real – just as the walkers are excluded from "being" the real they perform at the ball. While the walkers are not excluded ontologically, the forces of class, racism, and homophobia conspire to make their political–social exclusion seem ontological. The art of the walkers, however, is to illustrate how capricious such exclusions are, and how false the white heterosexual "real" is.

The balls aim to show that a flamboyant walk at the Imperial Elks Club is a ticket to passing for real outside of the club. Paradoxically, performing this real allows the walker to be passed over, not vulnerable to the hostile gaze of white heterosexual culture. The goal of the balls is to theatricalize the passage from excessive hyper-visibility attendant on the racialized and homosexualized "other" in white, affluent culture to the "invisibility" accorded to white heterosexual femininity within that same culture.

When the white couples appear in *Paris*, it is almost as if the film has become a commercial selling and exposing the commodity of white, heterosexual and economic privilege. These couples signal the distance between the ball's dream of the real – a dream full of concentration, energy, and focus – and the surface casualness of these couples' real. It is precisely this ease which is inimitable for the walkers. The balls are the manifestation of the yawning distance between symbolic identification and identity itself. The figure of the (white) woman as the cipher for that distance is then necessarily a figure of immense ambivalence. Had Livingston rigorously examined this subject she might have made an extraordinary film. The film's failure to take up that harder project is the failure to look closely at the political implications of appropriative epistemology and to examine the incredible allure of being unseen when visibility has meant (and continues to mean) violence, imprisonment, death.

IV

My friend keeps telling me to be sure I keep saying I'm only writing about Livingston's film of the balls and I'm not writing about the balls themselves. My friend knows how tempted I am to take Livingston's film as "the real." That's where the hook of the film (and perhaps of most ethnographic film) breaks my skin. Like Essex Hemphill, I want a film that substitutes for the performance itself – a transparent film that renders the performance in all its complexity. I know there's no such thing as transparent film, but that doesn't make my wish for it disappear. So my friend tries to remind me of the difference between what I know to be true and what I wish to be true. I half-listen and half-rant. I type and retype these old and new words, look at the clock, look at time moving across my own face. This typeface. Black ink on a white page. The projector is still on.

I want the film to be transparent so I can explain in lavish detail how the performance makes equivalencies between mopping (stealing) a St Laurent dress and "buying" breasts. Gender has a price tag – and once in the market, it can be bought and sold, manipulated by the surgeon's knife, deft clefts in the market of elegant signs. But there's something more behind my desire for the film to be "real." White women like myself have been encouraged to mistake performance for ontology – to believe that the role is real, and thus sufficient to constitute an identity, a sense of purpose, a reason for being. If performance can provide a substitute real, then "identity" can truly be an invention – not something susceptible to some external facts (biological, sexual, economic) which prohibit us access to "femininity," "beauty," "glamour," "power," "wealth," or whatever it is we desire. But the only way we can see if performance is an adequate substitute for ontology is through the staging of performances. In that enactment, however, we make conscious again the difference between performance and ontology: precisely what motivates the performance is that which ontology – the question of being itself – will not and cannot answer. In the variations on that reenactment, we can read the historical and political imperatives that prohibited Dorian Corey from seeing Lena Horne as his real idol twenty years ago, and allows someone today to see Patti LaBelle as his. Are these the "facts" that cannot be flicked away with the surgeon's knife? Is imagination the "real" limit? Or history? Or our imagination of history?

Racism and homophobia are seen in *Paris* as more hostile than the forces of sexism – and this I believe is partially because the informants are men and less astute about the impact of sexism on identity than they are about the impact of racism and homophobia. Pepper Labeija hints as much when he says that he thinks having a sex change operation is taking things "a little too far." After all, he points out, in many ways women have it a lot worse than men in this culture. But given the virulence of homophobia it may well be that for someone like Venus Xtravaganza surgically transforming her genitals promises a more satis-fying life than desiring a man from within the caverns of a biologically male body.

It is in the attitude toward self-invention that the relationship between the ideology of nation/culture and the ideology of gender can be most clearly seen. The stories told in *Paris* are compatible with the myths of American identity – myths which center on white men's struggle to invent and reinvent their identities. Part of the appeal of *Paris* for a white, straight audience is its ability to absorb and tame the so-called otherness of this part of black and Latino gay male culture. The dreams of economic success, fame, and security articulated by the performers are exactly the same dreams of "most American men." The means by which these dreams are realized – self-invention, hard work, and ingenuity – are the same methods celebrated in the careers of Ragged Rick and Rocky I through V. For the white American man, self (re)in-vention is an integral part of the mythos of success.[9]

Overlaid on this mythos is the American philosophical predisposition toward pragmatism; the sense that philosophy and jurisprudence must, above all, be practical and concern themselves with the questions and problems of "the ordinary guy." Philosophical positions and judicial decisions must, in other words, be responsive to the real.

Given the accents on pragmatism within the US, the judicial stance toward difference, most recently underlined by *Bowers* v. *Hardwick* (1986), has a startlingly clear relation to the streetlife and culture of "the ordinary guy." *Bowers* v. *Hardwick* effectively eliminated the notion of privacy for homosexuals: the state is legally permitted to survey and prosecute sodomy between same-sex partners, even in their own bed-rooms. By legally eliminating privacy for homosexuals, the Supreme Court extends the runway of the ball. There is no legal boundary to the gaze of the state and the "enforcers" of the law. Thus, if a gay man can get home on the subway dressed as a woman without having his head bashed in, he wins because he has managed to escape scrutiny and notice. That's pragmatism and self-invention at once. That is America. And that is living and surviving based on appropriative knowledge.

But it is here too that the most troublesome aspect of Livingston's film is revealed. (And this is precisely the problem of ethnography – once the "subject" is turned into the subject-supposed-to-know, the subject is misrecognized.) Livingston, like the Supreme Court in *Bowers*, also ex-tends the runway of the ball. She confuses performance with identity – and thus repeats the misrecognition which generates the American mythos of self-invention. The film makes it seem as if the balls are the focal point of these people's lives, but identities are never that singular. Livingston's reduction of this community serves the interest of dominant culture. (As hooks puts it: "What could be more reassuring to the white public than a documentary affirming that the victims [of racism] are all too willing to be complicit in perpetuating the fantasies of ruling class white culture?") The balls are certainly not socially or politically revolutionary. (Unless one believes shoplifting is a revolutionary act.) The power of the balls is psychic, which is to say they operate at the level of the political economy of the sign. The balls intervene in the smooth reproduction of physical images by using mimicry and appropriation both to point out the constructedness of that image and to replicate its power. Unavoidably complicitous with the thing they try to denounce, the walkers – like other post-modern artists such as Cindy Sherman, Sherrie Levine, and Richard Prince – find themselves caught in the tight logic of the commodified sign. It is virtually impossible to escape this logic, and Livingston's lucrative film – to appropriate Foucault's description of Freud – would have to be invented if it had not already appeared.

V

If the challenge of *Paris* is to find a filmic equivalent for the appropriative knowledge of cross-dressing, what is the challenge for writing, for the critical–political economy of the sign? It must require more than the insistent mentioning of "my friend." It must require more motility between the voices of critical authority and personal prose. Writing always requires scrutiny of the name; all signature is appropriation; writerly authority and identity are both announced by and through naming. "Venus Xtravaganza." "Willie Ninja." Names are the literal signs of appropriative knowledge. As metaphors of identity, these renamings serve to make present the absence of the "proper" name – for subjects and for objects. It is this absence which metaphor tries to hide.

By linking the appropriated, metaphoric name with the masquerade of stylized, performed identity, the balls underline the violence of language and, more specifically, the rhetoric of identity. Neither metaphor nor performance can summon the proper name which will reveal ourselves to ourselves as ourselves. Always we are stuck trying to find ourselves within and through the realm of the other, which is to say within the other-sign, the metaphor.

Between my own first and last names, my first name for my mother, my surname his name, is the symbolic identification that allows these words to be rewritten, written over, touched up, retouched, reprinted, revised. And here too is the inscription of violence. Circulated again in the economy of print, bleeding into another text, notating the choreography of another film. Falling in behind Barthes's *déjà-lu*, the always already read, the quoted words. That's always the (small) authority of girl talk. Nothing ever set in stone; nothing ever rigid. Fluid they usually say. Liquid assets. Rigid is boy talk. Reprint as is. Boys can teach girls to talk and walk. James Joyce writing Molly's version of Bloom's (second) coming. Willie Ninja teaching the girls to swing their hips wide for the boys. Incomplete choreography, the stutter step before the music fades. The open hand writing; the emptiness of the word carving a space for others to inhabit.

The dramatic climax of *Paris is Burning* is not, as the title suggests, the final and grandest ball of the season. It is rather the murder of Venus Xtravaganza. Petite and soft-spoken, the pre-transsexual Venus, dressed all in white and leaning back against a bed, says she wants only to be a "spoiled rich white girl" and live with the man she loves. As Venus speaks I am struck again with how deeply self-invention and reinvention structures the performance of identities. In abandoning the dream of being a spoiled white girl I paradoxically confirm the fact that I am spoiled enough and white enough to be able to afford to abandon it. Venus abandoned "being a man" in part because her version of masculinity gave her no currency (or even a negative currency, a perpetual debit) within the rigid economy of the sex–gender system. Livingston, through the single interview she conducts with Angie Xtravaganza, implies that Venus, found under a bed in a cheap hotel after four days, was murdered because she could not finally pass as a woman. Livingston wants that to be the message of her film – gender and sexuality are games played for keeps and no one who steps too far outside tradition-ally assigned roles is ever home free.

But it may well be that Venus was murdered precisely because she did pass. On the other side of the mirror which women are for men, women witness their own endless shattering. Never securely positioned within the embrace of heterosexuality or male homosexuality, the woman winds up *under* the bed, four days dead.

Paris is a city on the Seine. In the song Judy Collins sings her father always promised her they would live in France, go boating on the Seine, and she would learn to dance. In the myth, Paris is the one who must decide who among the three goddesses should get the enigmatically inscribed golden apple – "to the fairest" – thrown by Eris into the wedding feast of Thetis and Peleus. Eris' name announces the trans-formation of the unified circle of Er*os* to the singular "I" of Str*i*fe; that is why she alone among the divinities is not invited to the wedding. The apple is immediately given to Zeus who is asked to settle the question of rightful ownership – who should appropriate the apple? Zeus, a wise god, says Paris, the most handsome god, must be the judge. Pallas Athena promises Paris wisdom; Hera promises him power; but Aphrodite (Venus) promises that Helen, the most beautiful woman, will love him. Paris gives her the apple. She gives Paris Helen. And Troy burns.

From the Greek Aphrodite to the Roman Venus, the proper name is transformed. Textual emendation; sexual emendation. The proper name for woman may be always a transsexual, a sign forever "in process." The name of woman may always be susceptible to translation, reinterpretation, an endless cut in/to the mother tongue. Vulnerable to a master myth and laboring under the image of mastery, the image and the name of woman is metaphoric, substitutive. In the advertisements for the film Venus' image is frozen on the film ads (Plate 20). Her singular display portends her final absence. Venus' leg is propped up, you can see up her dress. Covered in white, her genitals are on display as mystery, as disguise, as revision. Reprinted, blown up, cropped back, Venus' transformations are textual and sexual. The desire enunciated by *Paris* is that what the walkers want is a life *on* film: a life which records the subtle transformations of physical surface by manipulating the light, changing the shutter speed, cropping this or that unnecessary surface detail. Such a life guarantees the production of the walkers' endless re/presentation, a reproduction which promises perfect copies. In a climate which aggressively and violently associates "imperfect" desire with death, the frozen image of a perfect copy maintained in the perpetual present seems more than an appeal to "surface."

While always entering representation disguised as an other, these walkers remain invulnerable to surveillance as themselves. As the possibility of "privacy" continually recedes in this culture of the documenting camera and legislating lens, this strategy of mis/representing has its own brilliant and tragic logic.

Projecting "the woman," the walkers manage at once to be the screen and the creators of that image. "And were it not for the assistance of a projection screen – a dead cave – which provides some goal for representation, no doubt representation would fall short" (Irigaray 1985: 355). That dead cave is the "real" body of the woman – she who is actually screened out of representation to assure men of their image.

Film's own ontology, its need for dark rooms and bright light, mitigates against the demise of privacy and participates in creating the distinction between the real and the phantom. Film's history is implicated in the impoverished politics of appearance that fuel the balls. Like old lovers who leave smoke in your eyes, film must always leave a ghost on the screen. This time her name is Venus. She died because she thought if she were a beautiful woman, a man might love her. But that's against all the rules. Zeus to Paris: the golden apple is always given by men to other men.

Acknowledgment: pages 160–9 are a condensed version of "The golden apple: Jennie Livingston's *Paris is Burning*" which appeared in *Unmasked: The Politics of Performance* (Routledge, 1993).

NOTES

1 Despite Barba's reiteration of his anti-psychologism, his insistence that each performer tell the story of his/her "first day of training" has more than a little in common with psychoanalysis's interest in the "primal scene," the "originary cause," and "earliest memories." "The first days of [the performer's] work leave an indelible imprint," Barba notes in the Conference Program. All quotations from Barba, unless otherwise indicated, come from the Program Notes.

2 See Avanthi Meduri (1991).

3 Žižek (1989) argues: "in symbolic identification we identify ourselves with the other precisely at a point at which he is inimitable, at the point which eludes resemblance" (109).

4 The best discussion of this can be found in Irigaray (1985): 58.

5 For Freud the fetish functions as a phallic substitute. For Lacan, woman must turn herself into the phallus in order to signify the desire of the other, the man. "Paradoxical as this formulation might seem, I would say that it is in order to be the phallus, that is to say, the signifier of desire of the Other, that the woman will reject an essential part of her femininity, notably all its attributes through masquerade. It is for what she is not that she expects to be desired as well as loved" (Lacan, in Rose Mitchell (1982: 84). These walkers exhibit the same relation to the masquerade, and to the attendant expectation that this masquerade will bring them love.

6 It may well be that as the internalized homophobia of gay male culture abates the appeal of the "showgirl woman" will decrease. In other words, the appeal of hyper-femininity may diminish as same-sex relations seem more pervasive and less unusual. Perhaps this is happening with the category "best bangee girl."

7 Marilyn Frye, *The Politics of Reality*, quoted in hooks (1991).

8 A brief list: Canby (1991); Crisp (1991); Brown (1991); Hemphill (1991).

9 This compatibility is reflected in the financial success of the film as well. In its first weekend limited release (23 screens in 17 cities) the film grossed more than $310,000. See Beale (1991).

BIBLIOGRAPHY

Abel, Sam (1991) "The emasculated hero: the changing image of woman-as-man on the operatic stage," paper delivered at the American Society for Theater Research Conference, Seattle, Washington, November 15.

Ackroyd, Peter (1979) *Dressing Up – Transvestism and Drag: The History of an Obsession*, New York: Simon & Schuster.

Agnew, Jean-Christophe (1986) *Worlds Apart: The Market and the Theater in Anglo-American Thought, 1550–1750*, New York: Cambridge University Press.

Allen, Robert (1990) "'The leg business': transgression and containment in American burlesque," *Camera Obscura* 23: 43–68.

Almaviva (1871) *The Figaro* (October 14): 14. London.

Althusser, Louis (1971) "Ideology and ideological state apparatuses," in *Lenin and Philosophy and Other Essays*, New York: Monthly Review Press, 127–86.

Anson, John (1974) "Female monks: the transvestite motif in early Christian literature," *Viator* 5: 1–32.

Ash, Peter (1958) "The first auctioneer: origin of sales by auction of real property," *Estates Gazette* (Centenary Supplement).

Aston, Elaine (1988) "Male impersonation in the music hall: the case of Vesta Tilley," *New Theatre Quarterly* 4, 15: 247–57.

—— (1989) *Sarah Bernhardt: A French Actress on the English Stage*, Oxford: Berg.

"Apollo, NY" (1964) Review of the Jewel Box Revue, *Variety* (March 18) (no page), from the Billy Rose Theater Collection at Lincoln Center.

Auerbach, Nina (1987) *Ellen Terry: Player in Her Time*, London: J. M. Dent.

Avery, Willard (1971) *Female Impersonation*, New York: Regiment Publications.

Babcock, Barbara A. (1978) *The Reversible World: Symbolic Inversion in Art and Society*, Ithaca: Cornell University Press.

Baker, Roger (1968) *Drag: A History of Female Impersonation on the Stage*, London: Triton.

Baker, Sheridan (1959) "Henry Fielding's *The Female Husband*: fact and fiction," *PMLA* 74: 213–24.

Balzac, Honoré de (1899) "Sarrasine," in *The Works of Honoré de Balzac XXXI–XXXII*, trans. W. P. Trent, New York: Thomas Y. Crowell.

Bamber, Linda (1982) *Comic Women, Tragic Men: A Study of Gender and Genre in Shakespeare*, Stanford: Stanford University Press.

Banner, Lois W. (1983) *American Beauty*, Chicago: University of Chicago Press.

Barba, Eugenio (1986a) *The Floating Islands*, New York: Performing Arts Journal Publication.

—— (1986b) "The female role as represented on the stage in various cultures," in the conference Program, compiled and edited by Richard Fowler. The

International School of Anthropology, Hostelbro, Denmark.

"Bare bosoms have Reno's tacit OK but would bar femme 'personators" (1962), *Variety* (Feb. 28) (no page), from the Billy Rose Theater Collection at Lincoln Center.

Barish, Jonas (1981) *The Antitheatrical Prejudice*, Berkeley: University of California Press.

Barker, Francis (1984) *The Tremulous Private Body: Essays on Subjection*, London: Methuen.

Barthes, Roland (1972) *Mythologies*, trans. Annette Lavers, New York: Hill & Wang.

—— (1974) *S/Z*, trans. Richard Miller, New York: Hill & Wang.

Bartlett, Neil (1988) *Who Was That Man? A Present for Mr Oscar Wilde*, London: Serpent's Tail.

Beale, Lewis (1991) "*Paris* has box-office appeal," *The Philadelphia Inquirer* (Aug. 15), 1C.

Becon, Thomas (1637) *The Displaying of the Popish Masse*, London.

Bell-Metereau, Rebecca (1985) *Hollywood Androgyny*, Irving, New York: Columbia University Press.

Belsey, Catherine (1985a) *The Subject of Tragedy: Identity and Difference in Renaissance Drama*, London: Methuen.

—— (1985b) "Disrupting sexual difference: meaning and gender in the comedies," in John Drakakis (ed.) *Alternative Shakespeares*, London: Methuen, 166–90.

Benjamin, Walter (1973) *Understanding Brecht*, trans. Anna Bostock, London: NLB.

Benson, Edward F. (1929) *The Male Impersonator*, London: Elkin Matthews & Marrot.

Berger, Harry, Jr (1981) "Marriage and mercifixion in *The Merchant of Venice*: the Casket Scene revisited," *Shakespeare Quarterly*, 32: 155–62.

Berggren, Paula (1983) "'A prodigious thing': the Jacobean heroine in male disguise," *Philological Quarterly* 62, 3: 383–402.

Berube, Allan (1979) "Lesbian masquerade," *Gay Community News* (November 17): 8–9.

—— (1990) *Coming Out Under Fire: The History of Gay Men and Women in World War II*, New York: The Free Press.

Betsko, Kathleen and Koenig, Rachel (eds) (1987) *Interviews with Contemporary Women Playwrights*, New York: Beech Tree Books.

Binns, J. W. (1974) "Women or transvestities on the Elizabethan stage?: An Oxford controversy," *The Sixteenth-Century Journal* 5: 95–120.

Blair, Rhonda (1993) "'Not . . . But'/ 'Not-Not-Me': musings on cross-gender performance," in Ellen Donkin (ed.) *Upstaging Big Daddy: Directing Theater as if Gender and Race Matter*, Ann Arbor: University of Michigan Press.

Blewitt, David (1984) "Records of drama at Winchester and Eton, 1397–1576," *Theatre Notebook* 38, 2: 88–143.

Boas, Guy (1955) *Shakespeare and the Young Actor*, London: Rockliffe.

Boswell, Terry E., *et al.* (1986) "Recent developments in Marxist theories of ideology," *Insurgent Sociologist* 13: 5–22.

Bournonville, August (1979) *My Theatre Life*, trans. Patricia N. McAndrew, Middleton: Wesleyan University Press.

Bratton, J. S. (1992) "Irrational dress," in V. Gardner and S. Rutherford (eds) *The New Woman and Her Sisters: Feminism and Theatre 1850–1914*, London:

Harvester Wheatsheaf.

Bratton, Jackie (1987) "King of the boys: music hall male impersonators," *Women's Review* 20: 77–91.

Brau, Lorie (1990a) "Reviews and resources – performance," *Women and Performance* 5, 1: 156–63.

—— (1990b) "The women's theatre of Takarazuka," *The Drama Review* 34, 4: 79–95.

Brians, Paul (1972) "The lady who was castrated," in *Bawdy Tales from the Courts of Medieval France*, New York: Harper & Row.

Brown, Georgia (1991) "Do the real thing," *The Village Voice* (March 19): 54.

Brown, Laura (1985) *Alexander Pope*, New York: Basil Blackwell.

Bulliet, C. J. (1933) *Venus Castina: Famous Female Impersonators – Celestial and Human*, New York: Covici, Friede Publishers.

Bullough, Vern L. and Bullough, Bonnie (1993) *Cross Dressing, Sex and Gender*, Philadelphia: University of Pennsylvania Press.

Burgess, Alan (1963) *The Lonely Sergeant*, London: William Heinemann Ltd.

Burke, Peter (1978) *Popular Culture in Early Modern Europe*, London: Temple Smith.

Buruma, Ian (1984) *Behind the Mask: On Sexual Demons, Sacred Mothers, Transvestites, Gangsters, Drifters and Other Japanese Cultural Heroes*, New York: Pantheon.

Butler, Judith (1990) *Gender Trouble: Feminism and the Subversion of Identity*, London: Routledge.

—— (1991) "Imitation and gender insubordination," in Diana Fuss (ed.) *Inside/ Out: Lesbian Theories, Gay Theories*, New York: Routledge, 13–31.

Canby, Vincent (1991) "*Paris is Burning*," *New York Times* (March 13): C13.

Candy, Edward (1983) "The coming of age of Peter Pan," *Drama-Quarterly Theatre Review* 147: 9–10.

Carson, James P. (1992) "Commodification and the figure of the castrato in Smollett's *Humphrey Clinker*," *The Eighteenth Century* 33, 1: 24–46.

Case, Sue-Ellen (1984) "Gender as play: Simone Benmussa's *The Singular Life of Albert Nobbs*," *Women and Performance* 1, 2: 22.

—— (1985) "Classic drag: the Greek creation of female parts," *Theatre Journal* 37, 3: 317–28.

—— (1988) "Materialist feminism and theatre," in *Feminism and Theatre*, New York: Methuen, 82–94.

—— (1989) "Toward a butch-femme aesthetic," in Lynda Hart (ed.) *Making a Spectacle*, Ann Arbor: University of Michigan Press.

—— (1990) *Performing Feminisms: Feminist Critical Theory and Theatre*, Baltimore: Johns Hopkins University Press.

Cassady, Ralph, Jr (1967) *Auctions and Auctioneering*, Berkeley: University of California Press.

Castle, Terry (1982) "Matters not fit to be mentioned: Fielding's *The Female Husband*," *ELH* 49: 602–22.

—— (1983) "Eros and Liberty at the English masquerade, 1710–90," *Eighteenth-Century Studies* 17: 156–76.

The Champion (1743) collection, London: H. Chapelle.

Charke, Charlotte (1969) *A Narrative of the Life of Mrs Charlotte Charke*, introduction by Leonard R. N. Ashley, Gainesville, Florida: Scholars' Facsimiles and Reprints.

Chauncey, George (1986) "The way we were: gay male society in the Jazz Age," *Village Voice* (July 1): 29–30, 34.

173

—— (1989a) "Christian brotherhood or sexual perversion? Homosexual identities and the construction of sexual boundaries in the World War I era," in Martin Bauml Duberman, Martha Vicinus, and George Chauncey, Jr (eds) *Hidden From History: Reclaiming the Gay and Lesbian Past*, New York: New American Library, 294–317.

—— (1989b) "From sexual inversion to homosexuality: the changing medical conceptualization of female 'deviance,'" in Kathy Piess and Christina Simmons (eds) *Passion and Power: Sexuality in History*, Philadelphia: Temple University Press, 87–117.

Cheney, Patrick (1983) "Moll Cutpurse as hermaphrodite in Dekker and Middleton's *The Roaring Girl*," *Renaissance and Reformation* 7, 2: 120–34.

Cheshire, David (1969) "Male impersonators," in J. Hadfield (ed.) *Saturday Book 29*, New York: Clarkson Porter.

Christon, Lawrence (1982) "Pierce's mirror on us all," *Los Angeles Times Calendar* (January 10): 54.

Churchill, Caryl (1984) *Cloud Nine*, New York: Methuen.

Churchill, Caryl and Lan, David (1986) *A Mouthful of Birds*, London: Methuen.

Clark, Anna (1987) "Popular morality and the construction of gender in London, 1780–1845," Ph.D. thesis, Rutgers University.

Clark, Sandra (1985) "*Hic Mulier, Haec Vir*, and the controversy over masculine women," *Studies in Philology* 82, 2: 157–83.

Cody, Gabrielle (1989) "David Hwang's *M. Butterfly*: perpetuating the misogynist myth," *Theater* 20, 2: 24–7.

Coffin, Tristram Potter (1978) *The Female Hero*, New York: Pocket Books.

Cohen, Walter (1985) *Drama of a Nation: Public Theater in Renaissance England and Spain*, Ithaca, NY: Cornell University Press.

"College theatricals" (1843) *Blackwood's Magazine* (December): 737–49.

Corathers, Don (1992) "Boys will be boys, or else: Samuel French says no to gender switching," *Dramatics*, 64, 3: 6–7.

Cowell, Marguerite (1934) *The Cowells in America being the Diary of Mrs Sam Cowell during her Husband's Concert Tour in the Years 1860–1861*, ed. M. Willson Disher, London: Oxford University Press.

Crisp, Quentin (1991) "*Paris is Burning*," *New York Times* (April 7), sec. 2: 20.

Croce, Arlene (1990) "Profiles: the Tiresias factor," *The New Yorker* (May 28): 41–64.

Cross, Wilbur L. (1918) *The History of Henry Fielding*, New Haven: Yale University Press.

Daugherty, Diane and Pitkow, Marlene (1991) "Who wears the skirts in Kathakali?" *The Drama Review* 35, 2: 138–56.

David-Neel, Alexandra (1981) *My Journey to Lhasa*, Boston: Beacon Press.

Davies, William Robertson (1964) *Shakespeare's Boy Actors*, New York: Russell & Russell.

Davis, Melton S. (1982) "Hale and hairy in Italian theater," *Sunday Times Calendar* (April 25): 5.

Davis, Natalie Zemon (1978) "Women on top: symbolic sexual inversion and political disorder in early modern Europe," in Barbara A. Babcock (ed.) *The Reversible World: Symbolic Inversion in Art and Society*, Ithaca, NY: Cornell University Press, 147–90.

Davis, Tracy C. (1991) *Actresses as Working Women: Their Social Identity in Victorian Culture*, London: Routledge.

Davy, Kate (1986) "Constructing the spectator: reception, context, and address in lesbian performance," *Performing Arts Journal* 10, 2: 74–87.

—— (1989) "Reading past the heterosexual imperative: *Dress Suits to Hire*," *The Drama Review* 33, 1: 153–70.

de Beauvoir, Simone (1952) *The Second Sex*, New York: Vintage Books.

Dekker, Rudolf M. and voor de Pol, Lottie C. (1989) *The Tradition of Female Transvestism in Early Modern Europe*, London: Macmillan.

D'Emilio, John (1983) *Sexual Politics, Sexual Communities: The Making of a Homosexual Minority in the US, 1940–1970*, Chicago: University of Chicago Press.

Devor, Holly (1989) *Gender Blending: Confronting the Limits of Duality*, Bloomington: Indiana University Press.

d'Israeli, Isaac (n.d) *Curiosities of Literature*, London: Ward, Lock.

Diamond, Elin (1985) "Refusing the romanticism of identity: narrative interventions in Churchill, Benmussa, Duras," *Theatre Journal* 37, 3: 273–86.

—— (1990) "Mimesis, mimicry, and the 'true-real,'" *Modern Drama* 32, 1: 58–72.

Dickens, Homer (1982) *What a Drag*, London: Angus & Robertson.

Dickson, P. G. M. (1967) *The Financial Revolution in England: A Study in the Development of Paper Credit 1688–1756*, New York: St Martin's Press.

Doane, Marianne (1982) "Film and masquerade: theorizing the female spectator," *Screen*, 23: 74–89.

Dolan, Jill (1985) "Gender impersonation onstage: destroying or maintaining the mirror of gender roles?," *Women and Performance* 2, 2: 4–11.

—— (1988) *The Feminist Spectator as Critic*, Ann Arbor: UMI Research Press.

—— (1989a) "In defense of the discourse: materialist feminism, postmodernism, poststructuralism and theory," *TDR* 33, 3: 58–71.

—— (1989b) "Desire cloaked in a trenchcoat," *TDR* 33, 1: 59–67.

Dollimore, Jonathan (1987) "Subjectivity, sexuality, and transgression: the Jacobean connection," *Renaissance Drama* n.s. 17: 53–81.

Dooley, J. A. (1979) "The re-emergence of the male tan in the Chinese theatre," *Theatre Quarterly* 9, 34: 42–7.

Dorff, Jay (1990) "Drag and empowerment: the erotics of the Radical Faeries," paper delivered at Performance Studies International Conference at New York University, October, 1990; Pleasure and Politics: the 4th Annual Lesbian, Bisexual, and Gay Studies Conference at Harvard University, November 1990; Flaunting It: The First Annual Lesbian and Gay Graduate Students Conference at University of Wisconsin/Milwaukee 1990.

Dougill, David (1991) "Takes your breath away," *The Sunday Times* (April 28), sec. 5: 5.

Drorbaugh, Elizabeth (1990) "The girls of Salome, Wilde and provocative," paper delivered at Performance Studies International Conference at New York University, October 1990; Pleasure and Politics: the 4th Annual Lesbian, Bisexual, and Gay Studies Conference at Harvard University, November 1990; Flaunting It: The First Annual Lesbian and Gay Graduate Students Conference at University of Wisconsin/Milwaukee 1990.

Duberman, Martin Bauml, Vicinius, Martha, and Chauncey, Jr, George (eds) (1989) *Hidden from History: Reclaiming the Gay and Lesbian Past*, New York: New American Library.

Duchartre, Pierre Louis (1966) *The Italian Comedy*, trans. Randolph T. Weaver, New York: Dover.

Dugaw, Dianne (1985) "Balladry's female warriors: women, warfare and disguise in the eighteenth century," *Eighteenth Century Life* 9, 2: 1–20.

—— (1989) *Dangerous Examples: Warrior Women and Popular Balladry, 1600–1850*, Cambridge: Cambridge University Press.

Durante, Jimmy and Kofoed, Jack (1931) *Nightclubs*, New York: Alfred A. Knopf.

Durova, Nadezhda (1989) *The Cavalry Maiden: Journals of a Female Russian Officer in the Napoleonic Wars*, trans. Mary Fleming Zirin, London: Angel Books.

Dusinberre, Juliet (1975) *Shakespeare and the Nature of Women*, London: Macmillan.

Eades, Gerald (1984) *The Profession of Player in Shakespeare's Time, 1590–1642*, Princeton: Princeton University Press.

Early, Alice K. (1955) *English Dolls, Effigies, and Puppets*, London: B. T. Batsford.

Eberhardt, Isabelle (1988) *The Passionate Nomad: The Diary of Isabelle Eberhardt*, Boston: Beacon Press.

Eccles, Christine (1990) "Switching the breeches parts," *The Guardian* (June 29).

Edmonds, Jill (1992) "Princess Hamlet," in V. Gardner and S. Rutherford (eds) *The New Woman and Her Sisters: Feminism and Theatre 1850–1914*, London: Harvester Wheatsheaf, 59–76.

Edwards, Charlene Frances (1957) "The tradition for breeches in the three centuries that professional actresses have played male roles on the English speaking stage," unpublished Ph. D. dissertation, University of Denver.

"Edwina" (1963) "Acceptance via the stage," *Transvestia* 19: 52–4.

Elias, Norbert (1939) *The History of Manners*, vol. I of *The Civilizing Process*, 2 vols, rpt 1978, New York: Pantheon.

Ellington, George (1870) *The Women of New York or Social Life in the Great City*, New York: New York Book Co.

Ellis, Havelock (1936) *Studies in the Psychology of Sex*, New York: Random House.

Eltinge, Julian (1913) "How I portray a woman on the stage," *Theatre Magazine* (Aug.): 57–8.

"An epistle to *John James H–dd–g–r*, Esq; On the Report of *Signior F–r–n–lli's* being with Child," (1736), London: E. Hill.

Evans, G. Blakemore, Levin, Harry, Baker, Herschel, and Shattuck, Charles H. (eds) (1974) *The Riverside Shakespeare*, Boston: Houghton Mifflin Company.

Feinbloom, Deborah Heller (1976) *Transvestites and Transsexuals*, New York: Delta Books.

Feingold, Michael (1992) "Lypsinka I: now it can be lip-synched," *The Village Voice* (Aug. 26): 99.

Ferguson, Margaret W., Quilligan, Maureen, and Vickers, Nancy J. (eds) (1986) *Rewriting the Renaissance: The Discourses of Sexual Difference in Early Modern Europe*, Chicago: University of Chicago Press.

Ferris, Lesley (1990) *Acting Women: Images of Women in Theatre*, London: Macmillan.

—— (1993) "The female self and performance: the case of the first actress," in Karen Laughlin and Catherine Shuler (eds) *Theatre and Feminist Aesthetics*, Farleigh Dickinson Press, forthcoming.

Fielding, Henry (1728) *The Masquerade*, "by Lemuel Gulliver, Poet Laureat to the King of Lilliput," London: J. Roberts.

—— (1902) *Love in Several Masques*, (rpt) New York: Croscup & Sterling Co.

—— (1903) *The Works of Henry Fielding*, 11 vols, ed. James P. Browne, London: Bickers & Son.

—— (1918) *The Tragedy of Tragedies*, ed. James T. Hillhouse, New Haven: Yale University Press.

—— (1960) *"The Female Husband" and Other Writings*, in Claude E. Jones (ed.) English Reprint Series, no. 17, Liverpool University Press.

—— (1966) *The Author's Farce*, ed. Charles B. Woods, Lincoln: University of

Nebraska Press.

—— (1967) *The Historical Register*, ed. William Appleton, Regents Restoration Drama Series, Lincoln: University of Nebraska Press, rpt.

Fineman, Joel (1980) "Fratricide and cuckoldry: Shakespeare's doubles," in Murray M. Schwartz and Copplia Kahn (eds) *Representing Shakespeare: New Psychoanalytic Essays*, Baltimore: Johns Hopkins University Press.

Fletcher, Kathy (1987) "Planché, Vestris, and the transvestite role: sexuality and gender in Victorian popular theatre," *Nineteenth Century Theatre* 15: 9–33.

Fo, Dario (1979) "Dialogue with an audience," *Theatre Quarterly* 35: 11–17.

Foster, Jeanette (1975) *Sex Variant Women in Literature*, Baltimore: Diane Press.

Foucault, Michel (ed.) (1980) *Herculine Barkin: Being the Recently Discovered Memoirs of a Nineteenth Century Hermaphrodite*, London: Harvester Press.

"Francis Renault, last of major femme mimics, dies of stroke at 62" (1955), *Variety* (May 25): 64, from the Billy Rose Theater Collection at Lincoln Center.

Freeburg, Victor Oscar (1965) *A Study in Stage Tradition*, New York: Bloom.

French, Marilyn (1991) "Shakespeare from women's eyes," *MS* (March/April): 68–70.

Furman, Nelly (1985) "The politics of language: beyond the gender principle?," in Gayle Green and Coppelia Kahn (eds) *Making a Difference: Feminist Literary Criticism*, London: Methuen.

Gainor, J. Ellen (1991) *Shaw's Daughters: Dramatic and Narrative Constructions of Gender*, Ann Arbor: University of Michigan Press.

Garber, Marjorie (1992) *Vested Interests: Cross Dressing and Cultural Anxiety*, New York: Routledge.

Gautier, Théophile (1932) *The Romantic Ballet as Seen by Theophile Gautier*, trans. Cyril W. Beaumont, London, rpt 1980, New York: Arno.

Gerould, Daniel (1981) "Madame Rachilde 'man' of letters," *Performing Arts Journal*: 117–22.

Gilbert, O. P. (1932) *Women in Men's Guise*, trans. J. Lewis May, London: John Lane.

Gilbert, Sandra M. (1980) "Costumes of the mind: transvestism as metaphor in modern literature," *Critical Inquiry* 7: 391–418.

Gildor, Rosamund (1960) *Enter the Actress: The First Women in the Theatre*, New York: Theatre Art Books.

Goldoni, Carlo (1982) *Mirandolira (La Locandiera)*, trans. and ed. Frederick Davies, *Goldoni: Four Comedies*, Harmondsworth: Penguin.

Goldsby, Jackie (1991) "Queens of language," *Afterimage* (May): 10–11.

Goodman, Walter (1895) *The Keeleys on Stage and at Home*, London: Richard Bentley & Son.

Gosson, Stephen (1579) *The School of Abuse*, rpt 1973, New York: Garland.

Graham, Franklin (1902) *Histrionic Montreal*, Montreal: John Lovell & Son.

Gramsci, A. (1971) *Selections from the Prison Notebooks*, ed. Quinten Hoare and Geoffrey Smith, New York: International Publishers.

Gray, George (1930) *Vagaries of a "Vagabond,"* London: Heath Cranston.

Green, Roger Lancelyn (1954) *Fifty Years of Peter Pan*, London: Peter Davies.

Greenblatt, Stephen (1983) "Murdering peasants: status, genre, and the representation of rebellion," *Representations 1*: 1–29.

—— (1985) "Shakespeare and the exorcists," in Patricia Parker and Geoffrey Hartman (eds) *Shakespeare and the Question of Theory*, New York: Methuen.

—— (1988) "Fiction and friction," in *Shakespearean Negotiations: The Circulation of Social Energy in Renaissance England*, Berkeley: University of California Press, 66–93.

Gregory, Sandra (1982) "The pantomime Dame – how long can the species survive?," *The Listener* 108: 20–1.

Gubar, Susan (1981) "Blessings in disguise: cross dressing as re-dressing for female modernists," *The Massachusetts Review* 22, 3: 477–508.

Guest, Ivor (1954) *The Romantic Ballet in Paris: Its Development, Fulfilment and Decline*, London: Phoenix House.

—— (1959) "The Alhambra Ballet," *Dance Perspectives* (autumn): 2–12.

—— (1962) *The Empire Ballet*, London: Society for Theatre Research.

—— (1974a) *The Ballet of the Second Empire*, Middletown: Wesleyan University Press.

—— (1974b) *Fanny Cerrito: The Life of a Romantic Ballerina*, 2nd rev. edn, London: Dance Books.

—— (1980) *The Romantic Ballet in Paris*, forewords by Ninette de Valois and Lillian Moore, 2nd rev. edn, London: Dance Books.

Guillory, John (1986) "Dalila's house: *Samson Agonistes* and the sexual division of labor," in Margaret Ferguson, Maureen Quilligan, and Nancy J. Vickers (eds) *Rewriting the Renaissance: The Discourses of Sexual Difference in Early Modern Europe*, Chicago: University of Chicago Press, 106–22.

Gurr, Andrew (1987) *Playgoing in Shakespeare's London*, Cambridge: Cambridge University Press.

Gussow, Mel (1976) "A Review," *New York Times*, October 13: n.p.

Haec-Vir or The Womanish-Man (1620) London.

Haller, William and Haller, Malleville (1942) "The Puritan art of love," *Huntington Library Quarterly* 5: 235–72.

Harbage, Alfred (1941) *Shakespeare's Audience*, New York: Columbia University Press.

Hardeman, Paul D. (1983) "Walter Bothwell Browne," *California Voice* (June 3): 16–17.

Harris, John (1991) "Gay activist or beauty queen?," *Theater Week* (Aug. 5): 18–23.

Harris, Laurilyn J. (1981) "'In truth, she has good cause for spleen': Madame Vestris' American tour," *Theatre Studies* 28/9: 41–58.

Harrison, William (1587) *The Description of England*, ed. Georges Edelen, rpt 1968, Ithaca, NY: Cornell University Press.

Hart, Lynda (ed.) (1989) *Making a Spectacle: Feminist Essays on Contemporary Women's Theatre*, Ann Arbor: University of Michigan Press.

Haskell, Molly (1973) *From Rape to Reverence*, New York: Holt, Rinehart & Winston.

Hayles, Nancy K. (1979) "Sexual disguise in *As You Like It* and *Twelfth Night*," *Shakespeare Survey* 32: 63–72.

Heilbrun, Carolyn G. (1973) *Toward a Recognition of Androgyny*, New York: W. W. Norton.

Heise, Ursula K. (1992) "Transvestism and the stage controversy in Spain and England, 1580–1680," *Theatre Journal* 44, 3: 357–74.

Helms, Lorraine (1989a) "Roaring girls and silent women: the politics of androgyny on the Jacobean stage," in James Redmond (ed.) *Women in Theatre*, Cambridge: Cambridge University Press.

—— (1989b) "Playing the woman's part," *Theatre Journal* 41, 2: 190–200.

Hemphill, Essex (1991) "*Paris is Burning*," *The Guardian* (July 3): 10–11.

Heriot, Angus (1956) *The Castrati in Opera*, London: Secker & Warburg.

Herrmann, Anne (1989) "Travesty and Transgression: transvestism in Shakespeare, Brecht, and Churchill," *Theatre Journal* 41, 2: 133–54.

—— (1991) "Passing women, performing men," *Michigan Quarterly Review* 30, 1: 60–71.

Hic Mulier or The Man-Woman (1620) London.

Highfill, Philip H., Jr, Burnim, Kalman A., and Langhans, Edward A. (eds) (1982) *A Biographical Dictionary of Actors, Actresses, [Etc.] in London, 1660–1800*, Carbondale: Southern Illinois University Press.

Hill, Ronald (1965) "Pants in the provinces," *Theatre World* 61 (January): 4–6.

Hippisley-Cox, Anthony (1969) "Review of *Enter Foot and Horse* by A. H. Saxon," *Theatre Notebook* (autumn): 39.

Hirschfeld, Magnus (1910) *Die Transvestiten*, Berlin: Alfred Pulvermacher.

Hirschorn, Clive (1992) "Letter from London: Moby Dick," *Theatreweek* (April 20–6): 23–7.

Hitchman, Janet (1975) *Such a Strange Lady*, New York: Avon.

Hoberman, J. and Rosenbaum, Jonathan (1983) *Midnight Movies*, New York: Harper & Row.

Hochswender, Woody (1992) "Strong suit," *New York Times*, (May 3): 10.

Holden, Stephen (1991) "Performance, illusion and obsession in *Sarrasine*," *New York Times* (September 9): 133.

Hollander, Anne (1978) *Seeing Through Clothes*, New York: Avon Books.

Hollibaugh, Amber and Moraga, Cherrié (1983) "What we're rollin' around in bed with: sexual silences in feminism," in Ann Snitow, Christine Stansell, and Sharon Thompson (eds) *Powers of Desire: The Politics of Sexuality*, New York: Monthly Review Press, 394–405.

Holmberg, Arthur (1992) "Hamlet's body," *American Theatre* (March): 12–17.

hooks, bell (1991) "Is Paris burning?," *Z Magazine* (June): 61.

Hooper, Wilfred (1915) "The Tudor sumptuary laws," *English Historical Review* 30: 433–49.

Horwitz, Simi (1991) "The substance of Fierstein," *Theater Week* 4, 42: 17–23.

Howard, Jean E. (1984) "The orchestration of *Twelfth Night*," in *Shakespeare's Art of Orchestration*, Urbana: University of Illinois Press.

Howard, Roland (1879) "Obituary," *New York Clipper*, undated clipping, Harvard Theatre Collection.

Howard, William Lee (1900) "Effeminate men and masculine women," *New York Medical Journal* 71: 686.

Howard-Howard, Margo (1991) *I Was a White Slave in Harlem*, New York: Four Walls Eight Windows.

Hughes, Holly (1991) "The Lady Dick," *The Drama Review* T131 (fall): 199–215.

Hull, Suzanne (1982) *Chaste, Silent and Obedient: English Books for Women 1475–1640*, San Marino, California: Huntington Library.

Hyland, Peter (1987) "'A kind of woman': the Elizabethan boy-actor and the Kabuki *Onnagata*," *Theatre Research International* 12, 1: 1–8.

Ingram, Martin (1985a) "The reform of popular culture? Sex and Marriage in early modern England," in Barry Reay (ed.) *Popular Culture in Seventeenth-Century England*, New York: St Martin's, 129–65.

—— (1985b) "Ridings, rough music and mocking rhymes in early modern England," in Barry Reay (ed.) *Popular Culture in Seventeenth-Century England*, New York: St Martin's, 166–97.

—— (1985c) "The taming of the scold: the enforcement of patriarchal authority in early modern England," in Anthony Fletcher and John Stevenson (eds) *Order and Disorder in Early Modern England*, Cambridge: Cambridge University Press, 116–36.

Irigaray, Luce (1985) *Speculum of the Other Woman*, trans. Gillian C. Gill, Ithaca, NY: Cornell University Press.

Iser, Wolfgang (1983) "The dramatization of double meaning in Shakespeare's *As You Like It*," *Theatre Journal* 35, 3: 330.

Jamieson, Michael (1968) "Shakespeare's celibate stage: the problem of accommodation to the boy actors in 'As You Like It,' 'Anthony and Cleopatra,' and 'The Winter's Tale,'" in Gerald Bentley (ed.) *The Seventeenth Century Stage: A Collection of Critical Essays*, Chicago: University of Chicago Press.

Jardine, Lisa (1983) *Still Harping on Daughters: Women and Drama in the Age of Shakespeare*, Totowa, NJ: Barnes & Noble.

Jay, Karla (1988) *The Amazon and the Page*, Bloomington: Indiana University Press.

Jeffries, Joe E. (1990) "Pansies: the flowers of burlesque," paper delivered at Performance Studies International Conference at New York University, October, 1990; Pleasure and Politics: the 4th Annual Lesbian, Bisexual, and Gay Studies Conference at Harvard University, November, 1990; Flaunting It: The First Annual Lesbian and Gay Graduate Students Conference at University of Wisconsin/Milwaukee 1990.

Jenkins, Linda Walsh and Ogden-Malouf, Susan (1985) "The (female) actor prepares," *Theatre* 17, 1: 66–9.

Jenkins, Ron (1992) "Downtown Kabuki," *The Village Voice* (July 14): 100.

Jensen, Ejner J. (1975) "The boy actors: plays and playing," *RORD* 18: 5–11.

"Jewel Box Revue winds up stay at Apollo Theater Tuesday night" (1973) *The New York Amsterdam News* (Mar. 3) (no page), from the Billy Rose Theater Collection at Lincoln Center.

Johnson, Barbara (1980) "The critical difference: BartheS/Bal Zac," in *The Critical Difference: Essays in the Contemporary Rhetoric of Reading*, Baltimore: Johns Hopkins University Press, 3–12.

Jonson, Ben (1966) *Epicoene* or *The Silent Woman*, ed. L. A. Beaurline, Lincoln: University of Nebraska Press.

Kaite, Berkeley (1987) "The pornographic body double: transgression is the law," in Arthur and Mary Louise Kroker (eds) *Body Invaders: Panic Sex in America*, New York: St Martin's, 149–68.

Kaplan, Gisela and Rogers, Lesley J. (1990) "Scientific constructions, cultural productions: scientific narratives of sexual attraction," in Terry Threadgold and Anne Cranny-Francis (eds) *Feminine, Masculine and Representation*, London: Allen & Unwin.

Katz, Jonathan Ned (1983) *Gay/Lesbian Almanac*, New York: Harper & Row.

Kavenik, Frances M. (1991) "Aphra Behn: the playwright as 'breeches part,'" in Mary Anne Schofield and Cecilia Macheske (eds) *Curtain Calls: British and American Women and the Theater, 1660–1820*, Athens: Ohio University Press.

Kelly, Joan (1984) "Did women have a renaissance?," in *Women, History, and Theory: The Essays of Joan Kelly*, Chicago: University of Chicago Press, 19–50.

Kelly, Katherine E. (1990) "The queen's two bodies: Shakespeare's boy actress in breeches", *Theatre Journal*: 81–93.

Kennedy, Brian (1984) "Men in frocks," *City Limits* (March 30–April 5): 21–4.

Kennedy, Patricia (1981) "Madame Vestris: a chronology," *Theatre Studies* 28/9: 53–8.

Kerr, Peter (1991) "Cosmetic makers read the census," *The New York Times* (August 29): D1.

Keyssar, Helene (1990) *Feminist Theatre*, New York: St Martin's.

Kimbrough, Robert (1982) "Androgyny seen through Shakespeare's disguise," *Shakespeare Quarterly* 33, 1: 17–33.

Kingsley, Omar (1879) "Obituary," *New York Clipper* (May 17).

Kingston, Maxine Hong (1977) *The Woman Warrior*, London: Pan Books.

Kirk, Kris and Heath, Ed (1984) *Men in Frocks*, London: GMP.

Kissel, Howard (1976) "The Club Review," *Women's Wear Daily* (October 15) n.p.

Knight, Arthur (1977) "Introducing Craig Russell – outrageous!," *The Hollywood Reporter* (September 30): 8.

Kobak, Annette (1989) *Isabelle: The Life of Isabelle Eberhardt*, New York: Knopf.

Kott, Jan (1972) "Shakespeare's bitter Arcadia," in *Shakespeare Our Contemporary*, London: Methuen.

—— (1984) *The Theater of Essence*, Evanston: Northwestern University Press.

Kuhn, Annette (1985) "Sexual disguise and cinema," in *The Power of the Image: Essays on Representation and Sexuality*, London: Routledge & Kegan Paul, 48–73.

La Belle, Maurice Mark (1980) *Alfred Jarry: Nihilism and the Theatre of the Absurd*, New York: New York University Press.

"Lads-in-drag and 1 mustachioed girl, or limp-wrist time on Broadway" (1958) *Variety* (December 10) (no page), from the Billy Rose Theater Collection at Lincoln Center.

Lahr, John (1985) "Dame Edna Everage," in *Automatic Vaudeville: Essays on Star Turns*, London: Methuen.

—— (1991) "Profiles: playing possum," *The New Yorker*, 67 19: 38–66.

—— (1992) *Dame Edna Everage and the Rise of Western Civilisation: Backstage with Barry Humphries*, New York: Farrar, Straus & Giroux.

Laqueur, Thomas W. (1986) "Orgasm, generation, and the politics of reproductive biology," *Representations*, 14: 1–41.

—— (1990) *Making Sex: Body and Gender from the Greeks to Freud*, Cambridge, Massachusetts: Harvard University Press.

Leavitt, M. B. (1912) *Fifty Years in Theatrical Management*, New York: Broadway Publishing Co.

Le Gallienne, Eva (1983) "Acting *Hamlet*," in Karen Malpede (ed.) *Women in Theatre: Compassion and Hope*, New York: Drama Books.

Legludic, H. (1979) "Splendeurs et misères d'une courtisane mâle, ou confidences et aveux d'un Parisien recueillies en 1874 par le Dr. H. Legludic" (1874), in Pierre Hahn (ed.) *Nos ancêtres les pervers*, Paris: Olivier Orban, 269–310.

Lenz, C. R. S., Green, G., and Neely, C. T. (eds) (1981) *The Women's Part: Feminist Criticism of Shakespeare*, Urbana: Indiana University Press.

"Leon, the female impersonator" (n.d.) *Cleveland Press*, undated clipping in Harvard Theatre Collection.

Le Roux, Hugues (1889) *Les Jeux du cirque et la vie foraine*, Paris: E. Plon.

Levine, Laura (1986) "Men in women's clothing: anti-theatricality and effeminization from 1579 to 1642," *Criticism* 28, 2: 121–43.

Lichtenstein, Jacqueline (1987) "Making up representation: the risks of femininity," *Representations* 20: 77–87.

Lithgow, John (1982) "My life as a woman," *Mademoiselle* (September): 46–47.

Logan, Olive (1875) "The ancestry of Brudder Bones," *Harper's* 58: 687–98.

"The London Hermit" (1875) "The epicene gender: a theatrical nuisance," *Dublin University Magazine* 506, 85: 248–54.

Loulan, JoAnn (1990) *The Lesbian Erotic Dance: Butch, Femme, Androgyny and Other Rhythms*, San Francisco: Spinsters Book Company.

Lucas, R. Valerie (1988) "*Hic Mulier*: the female transvestite in early modern

England," *Renaissance and Reformation* 24, 1: 65–84.

Ludlam, Charles (1992) "Charles Ludlam: in his own words," *Theatreweek*, March 2–8, 22–20.

McIntosh, Mary (1968) "The homosexual role," in *Social Problems* 16, 2: 182–92.

McKendrick, Melveena (1974) *Woman and Society in the Spanish Drama of the Golden Age: A Study of the Mujer Varonil*, Cambridge: Cambridge University Press.

McKendrick, Neil, Brewer, John and Plumb, J. H. (1982) *The Birth of a Consumer Society: The Commercialization of 18th Century England*, Bloomington: Indiana University Press.

MacKinnon, Catherine (1987) "Difference and dominance: on sex discrimination," *Feminism Unmodified: Discourses on Life and Law*, Cambridge, Massachusetts: Harvard University Press, 32–45.

McLuskie, Kathleen (1987) "The act, the role, and the actor: boy actresses on the Elizabethan stage," *New Theatre Quarterly* 3, 10: 120–30.

Maitland, Sara (1986) *Vesta Tilley*, London: Virago.

Malin, Stephen (1992) "The man woman," in *English Folk Theatre: Witch, Rite and Stage*, unpublished manuscript.

Mander, Raymond and Mitchenson, Joe (1965) *British Music Hall*, London: Studio Vista.

Marranca, Bonnie, Fuchs, Elinor, and Rabkin, Gerald (1991) "The politics of representation: New York theatre season, 1990–1991," '*Performing Arts Journal*, 39, 13: 1–19.

Maschio, Geraldine (1988/9) "A prescription for femininity: male interpretation of the feminine ideal at the turn of the century," *Women and Performance* 4: 1, 43–9.

Massinger, Philip (1964) *The City Madam*, ed. Cyrus Hoy, Lincoln: University of Nebraska Press.

Maus, Katherine Eisaman (1979) "'Playhouse flesh and blood': sexual ideology and the Restoration actress," *English Literary History* 46, 4: 595–617.

Mayer, David (1974) "The sexuality of pantomime," *Theatre Quarterly* 4, 13: 55–64.

Meduri, Avanthi (1991) "Western feminist theory, Asian Indian performance, and a notion of agency," *Women and Performance* 5, 2: 90–103.

Melicow, M.D., Meyer M. (1983) "Castrati singers and the lost 'cords,'" *Bulletin of The New York Academy of Medicine* (October): 744–64.

"Men as stage 'heroines'" (1909) *Strand* (December): 563–8.

Merriam, Eve (1987) in Kathleen Betsko and Rachel Koenig (eds) *Interviews with Contemporary Women Playwrights*, New York: Beech Tree Books, 294.

Merrill, Lisa (1985) "Charlotte Cushman: American actress on the vanguard of new roles for women," unpublished Ph.D. thesis, New York University.

Meyer, Morris (1991) "I dream of Jeannie: transsexual striptease as scientific display," *The Drama Review* 35, 1: 25–42.

Middleton, Thomas and Dekker, Thomas (1976) *The Roaring Girl*, ed. Andor Gomme, New York: W. W. Norton & Company.

Migel, Parmenia (1980) *The Ballerinas From the Court of Louis XIV to Pavlova*, New York: Da Capo.

Miles, Rosalind (1989) *The Women's History of the World*, London: Paladin.

Miller, Nancy K. (1981) "I's in drag: the sex of recollection," *Eighteenth Century* 22: 47–57.

Montrose, Louis Adrian (1986) "Renaissance literary studies and the subject of history," *English Literary Renaissance* 16: 5–12.

Moore, Frank (1866) *Women of the War: Their Heroism and Self-Sacrifice*, Hartford, CT: S. S. Scranton.

Morgan, Fidelis (1988) *The Well-Known Troublemaker: A Life of Charlotte Charke*, London: Faber & Faber.

Morgan, Robert (1987) "In the space of androgyny," *High Performance* 10, 3: 62–3.

Motter, T.H. Vail (1929) *The School Drama in England*, London: Longmans, Green.

Mulvey, Laura (1986) "Changes," Paper presented at New York University Humanities Institute Colloquium on Sex and Gender.

Munk, Erika (1976) "Only the uncomfortable few don't laugh," *The Village Voice* (Oct. 25): 78.

—— (1985a) "Cross left-drag: 1. Men," *The Village Voice* (February 5): 89–90.

—— (1985b) "Cross left-drag 2. Women," *The Village Voice* (March 12): 79–80.

—— (1986) "The rites of women," *Performing Arts Journal*, 29, X2: 35–42.

—— (1988) "Cross left: representation and its discontents," *The Village Voice* (September 6): 85–6.

Nanda, Serena (1990) *Neither Man nor Woman: The Hirjas of India*, Belmont, Ca: Wadsworth Publishing.

A Narrative of the Life of Mrs Charlotte Charke (1969) 2nd edn, introduction by Leonard R. N. Ashley, Gainesville, FL: Scholars' Facsimiles & Reprints.

Nathan, George Jean (1928) "The theatre," *American Mercury* (December): 500–3.

Nestle, Joan (1987) *A Restricted Country*, Ithaca, NY: Firebrand Books.

Neuls-Bates, Carol (ed.) (1982) *Women in Music*, New York: Harper & Row.

Newman, Karen (1986) "Renaissance family politics and Shakespeare's *The Taming of the Shrew*," *English Literary Renaissance* 6: 86–100.

—— (1987) "Portia's ring: unruly women and structures of exchange in *The Merchant of Venice*," *Shakespeare Quarterly* 38: 19–33.

Newton, Esther (1972) *Mother Camp: Female Impersonation in America*, Chicago: University of Chicago Press.

—— (1989) "The mythic mannish lesbian: Radclyffe Hall and the new woman," in Martin Bauml Duberman, Martha Vicinus, and George Chauncey, Jr (eds) *Hidden From History: Reclaiming the Gay and Lesbian Past*, New York: New American Library: 281–93.

Newton, Judith and Rosenfelt, Deborah (eds) (1985) "Toward a materialist-feminist criticism," in *Feminist Criticism and Social Change*, New York: Methuen, xv–xxxix.

Nicoll, Allardyce (1925) *A History of Early Eighteenth-Century Drama*, Cambridge: Cambridge University Press.

Noble, David F. (1992) *A World Without Women: The Christian Clerical Culture of Western Science*, New York: Alfred A. Knopf.

Nohain, Jean and Caradec, François (1969) *La Vie exemplaire de la femme à barbe*, Paris: La Jeune Parque.

Novy, Marianne (1984) *Love's Argument: Gender Relations in Shakespeare*, Chapel Hill: University of North Carolina Press.

O'Connor, Thomas (1982) "Mimic Charles Pierce still dressing the part," *Los Angeles Herald Examiner* (October 4): D2–D3.

Odell, George C. D. (1937) *Annals of the New York Stage*, vol. 9, New York: Columbia University Press.

"Old time circus attractions" (1899) Unidentified clipping (February 19) in Harvard Theater Collection.

Olsen, Kirstin (1988) *Remember the Ladies: A Women's Book of Days*, Pittstown, New Jersey: Main Street.

Omvedt, Gail (1986) "'Patriarchy': the analysis of women's oppression," *The Insurgent Sociologist* 13: 30–50.

Orgel, Stephen (1975) *The Illusion of Power: Political Theater in the English Renaissance*, Berkeley: University of California Press.

—— (1989) "Nobody's perfect: or why did the English stage take boys for women?" *The South Atlantic Quarterly* 88, 1: 7–29.

Paloma, Delores (1980) "Margaret Cavendish: defining the female self," *Women's Studies* 7: 55–66.

Park, Clara Claiborne (1980) "As we like it: how a girl can be smart and still popular," in *The Woman's Part: Feminist Criticism of Shakespeare*, Urbana: University of Illinois Press, 100–16.

Parkerson, Michelle (1987a) "Beyond chiffon: the making of Stormé," in Brian Wallis (ed.) *Blasted Allegories: An Anthology of Writings by Contemporary Artists*, New York: The Museum of Contemporary Art, 2–5.

—— (1987b) *Stormé: The Lady in the Jewel Box*, 21 minutes, color, 16 mm/video, film available from Women Make Movies Inc., 225 Lafayette Street 212, New York, New York 10012. For information/world rights: Eye of the Storm Productions, 1716 Florida Ave NW 2, Washington DC 20009, USA.

Parsons, Frank Alvah (1923) *The Psychology of Dress*, Garden City, NY: Doubleday.

Partridge, Eric (1961) *A Dictionary of Slang and Unconventional English*, London: Routledge & Kegan Paul.

Peacock, Shane (1990) "Farini the Great," *Bandwagon* (September–October): 13–20.

Pearsall, Ronald (1969) *The Worm in the Bud: The World of Victorian Sexuality*, New York: Macmillan.

Peavy, Charles D. (1969) "The chimerical career of Charlotte Charke," *Restoration and Eighteenth Century Theatre Research* 8, 1: 1–12.

Pepys, Samuel (1942) *The Diary of Samuel Pepys*, ed. with additions by Henry B. Wheatley, New York: Heritage Press.

Peschel, Enid Rhodes and Peschel, Richard E. (1986) "Medicine and music: the castrati in opera," *Opera Quarterly* 4: 21–38.

Phelan, Peggy (1988) "Feminist theory, poststructuralism, and performance," *The Drama Review* 32, 1: 107–27.

—— (1993) *Unmarked: The Politics of Performance*, New York and London: Routledge.

Phillips, Teresia Constantia (1735) *The Happy Courtezan: Or, the Prude demolish'd. An EPISTLE From the Celebrated Mrs. C – P –. TO THE Angelick Signior Far–n–lli*, London: J. Roberts.

Pisik, Betsy (1987) "In search of a lost legacy," *Washington Blade* (May 1), n.p. From Stormé DeLarverié's personal collection of reviews.

Pollak, Ellen (1985) *The Poetics of Sexual Myth: Gender and Ideology in the Verse of Swift and Pope*, Chicago: University of Chicago Press.

Powers, Kim (1983) "Fragments of a trilogy: Harvey Fierstein's *Torch Song*," *Theatre* 14, 2: 63–7.

Pronko, Leonard (1967) "Kabuki and Elizabethan theatre," *Educational Theatre Journal* 19, 1: 9–16.

—— (1971) "Learning Kabuki: the training program of the National Theatre of Japan," *Educational Theatre Journal* 23, 4: 409–30.

Puknat, Elizabeth M. (1951) "Romeo was a Lady: Charlotte Cushman's London triumph," *Theatre Annual* 9: 65.

Pultney, William (1731) *A Proper Reply to a late Scurrilous Libel; intitled, Sedition and Defamation display'd*, published under the pseudonym of Caleb D'Anvers, London: R. Francklin.

Quennel, Peter (1940) *Caroline of England*, New York: Viking Press.

Quinn, Frank (1958) "Frank Quinn's stage show: boys are girls at state," review of the Jewel Box Revue, *New York Mirror* (December 5): n.p. from the Billy Rose Theater Collection at Lincoln Center.

—— (n.d.) "Frank Quinn's nitelife: Jewel Box Revue is a gem," *New York Mirror*, from the Billy Rose Theater Collection at Lincoln Center.

Rackin, Phyllis (1972) "Shakespeare's boy Cleopatra, the decorum of nature, and the golden world of poetry," *PMLA* 87: 201–12.

—— (1987) "Androgyny, mimesis, and the marriage of the boy heroine on the English Renaissance stage," *PMLA* 102, 1: 29–41.

Ralph, James (1728) *The Touchstone*, photofacsimile edition, with a preface by Arthur Freeman, 1973, New York: Garland Publishing Inc.

Rastall, Richard (1985) "Female roles in all-male casts," *Medieval English Theatre* 71: 25–51.

Raymond, Gerard (1991) "The last castrato," *Theatreweek* (September 2–8): 20–3.

—— (1992) "Letter from Chicago: Neil Bartlett's *Twelfth Night*," *Theatreweek* (January 27–February 2): 34–5.

—— (1993) "The importance of being Bette: Bloolips in *Get Hur*, a Roman Epic," *Theatre Week* (February 8): 24–5.

Reay, Barry (1985) *Popular Culture in Seventeenth-Century England*, New York: St Martin's.

Reed, Rex (1976) "Review: Merriam's Club," *New York Daily News* (October 15): n.p.

Reilly, D. R. (1953) *Protrait Waxes: An Introduction for Collectors*, London: B. T. Batsford.

Rendle, T. McDonald (1919) *Swings and Roundabouts: A Yokel in London*, London: Chapman and Hall.

"Reno's Riverside Hotel drops femme impersonator show in face of ban" (1962) *Variety* (Mar. 21) (no page), from the Billy Rose Theater Collection at Lincoln Center.

Review of the Jewel Box Revue (1960) *Variety* (Mar. 9) (no page), from the Billy Rose Theater Collection at Lincoln Center.

Rice, Edward Le Roy (1911) *Monarchs of Minstrelsy from "Daddy" Rice to Date*, New York: Kenny.

Richardson, Albert D. (1867) *Beyond the Mississippi: From the Great River to the Great Ocean, 1857–1867*, Hartford, CT: American Publishing Co.

Richardson, Joanna (1977) *Sarah Bernhardt and Her World*, London: Weidenfeld & Nicolson.

Roach, Joseph R. (1989) "Power's body: the inscription of morality as style," in Thomas Postlewait and Bruce A. McConachie (eds) *Theatrical Past: Essays in the Historiography of Performance*, Iowa City: University of Iowa Press, 99–118.

Robertson, Jennifer (1989) "Gender-bending in paradise: doing 'Female' and 'Male' in Japan," *Genders* 5: 50–69.

Robinson, Brian (1991) "Nothing finer than Regina," *Square Peg* 31: 36–9.

Rogers, Pat (1982) "The breeches part," in Paul-Gabriel Boucé (ed.) *Sexuality in Eighteenth-Century Britain*, Manchester and Totowa, NJ: Manchester University Press, 244–58.

Rolley, Katrina (1990) "Cutting a dash: the dress of Radclyffe Hall and Una

Troubridge," *Feminist Review* 35: 54–66.

Rose, Jacqueline and Mitchell, Juliet (eds) (1982) *Feminine Sexuality and the "Ecole Freudienne*," trans. J. Rose, New York: W. W. Norton.

Rose, Mary Beth (1984) "Women in men's clothing: apparel and social stability in *The Roaring Girl*," *ELR* 14, 3: 367–91.

Rosenberg, Marvin (1968) "Elizabethan actors: men or marionettes," in Gerald Bentley (ed.) *The Seventeenth Century Stage: A Collection of Critical Essays*, Chicago: University of Chicago Press.

Rothstein, Eric (1968) "The framework of *Shamela*," *ELH* 35: 396.

Roughead, William (1931) *Bad Companions*, New York: Duffield & Green.

Rubin, Gayle (1975) "The traffic in women: notes on the 'political economy' of sex," in Rayna R. Reiter (ed.) *Toward an Anthropology of Women*, New York: Monthly Review Press, 157–210.

S, Dr med. W. (1901) "Vom Weibmann auf der Bühne," *Jahrbuch für sexuelle Zwischenstufen* 3: 313–25.

Sacks, David Harris (1988) "Searching for 'culture' in the English Renaissance," *Shakespeare Quarterly* 39: 441–60.

Sage, William F. (1889) "Impersonators of women," *Theatre*, 5, 13: 284–6.

Sawyer, Corinne Holt (1987) "Men in skirts and women in trousers, from Achilles to Victoria Grant: one explanation of a comedic paradox," *Journal of Popular Culture* 21, 2: 1–16.

Schochet, Gordon (1975) *Patriarchalism in Political Thought: The Authoritarian Family and Political Speculation and Attitudes, Especially in Seventeenth-Century England*, Oxford: Basil Blackwell.

Scott, Joan (1986) "Gender: a useful category of historical analysis," *American Historical Review* 91, 5: 1053–75.

Scouten, Arthur H. (ed.) (1961) *The London Stage 1660–1800, Part III, vol. 1, 1729–1747*, Carbondale: Southern Illinois University Press.

Senelick, Laurence (1976) "Dragging the Thames," *After Dark* (August): 70–1.

—— (1982) "The evolution of the male impersonator on the nineteenth-century popular stage," *Essays in Theatre* 1, 1: 30–44.

—— (1989) "Changing sex in public: female impersonation as performance," *Theater* 20, 2: 6–11.

—— (1990) "Mollies or men of mode: sodomy and the eighteenth-century London stage," *Journal of the History of Sexuality* 1, 1: 33–67.

—— (1992) "Lady and the tramp: drag differentials in the progressive era," in Laurence Senelick (ed.) *Gender in Performance*, Hanover, NH: University Press of New England.

"Sensation by a comic singer" (1872) *Dexter Smith's* (May): n.p.

Shafer, Yvonne (1981) "Women in male roles: Charlotte Cushman and others," in Helen Krich Chinoy and Linda Walsh Jenkins (eds) *Women in American Theatre: Careers, Images, Movements*, New York: Crown.

Shakespeare, William (1974) *The Riverside Shakespeare*, ed. G. Blakemore Evans, Harry Levin, Herschel Baker, and Charles H. Shattuck, Boston: Houghton Mifflin Co.

Shapiro, Michael (1969) "Children's troupes: dramatic illusion and acting style," *Comparative Drama* 3, 1: 42–53.

Shapiro, Susan C. (1987) "Amazons, hermaphrodites, and plain monsters: the 'masculine' woman in English Elizabethan satire and social criticism from 1580–1640," *Atlantis* 13, 1: 23–44.

Sharp, Buchanan (1980) *In Contempt of All Authority: Rural Artisans and Riot in the West of England 1586–1660*, Berkeley: University of California Press.

Shepherd, Simon (1981) *Amazons and Warrior Women: Varieties of Feminism in Seventeenth-Century Drama*, Brighton: Harvester.

Skloot, Robert (1990) "Breaking the butterfly: the politics of David Henry Hwang," *Modern Drama* 33: 59–66.

Slide, Anthony (1981) *The Vaudevillians*, Westport, CT: Greenwood.

—— (1986) *Great Pretenders: A History of Female & Male Impersonation in the Performing Arts*, Lombard, Illinois: Wallace-Homestead.

Smith, Bruce R. (1991) *Homosexual Desire in Shakespeare's England*, Chicago: University of Chicago Press.

Smith, Hilda (1976) "Gynecology and ideology in seventeenth-century England," in Berenice Carroll (ed.) *Liberating Women's History: Theoretical and Critical Essays*, Champaign: University of Illinois Press.

Smith, Ronn (1989) "Ethyl Eichelberger," *Theatre Crafts* (January): 28–33.

Smith-Rosenberg, Carroll (1989) "Discourses of sexuality and subjectivity: the new woman, 1870–1936," in Martin Bauml Duberman, Martha Vicinus, and George Chauncey, Jr (eds) *Hidden From History: Reclaiming the Gay and Lesbian Past*, New York: New American Library, 264–80.

Snyder, Charles McCool (1962) *Dr Mary Walker: The Little Lady in Pants*, New York: Vantage Press.

Solomon, Alisa (1992) "Queen for a day: Marjorie Garber's drag race," *Voice Literary Supplement* (June): 23.

Sontag, Susan (1966) "Notes on camp," in *Against Interpretation*, New York: Delta Books.

Sorge, Thomas (1987) "The failure of orthodoxy in *Coriolanus*," in Jean E. Howard and Marion O'Connor (eds) *Shakespeare Reproduced: The Text in History and Ideology*, London: Methuen, 225–41.

Squire, Geoffrey (1984) *Dress and Society, 1560–1970*, New York: Viking Press.

Stallybrass, Peter (1986) "Patriarchal territories: the body enclosed," in Margaret W. Ferguson, Maureen Quilligan, and Nancy J. Vickers (eds) *Rewriting the Renaissance: The Discourses of Sexual Difference in Early Modern Europe*, Chicago: University of Chicago Press, 123–42.

Staves, Susan (1979) *Players' Scepters: Fictions of Authority in the Restoration*, Lincoln: University of Nebraska Press.

Stedman, Jane W. (1972) "From Dame to woman: W. S. Gilbert and theatrical transvestism," in Martha Vicinus (ed.) *Suffer and Be Still: Women in the Victorian Age*, Bloomington: Indiana University Press.

Steegmuller, Francis (1969) "An angel, a flower, a bird," *The New Yorker* (September 27): 130–43.

—— (1970) *Cocteau: A Biography*, Boston: Nonpareil Books.

Stoker, Bram (1910) *Famous Imposters*, London: Sidgwick & Jackson.

Stokes, John, Booth, Michael R., and Bassnett, Susan (1988) *Bernhardt, Terry, Duse: The Actress in Her Time*, Cambridge: Cambridge University Press.

Stone, Lawrence (1966) "Social Mobility in England, 1500–1700," *Past and Present* 33: 16–55.

—— (1977) *The Family, Sex and Marriage in England 1500–1800*, New York: Harper & Row.

—— (1979) *The Family, Sex, and Marriage in England 1500–1800*, abridged paperback edition, New York: Harper & Row.

Strange, Sally Minter (1976) "Charlotte Charke: transvestite or conjuror?," *Restoration and Eighteenth-Century Theatre Research* 15, 2: 54–60.

"Stranger than fiction: the true story of Annie Hindle's two marriages" (1891) *New York Sun* (December 27): n.p.

Stuart, C. D. and Park, A. J. (1895) The Variety Stage: A History of the Music Halls from the Earliest Period to the Present Time, London: T. Fisher Unwin.

Stubbes, Phillip (1583) *The Anatomie of Abuses*, London.

Sudworth, G. (1984) *The Great Little Tilley*, Luton: Courtney Publications.

Thirsk, Joan (1978) *Economic Policy and Projects: The Development of a Consumer Society in Early Modern England*, Oxford: Oxford University Press.

Thompson, C. J. S. (1938) *Mysteries of Sex: Women who Posed as Men and Men who Posed as Women*, London: Hutchinson & Company.

Tilley, Vesta (1934) *Recollections of Vesta Tilley*, London: Hutchinson.

Tilney, Edmund (1587) *A briefe and pleasant discourse of duties in Mariage, called the Flower of Friendship*, London.

Toll, Robert C. (1974) *Blacking Up: The Minstrel Show in Nineteenth-Century America*, New York: Oxford University Press.

—— (1976) *On With The Show*, New York: Oxford University Press.

The Trial of Boulton and Park with Hurt and Fiske (1871), Manchester: John Heywood.

Trumbach, Randolph (1989) "The birth of the queen: sodomy and the emergence of gender equality in modern culture, 1660–1750," in Martin Bauml Duberman, Martha Vicinus, and George Chauncey, Jr (eds) *Hidden from History: Reclaiming the Gay and Lesbian Past*, New York: New American Library, 129–293.

Trussler, Simon (1966), "That's no lady," *Plays and Players* 13, 10: 52–7.

Tumbleson, Treva Rose (1981) "Three female Hamlets: Charlotte Cushman, Sarah Bernhardt and Eva Le Gallienne," unpublished Ph.D. dissertation, University of Oregon.

Twycross, Meg (1983) "'Transvestism' in the Mystery Plays," *Medieval English Theatre* 5, 2: 156.

Tyler, Carole-Anne (1991) "Boys will be girls: the politics of gay drag," in Diana Fuss (ed.) *Inside/Out: Lesbian Theories, Gay Theories*, Ann Arbor: University of Michigan Press.

Underdown, David (1985a) *Revel, Riot, and Rebellion: Popular Politics and Culture in England 1603–1660*, Oxford: Clarendon Press.

—— (1985b) "The taming of the scold: the enforcement of patriarchal authority in early modern England," in Anthony Fletcher and John Stevenson (eds) *Order and Disorder in Early Modern England*, Cambridge: Cambridge University Press, 116–36.

The Unnatural History and Petticoat Mystery of Boulton and Park (1871) London: George Clarke.

Van der Meer, Theo (1991) "Tribades on Trial: female same-sex offenders in late eighteenth-century Amsterdam," *Journal of the History of Sexuality* 1, 3: 424–45.

Veljkovic, Morag (1972) "Phyllis and Judy and Barbara and Mae and Peggy," *After Dark* (January): 48.

Walen, Denise A. (1991) "Female power and powerlessness: an all female production of Aphra Behn," *The Rover*, paper delivered to the Midwest Theater Conference, March.

Walker, Alexander (1969) "Marlene Dietrich: at heart a gentleman," in *The Celluloid Sacrifice: Aspects of Sex in the Movies*, Baltimore: Pelican Books.

Wandor, Michelene (1986) *Carry on, Understudies: Theatre and Sexual Politics*, London: Routledge & Kegan Paul.

Ware, J. Redding (1909) *Passing English of the Victorian Era: a Dictionary of Heterodox English, Slang and Phrase*, London: George Routledge & Sons.

Watt, Douglas (1976) "Eve Merriam's *The Club*," *New York Daily News* (October 15): n.p.

Watt, Ian (1957) *The Rise of the Novel*, Berkeley: University of California Press.

Weeks, Jeffrey (1979) "Movements of affirmation: sexual meanings and homosexual identities," *Radical History Review* 20: 164–79.

—— (1980/1) "Inverts, perverts, and Mary-Annes: male prostitution and the regulation of homosexuality in England in the nineteenth and early twentieth centuries," *Journal of Homosexuality* 6, 1/2: 113–34.

Wetzsteon, Ross (1990) "Queen Lear: Ruth Maleszech gender bends Shakespeare," *The Village Voice* (January 30): 39–42.

Wheelwright, Julie (1989) *Amazons and Military Maids: Women Who Dressed as Men in the Pursuit of Life, Liberty and Happiness*, London: Pandora Press.

White, Eric Walter (1983) *A History of English Opera*, London: Faber & Faber.

Wickes, George (1978) *The Amazon of Letters*, New York: Popular Library.

Wiedersheim, William A., 2nd (1941) *Some Fifty Odd Years of the Mask and Wig Club 1889–1941*, Philadelphia.

Wiestack, Frank (1903) "Stage beauties in male attire," *Washington Post* (July 26).

Wikander, Matthew (1986) "As secret as maidenhead: the profession of the boy-actress in *Twelfth Night*," *Comparative Drama* 20, 4: 349–63.

Wilhelm, Maria (1985) "San Francisco's no. 1 nun in drag, Sister Boom Boom, tries out a new habit: marriage to (gasp) a woman," *People* (October 7): 89–90.

Williamson, Judith (1984) "It's different for girls," *City Limits* (March 30–April 5): 24–5.

Wilson, Elizabeth (1990) "Deviant dress," *Feminist Review*, 35: 67–74.

Wilson, John Harold (1958) *All the King's Ladies: Actresses of the Restoration*, Chicago: University of Chicago Press.

Winford, Carlton E. (1954) *Femme Mimics*, Dallas: Winford Company.

Winter, Marian Hannah (1974) *The Pre-Romantic Ballet*, London: Pitman.

Wolff-Wilkinson, Lila (1989) "Gender is a hoot: an interview with Kate Bornstein," *Theatre* 20, 2: 28–35.

"A woman's mania for wearing male attire ends in death" (1876) *New York Clipper* (October 7): 221.

Woodbridge, Linda T. (1986) *Women and the English Renaissance: Literature and the Nature of Womankind, 1540–1620*, Chicago: University of Chicago Press.

Woodhouse, Annie (1989) *Fantastic Women: Sex, Gender and Transvestism*, London: Macmillan Educational.

Woods, Charles B. (1933) "Captain B——'s Play," *Harvard Studies and Notes in Philology and Literature*, 15: 243–55.

Worman, Martin (1990) "Midnight masquerade: the travesty theatre of the Cockettes," paper delivered at Performance Studies International Conference at New York University, October, 1990; Pleasure and Politics: the 4th Annual Lesbian, Bisexual, and Gay Studies Conference at Harvard University, November, 1990; Flaunting It: The First Annual Lesbian and Gay Graduate Students Conference at University of Wisconsin/Milwaukee 1990.

—— (1992) "Midnight masquerade: the history of the Cockettes," unpublished Ph.D. thesis, New York University.

Wrightson, Keith (1982) *English Society 1580–1680*, New Brunswick, NJ: Rutgers University Press.

Wyatt, Diana and Heap, Carl (1983) "Thoughts on 'Transvestism' by diverse hands," *Medieval English Theatre* 5, 2: 110–22.

Zeig, Sande (1985) "The actor as activator: deconstructing gender through gesture," *Women and Performance Journal* 2: 12–17.

Zeitlin, Froma I. (1981) "Travesties of gender and genre in Aristophanes' *Thesmophoriazousae*," in Helen P. Folley (ed.) *Reflections of Women in Antiquity*, New York: Gordon & Breach Science Publishers.

—— (1985) "Playing the other: theatre, theatricality, and the feminine in Greek drama," *Representations* II (summer): 63–94.

Zelenak, Michael X. (1989) "'Not of woman born,' gender politics in Greek tragedy," *Theater* 20, 2: 12–18.

Zirin, Mary Fleming (1984) "My childhood years: a memoir by Czarist cavalry officer, Nadezhda Durova," in Donna C. Stanton (ed.) *The Female Autograph*, Chicago: University of Chicago Press.

Zizek, Slavoj (1989) *The Sublime Object of Ideology*, London: Verso.

INDEX

191